Contents

Tourism and Small Entrepreneurs
Development, National Policy, and Entrepreneurial Culture: Indonesian Cases

Edited By

Heidi Dahles
and
Karin Bras

Cognizant Communication Corporation
New York • Sydney • Tokyo

Tourism and Small Entrepreneurs: Development, National Policy, and Entrepreneurial Culture: Indonesian Cases

Cognizant Communication Offices:

U.S.A.	3 Hartsdale Road, Elmsford, New York 10523-3701
Australia	P.O. Box 352 Cammeray, NWS, 2062
Japan	c/o OBS T's Bldg. 3F, 1-38-11 Matsubara, Setagaya-ku, Tokyo

Library of Congress Cataloging-in-Publication Data

Tourism and small entrepreneurs: development, national policy, and entrepreneurial culture: Indonesian cases / edited by Heidi Dahles and Karin Bras.
    p.   cm. — (Tourism dynamics)
    Includes bibliographical references (p.) and index.
    ISBN 1-882345-24-X (hard). — ISBN 1-882345-27-4 (soft)
    1. Tourism—Indonesia. 2. Tourism—Government policy—Indonesia. 3. Small business—Indonesia.
I. Dahles, Heidi. II. Bras, Karin. 1960-   . III. Series.
G155.I5T635   1999
338.4'791598043—dc21   99-22632
                                                                           CIP

Printed in the United States of America

Printing: 1 2 3 4 5 6 7 8 9 10 Year: 1 2 3 4 5 6 7 8 9 10

Cover designed by Lynn Carano

List of Figures

List of Tables

Preface

This book aims to offer a better understanding of the relationship between tourism development and small-scale entrepreneurship. It is the ambition of the authors to fill a gap in the literature with respect to those actors in the tourism industry generally denoted as petty, micro, or small-scale entrepreneurs, family businesses, or self-employed people. As Valene Smith (1994) points out, proprietorship of small-scale tourist enterprises in developing countries is a critical developmental issue that has been largely ignored. Development plans for tourism often ignore the needs of the people they are supposedly designed to help. These people are important not only because they come in large numbers, but also because they may play a vital role in the establishment of more sustainable forms of tourism.

This book is based on research conducted in the major Indonesian tourist areas, Yogyakarta (Java), Bali, and Lombok. The projects were established within the Department of Leisure Studies, Tilburg University (The Netherlands), as part of the departmental research program "Globalization: Tradition and Modernity." With the backing of her department, Heidi Dahles, staff member and lecturer, designed a program focusing on different local actors in tourism-related enterprises in Indonesia and integrating research at a postdoctoral, doctoral, and graduate level. The chapters on the Balinese small-scale accommodations (Chapter 4), the homestays in Yogyakarta (Chapter 6), the pedicab men of Yogyakarta (Chapter 7), and the Lombok mountain guides (Chapter 8) are based on M.A. thesis projects of graduate students of the Department of Leisure Studies. The chapters on the Balinese women entrepreneurs (Chapter 3) and entrepreneurs in romance (Chapter 9) are partly based on the Ph.D. project of Karin Bras, featuring the role of local tourist guides in the social construction of tourist attractions in Lombok, and partly on Dahles' research on heritage and the politics of tourism in Yogyakarta. The chapter on entrepreneurship in Lombok (Chapter 5) is a collaborative effort of Karin Bras and Theo Kamsma, and related to Bras' Ph.D. project. All the research on which this book is based was conducted in 1995–1996. The graduates' projects were conducted during a 4-month fieldwork period. Bras and Dahles worked in Indonesia for over a year. In accordance with the scientific approach to leisure and tourism as adhered to by the Department of Leisure Studies, the projects apply basically a multidisciplinary approach. Given the nature of the research population and the conditions under which the research was conducted, the emphasis is on qualitative methodology, centering around anthropological fieldwork and ethnographical interviewing.

The editors would like to acknowledge the support of the following persons and institutions:

- The department of Leisure Studies, Tilburg University (The Netherlands), for providing the institutional conditions to develop the research program and composing this book.

- The International Institute for Asian Studies (IIAS) in Leiden (The Netherlands), for granting a fellowship to Heidi Dahles, which enabled her to finalize the editing process.

- The institutional support and hospitality of Udayana University, Denpasar, Bali (Indonesia), and in particular, Professor I Gusti Ngurah Bagus, acting as sponsor for a number of participants in this program.

- The institutional support and hospitality of Sanata Dharma University, Yogyakarta (Indonesia), and in particular Professor Dr. James Spillane, S.J. and Dr. Theo Gieles, S.J. for acting as sponsors for a number of participants in this program and for making their library accessible to the researchers.

The editors would like to express their gratitude to Anne-Marie van Schaardenburgh, graduate student and student assistant of the Department of Leisure Studies of Tilburg University, who compiled an annotated bibliography on small entrepreneurs on behalf of this volume; to Jeremy Boissevain, emeritus professor of Anthropology of the University of Amsterdam, who provided valuable comments on an earlier draft of this volume; and Valene Smith, professor of Anthropology at California State University in Chico for her ongoing support throughout this project. A special word of thanks is due to John Kuppens for his meticulous editorial work on the authors' English.

Heidi Dahles

Karin Bras

Chapter 1

Tourism and Small Entrepreneurs in Developing Countries: A Theoretical Perspective

Heidi Dahles

Introduction

Since the mid-1980s industrial systems in the advanced capitalist economies have undergone a profound transformation from Fordist to post-Fordist modes of production (Harvey, 1989). Upadhya and Rutten (1997) point out that "this transformation has been characterized by two seemingly contradictory tendencies: the increasing centralization and monopolization of capital by huge transnational corporations, and a flourishing of small businesses at the other end of the scale" (p. 20). The changing nature of industrial systems in advanced capitalist economies has implications for developing countries, which make it necessary to examine changing intra- and inter-firm relationships between enterprises operating at different scales in developing economies. In this book, the focus is on the manifold interlinkages between small-scale enterprises in the tourism industry.

The tourism sector is expanding on a global level and this expansion results in an organization of international tourism that S. Britton (1989) conceptualized as a three-tiered hierarchy. At the apex are those tourist companies that have their headquarters in the metropolitan market countries and that dominate international tourism. At the intermediate level are the branch offices and local associates of these transnational companies organizing most of the tourism in developing countries. And at the base lie those small-scale tourism enterprises of the destination area that are marginal, but dependent upon the transnational companies (S. Britton, 1989). Many governments of developing countries give priority to large-scale investments in tourism as they expect tourism to contribute significantly to national income and employment. The growth scenarios in tourism developed by government agencies are fed by the projections of economists in terms of profits and multiplier effects. However, liberal economic models often overstate the direct benefits of tourism expenditures. It has been pointed out that large-scale transnational enterprises are often not as effective in increasing foreign exchange earnings and job opportunities as originally believed. This is because there is significant economic leakage due to the purchase of foreign supplies and labor and to the channeling of profits out of the developing countries. In poor states tourists frequently pay for imports, creating a massive leakage that undermines the validity of some basic econometric analysis of the value of tourism for developing countries (S. Britton, 1989; Leheny, 1995; Rodenburg, 1980).

Within the body of literature on tourism's economic potential, little attention has been paid to the role of entrepreneurial activity and, in particular, to the entrepreneurial culture that emerges in different economies (Shaw & Williams, 1994). Apart from general discussions of the impact of transnational organizations, the literature is remarkably uninformative about the role and position of small and medium-sized businesses in the tourism industry. Scholars have repeatedly pleaded for more research on small-scale entrepreneurship in tourism, and in particular its cultural dimensions. For developing countries, Jafari (1989) has indicated the importance of a tourism business culture while, more generally, Cooke (1983) and Massey (1983, 1984) have stressed the role of local cultural systems in economic development. More recently this plea seems to be heard. There is an increasing interest in micro businesses and small entrepreneurs operating in the tourism industry in developing countries. This new interest is related to investigations into the potential of tourism for sustainable developments. "To adequately respond to the need for more sustainable developments on the one hand and changing consumer tastes in the tourist-generating areas on the other hand, new forms of tourism are required that consist of smaller-scale, dispersed, and low density tourism developments located in and organized by communities where it is hoped they will foster more meaningful interaction between tourists and local residents" (Brohman, 1996, p. 64). These forms of tourism depend on ownership patterns that are in favor of local, often family-owned, relatively small-scale businesses rather than foreign-owned transnationals and other outside capital. By stressing smaller scale, local ownership, it is anticipated that tourism will increase multiplier and spread effects within the host community and avoid problems of excessive foreign exchange leakages. It is assumed that small-scale tourism developments and active resident involvement in the ownership and operation of facilities are "much less likely to produce negative sociocultural effects associated with foreign ownership, are much more likely to enhance local tolerance to tourism activities, and can respond more effectively to changes in the market place and fill niches overlooked by larger, more bureaucratic organizations" (Echtner, 1995, p. 123).

In addition to the concern for small-scale tourism as a strategy in sustainable developments, much of the recent literature deals with the question whether petty entrepreneurship in tourism provides feasible employment opportunities (Cukier, 1996). As much of the employment generated by tourism is in the form of self-employed, petty entrepreneurs, the debate is between those who believe that capitalism sweeps away precapitalist modes of production and those who believe that capitalism exists side-by-side with precapitalist economies. Neo-Marxist scholars hypothesize that the capitalist mode of production would eventually replace the precapitalist modes of production (Van Diermen, 1997). Applied to tourism, the argument would be that as a destination's tourism industry evolves, the petty economic sector would initially grow in response to increased employment opportunities. But as the destination develops, the petty economic sector, largely as a result of government policies that favor the formal sector, would either be forced out of the tourism area or else would be absorbed into the formal sector (Kermath & Thomas, 1992). However, as development sociologists and anthropologists have shown, "traditional" modes of production do not disappear because of modernization, but exist alongside the capitalist economy and often even grow and become more important in the process (Drakakis-Smith, 1987; Hart, 1993; Van Diermen, 1997; Verschoor, 1992). The same thing seems to happen to tourism: "in developing countries, where the presence of the small-scale sector is well established, it continues to increase and diversify as the tourism industry develops" (Cukier, 1996, p. 55). However, there is a difference between employment opportunities and enterprises. The latter, according to the classical economic definition, are instruments for transforming and improving the economy and society. Entrepreneurs are innovators and decision makers pursuing progressive change (Schumpeter, 1942). The issue that has to be raised is to what extent the small-scale tourism enterprises actually constitute a vital, innovative force in the tourism industry of developing countries. Do these enterprises just absorb a labor force that would otherwise be unemployed, or do they allow enterprising individuals to explore new economic activities? In other words, is the tourism-related sector of petty businesses a productive and creative part of the economy or just a redistributive mechanism (Hart, 1993)?

There is a consensus among scholars regarding the basic characteristics of entrepreneurship and entrepreneurs. However, ideas diverge when it comes to demarcating the categories of petty, small, and micro entrepreneurs. In general, an entrepreneur is regarded as a person who builds and manages an enterprise for the pursuit of profit in the course of which she/he innovates and takes risks, as the outcome of an innovation is usually not certain (Boissevain, 1974; Chan & Go, 1996; Greenfield, Strickon, & Aubey, 1979; Schumpeter, 1942). Small entrepreneurs seem to distinguish themselves from other entrepreneurs simply by their scale of operation. Scholars are debating the maximum number of employees that defines an enterprise as a small enterprise. Some definitions establish a general limit to small enterprises, disregarding the specific structural and cultural context in which a business operates. According to Verschoor (1992), a small-scale enterprise covers all economic activities or businesses deploying a labor force of no more than about 10 individuals, dependent on commodity markets, and with no legal claim to be part of a larger enterprise. For Boswell (as quoted by Boissevain, 1997), a small firm is one with less than 5000 employees, whereas for others small generally means less than 200. However, as Van Diermen (1997) points out, "small" is a relative concept that varies between countries—and between different industries in these countries, we should add. For the whole of Southeast Asia and all kinds of industries in this area, Van Diermen defines as "small" establishments with less than 100 employees. Within the globalizing economy, companies with more than 100 employees are still regarded as small in scale, whereas the Indonesian government, for example, refers to an enterprise with a maximum of six employees as being small scale and with less than 50 as medium sized (Clapham, 1985). We will return to the issue of numbers in the next chapter of this volume. For the time being it should suffice to point out that such generalizations are of little use in understanding the specific character of small enterprises. The wide variety of concepts used for small-scale entrepreneurs (i.e., small, micro, or petty entrepreneurs, family businesses, self-employed people, home and cottage industries) may be regarded as a symptom of the lack of consensus about the definition of the concept "small entrepreneur." At a closer look, we are not dealing with synonyms that can be used interchangeably. The differences between these categories are considerable, demanding more precision as far as the size, the scope, the organization of, and the context within which an enterprise operates is concerned.

To understand the conditions under which this sector operates and what it accomplishes in terms of employment and sustainable development, we need to combine an analysis of "external" factors influencing the people who make up this sector (i.e., the "macroanalysis" of national economies and policies, the state, and the market) with an "actor-oriented" perspective. In addition, to understand the structural opportunities and restrictions of the tourism sector, we need to approach the people involved in the small-scale tourism sector as reasoning actors and not just as reactors, to understand the social meanings embodied in the different aspects of production, exchange, and consumption of the tourism product. As the activities of small-scale tourism enterprises do not unfold in a vacuum, we need to analyze their definition of the situation, the arenas of their actions, their routines of social interaction, social networks, and the kind of resources they control (Verschoor, 1992). To analyze the processes by which small entrepreneurs manage their everyday social worlds, this introductory chapter deals with the following interrelated questions:

1. What is the relationship between development and tourism in developing countries according to the dominant theoretical paradigms? What role is attributed to small-scale entrepreneurship according to these paradigms?

2. What are the characteristics of small-scale entrepreneurship in the tourism sector of developing countries and how does this concept relate to the "informal" economy?

3. What resources do small entrepreneurs in tourism control, and how do they operate their business and interact with other entrepreneurs in this sector?

4. What theoretical perspectives are needed to offer an appropriate framework of reference to understand the position of small entrepreneurs in tourism development in developing countries?

Subsequently, each of the above questions will be dealt with in a separate paragraph. This chapter is concluded with a brief outlook on the following chapters of this book and their contribution to a more profound understanding of small entrepreneurship in tourism development.

Tourism and Development

Whereas national governments in many developing countries promote tourism as a passport to development, the role that these governments attribute to the participation of small and micro entrepreneurs in this development is highly limited. Government policies towards the local tourism sector vary widely, and there is no consensus regarding the ways in which tourism should be developed and the major objectives that this development should pursue. In terms of Midgley (1986), state involvement in community development can range from an overtly antiparticipatory to a participatory mode. Where state bureaucracies expect tourism to contribute significantly to national development, tourism policy is directed towards large-scale investments in cooperation with transnational enterprises and project developers. According to the classical economic definition, entrepreneurs are instruments for transforming and improving the economy and society, as entrepreneurs are regarded as innovators and risk takers pursuing progressive change (Go, 1997). Liberal market theorists believe that prosperity is the outcome of successful individual entrepreneurship (Mazumdar, 1989). Although in the modernization paradigm small entrepreneurship may flourish in the early stages of capitalist development, it will soon be absorbed by large-scale business agglomerations. Small-scale businesses surviving under these circumstances are regarded as an obstacle rather than a vigorous force in tourism development. In that case, governments are characterized by an overtly antiparticipatory attitude: local participation in general, and business initiatives of small-scale entrepreneurs in particular, do not meet with supportive policies. Instead, governments often counter deregulatory measures at the top with more regulation and control below. Although deregulation facilitates large-scale and transnational investments, the petty business sector is subdued to formalization.

The economic and political implications of promoting development strategies that favor large-scale developments and foreign participation are but part of a still wider problem (i.e., the unequal relationship between large-scale and small-scale businesses in the tourism industry). Dependist theorists like S. Britton (1989) point out that the tourism industry is part of the set of unbalanced linkages between developed and developing countries, the core and the periphery. The economic organization and associated political institutions of developing countries can be identified as a distinct type of social formation—that of a peripheral capitalist economy, to use Britton's words. This scenario applies where a capitalist sector, consisting of monopolistic firms, is deeply integrated in an economy and linked to a variety of noncapitalist ("traditional") subsistence sectors. The resulting linkages between the two sectors are primarily a response to the needs and pace of expansion of the capitalist sector: peripheral capitalist economies are characterized and defined by a combination of capitalist and noncapitalist forms of production under the domination of the former. As governments in the periphery are dependent on the dominant sectors for the economic development of the state (and their own political legitimacy), the operation and expansion of these capitalist interests are given free reign. The allocation of financial aid, the provision of infrastructure, the orientation of administrative services and the passing of licensing, labor and marketing regulations all proceed in accordance with the requirements of the dominant sectors.

Because foreign companies are most important in defining what constitutes a tourist product, tourist services in a peripheral destination are likely to be owned and provided by these firms. The role that small-scale entrepreneurs are assigned in this dependist scenario is rather limited as "external" forces largely determine their success and failure. Local small-scale enterprises are involved in tourism only in marginal ways. S. Britton (1989) defines three market niches for small-scale tourism businesses in the shadow of large firms: (1) They may provide services which lie outside the commercial interests of dominant sector firms. Options here would include handicraft production and petty transport services. (2) They may attempt to provide services similar to those offered by dominant sector firms. But because of their smaller scale, limited access to key inputs, and entrepreneurial inexperience, only services of poor quality, limited appeal, and low cost are provided, like budget accommodation, localized tours, village-organized tourist attractions, and the retailing of cheap souvenirs. (3) They may provide services that complement tourist services and attractions controlled by the dominant sector and other enterprises, like shopping guides or retailing duty-free consumer goods supplied by large wholesaling and importing companies.

The nature of the international tourism industry and the marginal niche that local businesses are filling seem to support the idea of small-scale entrepreneurs acting in a "traditionalist" way and representing the underdeveloped and stagnant part of society. Developmental organizations strongly reflect this image. Tourism was and still is largely rejected as a development strategy as it is regarded as a neocolonial instrument enforcing inequality and exploitation through the international tourism industry (Van der Duim, 1997). And as far as tourism projects were initiated at all, they were NGO led and oriented towards community development or nature conservation. Strategies and practices of small entrepreneurs were and still are considered detrimental to these goals. This image of small entrepreneurs reflects the impasse in development studies. Although the effectiveness of programs to improve the economic and social position of the poor have become a subject for debate, the liberal market model is not regarded as a solution either (Schuurman, 1993). Despite the neglect by developmental practice and theory, small-scale entrepreneurial classes have shown a remarkable growth throughout the world (Upadhya & Rutten, 1997). It seems that small-scale tourism prospers in those developing countries where tourism has not yet entered the government's agenda of development, leaving entrepreneurial initiatives largely to the private sector.

The Dual Economy

The original concept of the informal sector was first used in the 1960s by Hart (1973), an anthropologist who studied rural–urban migration and employment opportunities for Ghana's growing urban work force. His work was followed by International Labor Organization (ILO) studies of different developing countries that popularized the dichotomy between the formal and the informal sector. According to the ILO findings, the informal sector is characterized by large numbers of very small-scale producers or service units that are family owned and use very simple, labor-intensive technology. Informal businesses are generally excluded from formal credit facilities. In addition, these units are not registered or regulated, their workers are paid low wages and are assumed to have little formal education. They experience high insecurity of employment. Moreover, the informal sector serves local markets and produces cheaper and/or lower quality goods than the formal sector or, alternatively, produces goods and services that the formal sector does not provide. Moreover, the informal sector is characterized by a lack of power to influence government decision-making processes, due to the fact that this part of the economy functions largely outside government control, lacking the proper licenses and operating in places not zoned for such use (Van Diermen, 1997).

As empirical evidence has shown, capitalist development does not absorb the traditional economy, but both economies simply exist side-by-side in a dual system (Drakakis-Smith, 1987; Gilbert & Gugler, 1992; Van Diermen, 1997). The idea of dualism gave rise to a dichotomical way of thinking in terms of modern versus traditional modes of production, formal versus informal sectors, the "firm type" economy versus the *pasar* or bazaar economy (Geertz, 1963), the capitalist versus the "second," "black," "hidden," "shadow," "underground," or "clandestine" market, the activities of which are concealed from the state and withdrawn from government regulations for a variety of reasons (Clapham, 1985; Evers, 1981, 1991; Hart, 1993). The entire field covered by the informal economy is associated with things illegal, preindustrial, "traditional" (Evers, 1991), or "involute" as described by Geertz (1963). Paramount to this is the definition of the informal sector as the unorganized, underdeveloped, and stagnant part of economy and society. As Evers and Mehmet (1994) have pointed out, this view is still widely and erroneously held despite a number of studies that have tried to challenge it. Moreover, the informal sector demonstrates the weakness of the "formal" economy that seems to be unable to absorb the majority of the workforce. As a consequence, informal sector workers have been regarded as unemployed, contributing little to national income, while adding to health, fire, and political hazards (Timothy & Wall, 1997). Governments have often taken a negative position towards the informal sector and measures have been designed to eliminate informal activities (Dahles, 1998b). However, informal does not refer to a self-contained market that escapes capitalist modes of production and reproduction. Rather, it is linked to the rest of the capitalist economy. Instead of seeing the informal sector as a hindrance to economic expansion, some governments in developing countries have started to regard this sector as very productive, offering employment opportunities to the poor and less educated with little state intervention (Drakakis-Smith, 1987; Hart, 1993).

The tourism-related sector is particularly illustrative of the manifold economic relationships that encompass formal as well as informal modes of employment. As tourism is seasonal and changeable due to volatile consumer preferences, it may involve incidental windfalls, but the individual entrepreneur may go without income for days or even weeks during the low season. However, the informal sector cannot be exclusively associated with poverty because many tourism-related activities provide higher incomes than the lower paid formal jobs. Making a living in the tourism sector may demand long working hours, unpaid labor by household members, accumulated experience on the job rather than formal training, access to restricted working areas as well as unprotected labor and competitive markets, reliance on personal networks and patronage, and the flexibility to switch between activities responding to changing demands in the market. Owing to all kinds of interlinkages between formal and informal sectors, it is difficult to identify what and who constitute the informal economy, as such. A broad range of jobs is found both in the formal and informal sectors; and many jobs and businesses exhibit characteristics of the formal as well as informal economy. It is often the lack of an official license, and not its organization or function, that classifies the activity. Household incomes may come from varied sources, as their individual members work in different sectors and change their working patterns many times during their lifetime or even on a monthly or daily basis. Their labor may not be protected by unions or the state, but often they establish protective organizations themselves that are tolerated by the authorities, or become accepted representatives of informal occupational groups. For these reasons it may be more appropriate to present local economy as a continuum with a formal and an informal end, whereas most business activities are characterized by a combination of formal and informal traits, depending on the specific context and the business under examination. Although informal tourism-related activities offer a substantial income to part of the population in developing countries, it remains unclear whether the people involved constitute a marginal layer in the social fabric of emerging as well as more established tourism areas or whether they form a creative and innovative force that rightly deserves to be called entrepreneurial.

Small Entrepreneurs

Boissevain (1997) defines as one of the most striking characteristics of small entrepreneurs that they form a very heterogeneous category with a wide range of incomes and performances, and large differences in lifestyles. Despite these differences there are characteristics that are broadly shared by small entrepreneurs as a category. An important feature is the value small entrepreneurs attach to (the feeling of) independence and freedom, of being able to build and implement one's own ideas. The disadvantages of this position are hard work, long hours, often a modest standard of living, and—particularly in developing countries—great vulnerability and lack of alternatives. The ethos of independence and freedom favors a laissez-faire economic policy and a deep distrust towards government authorities that are associated with interfering regulations and, above all, taxation. The overwhelming majority of small enterprises being family-run businesses, the role of gender is a vital one. As Boissevain (1997) points out, the public arena, in general, and the business arena, in particular, is dominated by men, the domestic by women. There is some evidence, however, that in tourism enterprises women often play a leading—not merely a supporting—role. This is especially the case in hotel-keeping and catering as extensions of domestic activities. In the developing world the most important determinant of success or failure in business is the skill and initiative of the individual entrepreneur.

An important question is how small entrepreneurs, lacking the knowledge and capabilities to understand and anticipate trends, can operate successfully in a tourism industry that is dominated by transnational corporations. The answer is provided by the interlinkages that exist between small-scale and large-scale enterprises and among small-scale enterprises with access to identical as well as diverging resources. Exploring the interlinkages between firms of different scales, Go (1997) pleads for a market model in which the transnational enterprises cooperate with the small ones. Many of the small enterprises, both manufacturing and service oriented, are linked to larger companies through subcontracting relations. "Such complex networks of interlinked firms typify the 'postmodern' pattern of industrial organization known as flexible accumulation," as Upadhya and Rutten (1997, p. 21) have pointed out. This shift in industrial organization has given rise to new opportunities of independent entrepreneurship by those who have small amounts of capital to invest and who, under a Fordist production regime, would likely have been employees. It is these interlinkages that Go (1997) outlines as an opportunity for small tourism-related enterprises. Linkages between resorts and the local community can, for instance, be found in the area of labor or agriculture. A case study of a beach resort in Lombok working closely with local food producers offers an example of a large tourism development attempting to increase the linkages with local farmers and fishermen for their mutual benefit (Telfer & Wall, 1996). But these linkages are rather exceptional and, generally, star-rated hotels are only marginally integrated in the overall regional economic development. Moreover, as the Lombok case showed, the projects required constant supervision and a large commitment from the resort management whose primary business is running a hotel, not coaching local entrepreneurs.

However, the development of subcontracting relations among firms is not restricted to a regime of flexible accumulation led by large multinationals. Small businessmen in different settings tend to develop various kinds of linkages not only with larger firms but also among themselves. Interfirm horizontal linkages benefit these small businesses in a multitude of ways. The minimization of distance, specialization of functions, large-scale purchasing of supplies, services and labor, and spatial concentration that allows a quick response to changes in consumer demand are among the noted advantages (Van Diermen, 1997). The creation of complex networking relations among entrepreneurs appears to be the central strategy in the development and operation of small enterprises. Networks are used to develop not only business contacts but also to raise social standing and enhance political influence, which in turn contribute to economic success. Networks—a source of "social capital"—are essential not only for successful business dealings and the enhancement of prestige, but also as insurance against an uncertain future.

Finally, there are strategic interlinkages between small entrepreneurs exploiting diverging but at the same time complementary resources. Following Boissevain (1974), we have to distinguish between two distinct types of resources that are used strategically in this competition: first-order and second-order resources. The first order includes resources such as land, equipment, jobs, funds, and specialized knowledge that the entrepreneur controls directly. The second order consists of strategic contacts with other people who control first-order resources directly or who have access to people who do. Entrepreneurs who primarily control first-order resources are denoted as *patrons*; those who control predominantly second-order resources are known as *brokers*. Patrons manipulate the private ownership of means of production for economic profit. Brokers act as intermediaries, they put people in touch with each other directly or indirectly for profit, they bridge gaps in communication between people. Entrepreneurs can become brokers if they occupy a central position that offers them a strategic advantage in information management. A broker's capital consists of his personal network of relations with people, his communication channels, his role relations, which are governed by notions of reciprocity and transaction. Brokers are network specialists. The value that the broker derives from the transaction can consist of services, information, status, good will, even psychological satisfaction. The broker's capital consists of his actual communication channels, his credit of what others think his capital to be; he is dealing in expectations and possible future services.

Strategic contacts as well as temporal and spatial flexibility to maintain and expand these contacts are essential conditions for brokers to operate successfully. Depending on the specific local context, this applies especially to taxi and bus drivers, pedicab men, lottery sellers, street and beach vendors, informal guides, and touts. They are the most flexible and mobile people moving around freely in a tourist area. They can usually dispose of a large network and up-to-date information. Most people who are employed in tourism-related enterprises are more limited in their freedom because of a permanent or part-time job tying them down at set times, but nevertheless offering them free access to tourists and connections in the local tourism industry. Often, the employees of small accommodations and travel agencies (drivers, bellboys, desk clerks, the cleaning personnel), waiters and bartenders, formal guides, shop assistants, and security men are able to leave their jobs during working hours to attend to other business. Moreover, employees are frequently encouraged or even summoned to take on different kinds of tasks and activities as their jobs are not performed at a professional level. This phenomenon has been referred to as the "de-skilling" of tourism-related employment (Crang, 1997). Although the de-skilling has been regarded as a major obstacle to the formalization and professionalization of the tourism sector, it also enables employees to exploit second-order resources beyond their employment (i.e., activities that offer additional sources of income).

Small entrepreneurs, getting involved in tourism because they control first-order resources, seem more likely to function as a significant actor in community-based tourism. Due to the fact that their business is based on some form of ownership, they are closer to the formal than the informal end of the local economy. They may pay their taxes, though they may be supposed to pay more according to the size and profit of their business; they may dispose of the required licenses, though some may have expired years ago; they may employ personnel, but the bulk of work may still be cleared by unpaid household members or underpaid family members; the owners may have gone through formal training, but not in the appropriate schools and programs; they may keep some records of their costs, income, and profit, but may do so irregularly; they may expand their business, but only with marginal additions and never change their basic product; and they still may largely rely on personal networks.

Small and micro establishments find it hard to attract individual tourists and, because of the fragmentation of the industry, they are in a weak bargaining position vis-à-vis the large tour operators, the more so as they are operating under the fluctuating conditions of an unpredictable tourism market. This has led to suggestions that small and micro enterprises should get together and market their products jointly (De Kadt, 1995). By establishing cooperative networks and banding together, small firms could afford the consultancy services that are beyond their reach as individuals; they could also market their products jointly, blending sectoral cooperation with enterprise competition. Networks and systems have become the fundamental survival route of small tourism firms because of the benefits they offer in terms of cost advantages, marketing, information access, and, ultimately, flexibility (De Kadt, 1995). Among small owners of accommodations, restaurants, and travel agencies informal self-help organizations do emerge, but they do not yet represent a vigorous force. Independent patrons seem to fear the loss of their autonomy if they get involved in any organization, including private local initiatives.

However, there is—informal—cooperation among these entrepreneurs in order to enhance their profit. There are occasional examples of small enterprises cooperating with multinational firms: for example, local food producers selling their product directly to big hotels (Telfer & Wall, 1996), local pedicab men organizing themselves to protect their working areas from outside competition (Chapter 7), local guesthouses establishing a pricing system to prevent underpricing by competitors (Chapter 4), the emergence of an association for local mountain guides in Senaru, Lombok (Chapter 8). Accommodation owners help other compatible businesses in a particular area to market their products. They distribute flyers containing information about excursions and trips organized by local travel agencies or the menus of local restaurants. Sometimes they offer brochures of other homestays or *losmen* in what will most probably be the next destination of their guests. There are notice boards with the business cards of local masseurs, beauty salons, transport services, and souvenir shops. Many accommodations are visited daily by the owner's family or friends from a compatible business to check on new guests and offer their products (Dahles, 1998b).

The establishment of elaborate networks of cooperation can be regarded as a risk-avoiding strategy of which small entrepreneurs have developed a number, as has been shown by Evers (1981), Evers and Mehmet (1994), and J. Alexander (1987). Following Evers and Mehmet, risk is defined here as the "unintended consequences of rational action" (p. 1). Applied to the small-scale economic sector, risk is the probability for small businessmen to achieve a sustainable level of income (i.e., emerging as successful entrepreneurs, making profits on a permanent basis, and eventually formalizing their enterprise). When such a level of sustainability is reached, the economic activities of the small entrepreneur are characterized by a reduction of risk. In this case, sustainability comes within reach not only for the entrepreneur but also for his or her community, hence the claim made by many scholars that local ownership of tourism enterprises will result in benefits for the local community as a whole. However, if entrepreneurial activity is unsuccessful, the business will be destroyed. To enhance the chances of staying in business, small entrepreneurs are inclined towards risk avoidance strategies. Among these strategies are: working long hours, diversifying their operations, seeking supplementary income, producing or trading in small quantities, imitating the product and services of others, assuming many business costs themselves, sharing profits among family members instead of reinvesting them, and being reluctant to grow. But the basic risk-reducing strategy that is found in a large variety of (tourism) enterprises is imitation. Once a product or service, an accommodation form or menu, a tour program, or even a mode of addressing tourists turns out to be successful, others try to copy the formula. Often one finds that former employees of a business or family members open a similar business right next door. The ever-present threat of generating their own competition is one of the reasons why patrons are reluctant to organize themselves and/or innovate their product. As a consequence, small enterprises often yield only a marginal profit and show a lack of innovation, which reduces their chance of reaching sustainability for the business. From this perspective, we have to question the proposition that small-scale entrepreneurship can be the major contributor to sustainable community development.

Although economic considerations are the basis for much of the cooperative efforts, personal networks, family obligations, and friendship are necessary for mutual support. This is where local brokers are integrated into the local tourism industry. At first sight, these locals who get involved in tourism by means of second-order resources seem to have a weak position. As one of their main resources, the tourist, is accessible only for a limited span of time, many brokers are pressed to benefit as much and as quickly as possible from the tourists. They are perpetually looking for a chance to make a smaller or larger killing, not able to build up a stable clientele or a steadily growing business. If large-scale tourism development implies the formalization of the tourism industry, these local brokers will be pushed further into marginality. However, within the local tourism business, the role of some individuals can become rather prominent, provided they possess considerable amounts of flexibility in terms of time, space, and social contacts among local owners and other brokers. Local patrons suffer from the same fluctuating customer–provider relationships as brokers do, as tourism flows are irregular and unpredictable. Whereas most patrons have only limited opportunities to control these flows, brokers are in the middle of the action. They have free access to tourists, they are informed about where and when tourists arrive, where and how long they stay, where they will go next, their activity patterns, their expectations and needs, and their spending power (Dahles, 1998a). Moreover, they are familiar with the local market and the opportunities to match demand with supply in a way that enables them to make a profit. That is why local businesses often rely on brokers to provide them with tourists. Taxi and bus drivers, touts, and informal guides are paid a commission to redirect the tourist flows to small accommodations and restaurants in back alleys; bellboys, waiters, and shop assistants are instructed to pick tourists from the street and direct them to a restaurant or souvenir shop.

Small entrepreneurs—patrons and brokers—form an integral part of the tourism industry and are becoming more and more important to governments in search for new forms of tourism to develop a product that is competitive in the global market. Small-scale entrepreneurs are neither representatives of a traditional, informal, "involute" economy, nor do they fit definitions of the completely modern, formal, capitalist sector. They participate in both economies. Depending on the kind of resources, some (the patrons who rely predominantly on private property) operate more in the formal sector, others (the brokers who rely predominantly on personal networks) participate more in the informal sector. The relations between the formal and informal spheres are complex. Patrons depend on brokers for the advertising and marketing of their accommodation, restaurant, or shop. Brokers, in turn, depend on patrons for their commission and access to tourists. Patronage and brokerage actually constitute a safety belt that allows small entrepreneurs to operate in a rather flexible manner. Both patrons and brokers depend heavily on networks based on personal friendships, business transactions, family relations, marriage, ethnic, and religious bonds. These networks often constitute more meaningful units than formal organizations and state-controlled associations.

The most effective forms of cooperation are those that meet the need for income security, insurance and protection, marketing, advertising, and information. However, this does not mean that petty entrepreneurs are innovative and risk taking. They are enterprising and inventive in the exploitation of new market niches and means of orientation, but they are less so in the product they offer. Once a product or formula has proven successful, everyone is willing to share in the success. Petty entrepreneurs fail to establish themselves in the tourism industry in a way that enables them to make a sustainable profit. Although they do not react passively to external forces, they are not independent and self-sufficient actors either. They act within certain parameters defined by the entrepreneurial culture they depend on. Risk-reducing and risk-avoiding strategies may be an integral part of this culture.

The hustle and bustle of petty enterprises that is dominating life in many tourist areas in developing countries is not necessarily an indicator of a vibrant economy. In these areas the competition among small entrepreneurs is frequently tough, causing irritation among tourists and leaving the competitors with less and less income. Tourism development cannot rely exclusively on free-market principles, but has to be supported and to a certain extent controlled by the state. If provisions are not made to increase local economic participation, this greatly increases the likelihood of the domination of the tourism sector by transnational capital from the metropolitan core. Processes of increased formalization that run parallel with the transnationalization in the tourism sector destroy the opportunities of petty entrepreneurs. Instead of focusing on regulatory measures, governments need to facilitate tourism development by making available public goods like credit facilities, education, and information, necessary for entrepreneurs to generate a tourism product and to set out rules and legal measures without stifling the entrepreneurial initiatives. Only then can innovative and risk-taking behavior be expected in the petty tourism sector that will result in more sustainable developments.

Theoretical Framework

Most studies of entrepreneurs define social networks to be central to our understanding of their functioning. As Upadhya and Rutten (1997) argue: "If networks are viewed in a broader sense as a kind of 'social capital,' then their ubiquity among business entrepreneurs can be better understood. The creation of social capital is essential not only for the successful business dealings and the enhancement of prestige, but also as insurance against an uncertain future" (p. 25). The significance of social capital in the strategies of small entrepreneurs underlines that "entrepreneurs are not merely economic agents but most of all social actors" (p. 30). Small entrepreneurs are not driven solely by the profit motive; goals such as desire for prestige, and constraints such as obligations toward kin, also determine their actions. The economic transactions of small entrepreneurs are also "social transactions, in the sense that they are usually embedded in social relations and not just determined by impersonal market forces" (p. 33).

To acknowledge and adequately explain this phenomenon, we need to focus on the interrelationships between the interests, motivations, and desires of individual actors and the wider context wherein access to power and resources is allocated (Schuurman, 1993). Or, according to Upadhya and Rutten (1997), we need to position entrepreneurial culture within the context of structural power relations. What is needed, then, is a theoretical framework that integrates the analysis of political and economic structures and an understanding of cultural context with a concept of human agency. Such a model should enable individual action (the innovating risk-taking entrepreneur) to be related to the macroeconomic processes that constitute development. Implications for the analysis of small-scale enterprise in the context of capitalist relations are to approach entrepreneurs as reasoning actors and not just as reactors, to understand the social meanings embodied in the different moments of production, exchange, and consumption, and to conceive their activities as strategic action (Verschoor, 1992).

From an economic perspective, one looks at the activities of individual entrepreneurs as actors within an economic system and at their contributions to the economy in terms of innovation and organization. From a sociological perspective, entrepreneurs are regarded as collectively constituting a "business community"; the focus is on their development, social organization, and entrepreneurial or "class" culture (Upadhya, 1997). "Much of entrepreneurship theory in sociology continues to subscribe to some sort of modernization model, ignoring the fact that political, economic and cultural studies of development have gone much beyond that paradigm in their understanding of the interaction of local cultural and economic formations with the expanding world capitalist economy" (Upadhya & Rutten, 1997, p. 48). As a consequence, we need to examine economic as well as cultural factors in explaining this development. An appropriate tool to analyze the interlinkage of economy and culture is offered by the concept of network analysis as developed by the school of transactionalism that puts the actor center stage. It started out from the idea that individuals are rational, strategizing actors instead of just bearers of social norms and values. To emphasize how actors strategically manipulate social relations to attain their goals, its proponents focused on temporary social configurations such as coalitions, cliques, and factions (Boissevain, 1974). Through the work of Bourdieu (1977), the relevance of social networks received a new impetus. Bourdieu's theory focuses on the concepts of capital, strategy, and "habitus." According to Bourdieu the accumulation of capital constitutes the main structuring principle of society, but contrary to common usage he does not restrict the term capital to the economic (i.e., the exchange of commodities). In addition to economic capital, he refers to other forms of capital (i.e., social, cultural, and symbolic capital). In Bourdieu's work cultural capital is constituted by the whole of (formal) education and upbringing. Symbolic capital refers to a person's social status and the prestige that accompanies this status. Both economic and cultural capital can function as symbolic capital, as they may imply prestige. Social capital refers to the resources people are able to mobilize through their networks of social relations; social capital always acts as symbolic capital. The accumulation of economic, social, cultural, and symbolic capital involves struggle. The goals pursued and the strategies applied depend on the available capital and on the entrepreneur's habitus.

According to Bourdieu, habitus refers to views and preferences held by individuals, which are molded within specific contexts of nationality, ethnicity, gender, age, and class.

As Gorter (1997) argues, Bourdieu's theory may offer the appropriate theoretical underpinnings to network analysis. By linking strategy to both the available forms of capital and a specific habitus he places the study of social networks in a political-economic tradition. Following this argument, the concept of social capital seems to be especially useful when analyzing economic and political relations among entrepreneurs on the one hand and between (small-scale) entrepreneurs and the state on the other hand. The presence of large numbers of small-scale businesses leads to the formation of dense social networks. Such relations reduce the dependence of small firms on larger ones and increase their possibilities for independent access to markets and supplies of raw materials. But apart from such business relations, entrepreneurs socialize in their neighborhoods and have a voice in local politics. On the basis of this interaction social figurations emerge that are characterized by similarities in economic position as well as similarities in outlook and lifestyle. Depending on the role of the state and the availability of other forms of capital, in particular "cultural" capital, a formalization of such figurations may emerge. "Formal organizations rise which represent the interests of the entrepreneurs vis-à-vis the state. Membership in and control over such bodies represent important assets as far as social capital is concerned. It offers not only economic benefits in terms of privileged access to the bureaucracy and the possibility of influencing state policies, but also a means of upward social mobility" (Gorter, 1997, p. 87). As small entrepreneurs do not constitute a homogeneous group with similar economic positions, social backgrounds, training, outlook, and so forth, the accumulation of social capital implies social struggle. As a heterogeneous category, they continuously compete for enhancing their access to different forms of capital.

About This Book

This book deals with different local entrepreneurs operating "under the tourist gaze" (Urry, 1990) in Indonesia's state bureaucracy that advocates tourism as part of its modernization strategy. The national tourism policy in Indonesia prioritizes the large-scale economic sector, in particular resort development, the star-rated hotel sector, and so-called "quality" tourism. Small-scale tourism business operating both in the formal and informal sectors are not subject to national government policy. Instead, these businesses range under local and provincial governments, which are less well equipped in terms of power and money to make provisions for these tourism enterprises. Moreover, as local governments are supposed to reach goals set by the central state in terms of economic growth, local policies easily favor the large-scale sector and foreign investors over small-scale economic activities. The national policy of deregulation in the large-scale sector is countered by more and stricter regulations in the small-scale sector. All the chapters in this book investigate a specific category of tourism-related small-scale entrepreneurs in a particular local setting against the background of the antiparticipatory national policies.

Projections of future tourism growth—the number of international tourists is supposed to double and the revenues from international tourism are expected to triple during the next few years (Parapak, 1995)—force the government to enhance and diversify Indonesia's tourism product. The sixth Five-Year Plan provides for the development of new tourism destination areas, especially in the eastern part of the country, in Nusa Tenggara Barat and Sulawesi. Promotional campaigns like *Beyond Bali* support this policy. Older and more established tourism areas (i.e., Bali and Java) have to be self-supporting and cannot count on special favors from the Jakarta government. As a consequence, there are basically three types of tourism destination areas in Indonesia. First, the old established ones that are performing well in the global tourism market and will most probably continue to do so in the future. Bali is a perfect example. Second, the older ones that suffer under the changed tourism policy as more substantial investments are badly needed to save them from stagnation and decline. Symptomatic for these areas are a declining growth rate, stagnating length of stay, low occupancy rates, and an increasing crime rate and violence against tourists. Yogyakarta is illustrative for this category. Third, the newly established areas, like Lombok, where tourism is booming, in particular in terms of resort development and large-scale foreign investments.

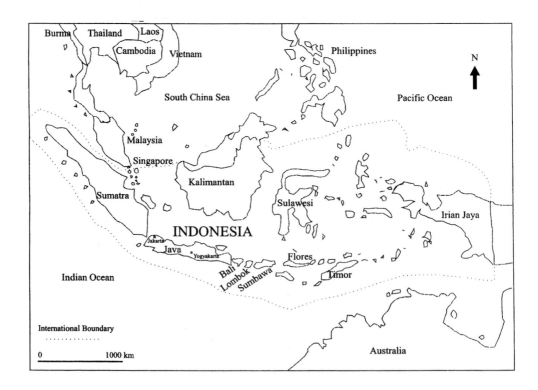

Figure 1.1. Location map of Indonesia.

The chapters in this book cover these three stages of tourism development by investigating forms of local entrepreneurship in tourism in either Bali, Yogyakarta, or Lombok (Figure 1.1).

The chapters are based on anthropological fieldwork. The authors lived in villages and neighborhoods in Bali, Yogyakarta, or Lombok that can be classified as popular tourist areas. They stayed in small-scale accommodations, traveled by pedicab, and hired local guides. Through the choice of these field sites the authors were able to observe and participate in tourist practice. Field data were obtained through informal and structured interviews with different actors in the local tourism industry and by recording life histories of a number of local key informants. Where relevant, the authors participated in a number of local tourist events and excursions. These excursions and events, like taking up temporary residence in local accommodations, formed the arena for the examination of the interaction between the local population and tourists. Although four of the seven research projects did not focus on tourist behavior, the authors considered it of importance to observe the local actors "on the job," giving information about the attractions, telling tales, and interacting with tourists. For Chapters 6 and 8 a survey was done among tourists. The data obtained were analyzed with SPSS (Statistical Package for the Social Sciences). The information generated by participant observation was supplemented by interviews with government representatives, respondents working in the tourism industry and in tourism education, and other experts in the field of tourism in Bali, Yogyakarta, and on the island of Lombok. Additionally, secondary data, statistics and case studies, were obtained from government agencies, educational institutions, and consultancies.

Chapter 2 discusses the characteristics of Indonesian government policy towards the development of tourism in general and small-scale tourism in particular. The priority given to tourism in the national development policy generated a rapid growth in tourist arrivals and earnings from tourism that have become a major source of foreign exchange for the Indonesian economy. This sector has benefited from the government policy of deregulation. The lower echelons of Indonesian economy, however, do not benefit from these measures. Instead, the government counters the deregulatory measures at the top with more regulation and control below. As a consequence, small-scale enterprises have to operate under harsher conditions, either conforming to increasing government regulations or facing destruction.

Chapter 3 deals with the impact of tourism and tourism policy on the employment opportunities of women in the informal sector in Sanur, Bali. Whereas all small entrepreneurs are subject to the government regulations that are aimed at the upgrading of tourist destinations, the effects of these regulations differ along gender lines. To demonstrate under which conditions women either benefit or suffer from government interventions in tourism development, this chapter investigates the way in which women entrepreneurs operate and make a living from tourism. In Sanur the government regulations did not destroy the opportunities for lower class women to profit from tourism. Some women benefit from these changes by finding their activities to be "upgraded" and "formalized." Although these activities are submitted to many restrictions, the government measures still leave enough room for the women to exploit new niches in the tourism market.

The Indonesian government has enforced regulations to restrict the uninhibited growth of the small-scale accommodation sector. A classification system for budget accommodations was introduced and owners were obliged to register their enterprise with the local government. Chapter 4 shows that this system has failed in Bali, where owners and managers circumvent the rules, government action being inconsistent. Within the small-scale accommodation sector in Bali broad differences occur. The differences are not related to government intervention but to locally constructed images, as a comparison between the budget accommodations in Kuta (beach tourism) and Ubud (cultural tourism) illustrates. Although the development of the budget accommodation sector in Ubud is as unplanned and uncontrolled as in Kuta, locally initiated measures to maintain the small-scale and "local" character of the village affect the construction and management of the accommodations.

Chapter 5 analyzes the tourism development on Gili Trawangan, a small island located at the northwest coast of Lombok. This case study provides a better understanding of the ways in which the local population tries to improve their living conditions and raise their standard of living through operating private, small-scale enterprises. Their success in tourism did not remain unnoticed. Growing competition, from outside investors and the new elite from the West Nusa Tenggara region, and upgrading activities put the existing tourism entrepreneurship under pressure and shows which different interests are at stake.

Yogyakarta is capitalizing on the image of a relaxed city offering its visitors a glimpse of the real Javanese life. How this strategy is implemented locally is discussed in Chapter 6, focusing on the numerous small-scale accommodations that seem to sustain the image of the city as a village community. Many local people make a living from running such an accommodation, especially in the busy tourist areas of Sosrowijayan and Prawirotaman. In contrast to the star-rated hotels, the small-scale accommodation sector that caters predominantly to budget travelers is not supported by the government. More efforts are put into the development of large-scale tourism. These efforts will inevitably lead to the destruction of the old neighborhoods and affect detrimentally the small-scale accommodations. So far attempts among the small owners to organize themselves have not been very successful.

Chapter 7 examines the impact of tourism on the daily life of pedicab men in Yogyakarta. As tourism has expanded rapidly since the 1980s, pedicab men who have traditionally been entrepreneurs in local transport increasingly have been involved in the transport and entertainment of tourists. In tourist areas tourist transport forms an important source of income for pedicab men. However, these men remain passive beneficiaries from tourism; they do not have any influence on local tourism development. They are at the mercy of shop owners, pedicab-owning companies, and the local police, and they are threatened to be expelled from the inner city by a governmental policy to "revitalize" Yogyakarta for tourism. Recently pedicab men in most of the tourist areas have established their own organizations to protect their position against intruders and to assure themselves of the scarce but lucrative opportunities tourism provides.

Tourism on Mount Rinjani, one of the highest volcanoes in Indonesia, is developing rapidly. Every year more tourists find their way to the village Senaru, one of the starting points of the climb. Chapter 8 focuses on the local tourist guides and porters from Senaru who accompany the tourists to the rim or to the top of the volcano. Although 10 years ago anyone who could speak a foreign language could become a tourist guide, nowadays guiding is developing into a profession with specific standards and requirements. Despite the Senaru guiding program organized by a local NGO, the local guides are often expelled from participating in trekkings as their professional standards are not found sufficient by Lombok tour operators. Their knowledge of the Rinjani area, however, would make them valuable intermediaries in this unique, but also vulnerable, area. In this chapter the activities and strategies of the Senaru guides and porters will be examined against the background of the government guiding regulations.

Chapter 9 addresses the extent to which the ever-present opportunity to enter into a sexual relationship with Western female tourists poses a challenge to the vast number of self-employed young men in Indonesian tourist destination areas. The areas that are compared in this chapter—a beach resort in Lombok and the downtown area of the city of Yogyakarta—differ in terms of Butler's resort area cycle. Whereas Yogyakarta is about to enter the consolidation phase, Lombok has only started to develop tourism. The position in the area life cycle affects the opportunities and restrictions that self-employed young males encounter in their participation in small-scale economic activities and, as a consequence, in their relationships with female tourists. In both areas, romancing the tourist is basically one of the manifold economic activities of young males that have to be understood in terms of small-scale entrepreneurship. However, in Yogyakarta, where tourism growth is declining, the future perspectives of self-employed males are gloomy and their aim is to use the tourist to get access to a better life in a foreign country. On Lombok there are still plenty of opportunities for petty entrepreneurs, and a relationship with a Western woman is regarded as a capital investment that can lead to a successful business career at home.

Chapter 2

Small Businesses in the Indonesian Tourism Industry: Entrepreneurship or Employment?

Heidi Dahles

Introduction

A major development in the Indonesian economy since the 1980s has been the expansion of non-oil sectors and especially the tourist industry. This sector has benefited from the government policy of deregulation (i.e., measures intended to facilitate private sector activities), particularly in the export sector (Booth, 1990). Examples of deregulatory measures are tax incentives for big companies, cutting tariffs, simplifying export procedures, eliminating permits, and introducing tax holidays for newly established companies. Measures designed specifically to benefit the foreign tourist sector have included the partial abolition of visa requirements, the granting of additional landing rights to foreign airlines in the major ports of entry, the establishment of more international airports, the reduction in the number of licenses required to build new hotels, and the definition of new tourist destination areas outside the islands of Java and Bali (Booth, 1990). The high priority given to tourism in the national development policy generated a rapid growth in tourist arrivals and in earnings from tourism, which have become a major source of foreign exchange for the Indonesian economy.

The lower echelons of Indonesian economy, however, have not benefited from the measures to facilitate this growth in tourism. The government, in fact, meets the deregulatory measures at the top with more regulation and control below. The Indonesian government does not regard small entrepreneurs as a force in Indonesian economic development in general, nor in tourism development in particular. Instead they are seen as an obstacle (Clapham, 1985). Petty commodity producers retain many features of social and cultural behavior identified as tradition. Markets all over Indonesia are characterized by complex bargaining procedures among petty traders and their customers. However, it seems that the tolerance towards small-scale economic activities is declining, causing even further negative associations with the uncontrolled "informal" sector. The government strongly believes that the country's ambition to join the Asian Tiger Economies necessitates interventionist policies directed towards the domestic economy, while applying a more liberal approach towards export and trade-related sectors (Chowdhury & Islam, 1993). Deregulation at the top and regulation at the bottom are both strategies that fit the government's objective to become a major actor in Asia. As a consequence, the position of small-scale enterprises in Indonesia is changing. They have to operate under harsher conditions and conform to increasing government regulations, or face destruction. The Indonesian government has attempted to shift petty traders into multistoried buildings and formalize trading arrangements (Guinness, 1994), to demolish the squatter housing in Jakarta, and to banish pedicabs in many large cities in Java and *bemos* from Jakarta (Jellinek, 1991). Food sellers are losing their businesses because of the authorities' reluctance to issue licenses, and lottery sellers and street guides have to hide because of occasional police raids (Dahles, 1996, 1997a). The recent blows that tourism in Bali and Yogyakarta has suffered have been blamed on the informal sector, leading to harsher government measures against hawkers, pedicab men, food sellers, and street guides.

Outside the formal markets, traditional business still flourishes, and as soon as the police turn their backs, hawkers, lottery sellers, and street guides carry on with their activities. The small-scale enterprises are a vigorous and visible element in the tourist sector, employing a large proportion of the labor force. Manifold opportunities for informal employment are emerging within the industry. Cukier (1996) argues that "much of the employment generated by tourism is in the form of self-employed, small-scale entrepreneurs, such as street guides and vendors. The employment effects of this small-scale sector are often excluded in the assessment of employment in tourism because no accurate data are available" (p. 54). As is discussed in the previous chapter, "traditional" modes of production do not disappear because of modernization, but exist alongside the capitalist economy and often even grow and become more important in the process. The same thing happens to tourism: in developing countries, where the presence of the informal sector is well established, it continues to increase and diversify as the tourism industry develops (Cukier, 1996; Timothy & Wall, 1996).

It may be obvious that tourism is thriving and absorbing many people who would otherwise be unemployed; however, there is a difference between employment opportunities and enterprises. The latter, according to the classical economic definition, are instruments for transforming and improving the economy and society. Entrepreneurs are innovators and decision makers pursuing progressive change (Schumpeter, 1942). Following this definition, entrepreneurs can only thrive under minimal state intervention (Clapham, 1985). In Indonesia, the informal sector consists of self-employed individuals and small family enterprises operating under strong restrictions set by the government. The issue that has to be raised is to what extent the small-scale tourism enterprises actually constitute a vital, innovative force in the Indonesian tourism industry. Do these enterprises just absorb a labor force that would otherwise be unemployed, or do they allow enterprising individuals to explore new economic activities?

To understand the conditions under which people in this sector operate and how they cope with increasing government interference, we need to understand the social meanings embodied in the different aspects of production, exchange, and consumption of the tourism product. In line with the theoretical perspective, as outlined in the previous chapter, we need to analyze both the "external" factors (i.e., national economy and policies, the state, and market) and the small entrepreneurs' definition of the situation, the arenas of their actions, their routines of social interaction, social networks, and the kind of resources they control (Verschoor, 1992). Although in this book the emphasis is on the social and cultural practices of small entrepreneurs in the Indonesian tourism industry and their strategic use of "capital" in the Bourdieuan sense, in this chapter the discussion will revolve around the political and economic conditions that restrict as well as benefit small entrepreneurs. To analyze the processes by which small entrepreneurs manage their everyday social worlds and the ways in which they cope with increasing government regulations, this chapter deals with two clusters of interrelated questions:

- What is the Indonesian government's policy towards tourism in general, and small-scale tourism in particular? What opportunities and threats radiate from government policy towards small-scale entrepreneurs in the tourism sector?

- What are the characteristics of small-scale entrepreneurs in the Indonesian economy in general and in the tourism sector in particular? What are their modes of operation? What resources do they control? To what extent and in which ways do they cooperate with other entrepreneurs in this sector, both small and large? How do small-scale entrepreneurs deal with government regulations that either benefit or stifle their activities?

Tourism Development and Government Policy in Indonesia

International tourist arrivals in Indonesia have shown a considerable growth from the 1980s onwards. The number of foreign visitors has increased more than 200% between 1988 and 1995, and the income from foreign tourism has more than doubled between

Table 2.1. Number of Foreign Visitors and Revenues

Year	Number of Visitors	Revenues (in US$)
1988	1,254,000	1.0 billion
1989	1,569,000	1.3 billion
1990	2,734,000	2.1 billion
1991	2,964,000	2.5 billion
1992	3,205,000	3.3 billion
1993	3,455,000	4.0 billion
1994	3,731,000	4.8 billion
1995	4,030,000	5.2 billion

Source: BPS (1995, 1996a).

1990 and 1994 (Table 2.1).The government estimates that in the year 2000 about 6.5 million foreign tourists will visit Indonesia, yielding US$9 billion of foreign exchange earnings. Growth scenarios for the next 10 years anticipate visitor arrivals to double and income from foreign tourism to triple (Parapak, 1995).At first sight, then, the politics and policies of the central government were quite successful in generating a rapid growth in and earnings from tourism, which has become a major source of foreign exchange for the Indonesian economy.

However, as Gunawan (1997) argues, Indonesia has not been able to attract a substantial proportion of the international tourism market.The number of tourist arrivals— comprising less than 1% of the world total—is small, considering the size of the country. But Indonesia has experienced the highest growth rate in the Southeast Asian region and, as a result of the shifting market composition, enjoys the longest length of stay. Moreover, the size of the Indonesian population, which is close to 200 million, constitutes a huge potential domestic market.The actual growth potential of both the international and domestic market is insecure, as the economic crisis in 1998 demonstrates.

In Indonesia, tourism, like the other economic sectors, is regulated by Five-Year Development Plans (*Rencana Pengembangan Lima Tahun, Repelita*).Although tourism in Indonesia dates back to the colonial period, tourism planning only started after the period of political and economic instability in the early 1970s under the first Five-Year Plan (*Repelita* I, 1969/70–1973/74). Few destination areas emerged spontaneously. In most cases, tourism development followed strict regulations from "above." In the early 1970s the government mapped out a national strategy to counteract unregulated and uncontrolled growth.This strategy was established in collaboration with international agencies such as United Nations Development Program (UNDP), World Tourist Organization (WTO), and ILO, and the Indonesian Ministry of Tourism, Post, and Telecommunications (*Parpostel*). Subsequently a national master plan for tourism was developed in the 1980s (to be succeeded by a new master plan before the turn of the century). In areas where tourism already played a prominent role, provincial master plans were established to guide tourism growth (Sammeng, 1995). Ever since, Indonesia's strategic Five-Year Plans have attached increasing importance to tourism regarding national and regional development (Gunawan, 1997).As Indonesia was almost nonexistent on the international tourism map in the 1960s, receiving less than 100,000 visitors per year (Gunawan, 1997), the main objective of the first Five-Year Plan was to attract more visitors. Originally Bali was identified as the main tourist area, followed by Jakarta and Yogyakarta. In the second Five-Year Plan (1974/75–1978/79), the simplistic growth scenario became more sophisticated, as the benefits for local communities and the quality of the tourism product were specified.The third Five-Year Plan (1979/80–1983/84) marked the era of deregulation, opening Indonesia to foreign investors and visitors by facilitating access to the country (establishing new ports of entry and reducing license and visa requirements) and expanding tourism development plans to areas other than Java and Bali. Under the fourth Five-Year Plan (1984/ 85–1988/89) resort development, mostly in Bali and Java, and the worldwide promotion of Indonesia as a tourist destination were the main target.The period covered by the fifth Five-Year Plan (1989/90–1993/94) was intended as a climax in tourism development, as major events were on the agenda. Whereas the 1991 *Visit Indonesia Year* promotional campaign failed in terms of visitor arrivals (because of the Gulf War), in 1992 Indonesia joined the *Visit ASEAN Year* campaign, and after that declared the *Visit Indonesia Decade*. In terms of international tourist arrivals and revenues, these and other promotional campaigns boosted tourism in Indonesia. Building on the success of the previous period, the sixth Five-Year Plan (1994/95–1998/99) identified new destinations and edicted financial measures channeling money to and stimulating investments in the areas to be developed. These initiatives were supported by a thorough analysis of the development of tourism in different areas (Sofield, 1995) and by promotional campaigns like *Bali and Beyond, There Is More to Indonesia Than Bali*, and *Indonesia—A World of its Own* (Picard, 1993; Sammeng, 1995). These campaigns mark the emergence of regionalization processes in Indonesian tourism with the purpose of enhancing its competitiveness in the global market (Gunawan, 1997). The explicit objective of national tourism policy is the reduction of regional disparities in the quantity and quality of tourism facilities. In practice this means that financial support for tourism development and promotion will be channeled towards regions that lag behind those areas that have a well-established tourism industry. The *Beyond Bali* campaigns imply that those destinations once favored and pampered by the Five-Year Plans in the 1970s and 1980s (i.e., Bali and Yogyakarta) cannot count on government support and have to maintain their position in tourism development themselves. Although the regionalization offers promising prospects for the tourism development in Indonesia, it is yet unclear how the new destinations will be differentiated in the marketplace so that they become complementary rather than competitive (Wall, 1997).

The basic model for the provincial tourism planning has been the *Bali Tourism Provincial Master Plan* from the early 1970s. The *Bali Provincial Master Plan* emphasized the construction of integrated resorts and designated limited zones for tourism development, controlled through the state-owned Bali Tourist Development Corporation (Picard, 1993). The most celebrated result of these government efforts to boost international tourism is Nusa Dua, an isolated area in south Bali boasting the highest concentration of carefully monitored five-star luxury resorts in Indonesia. In the meantime, Bali has experienced a booming semi- and unplanned tourism development all over the island, indicating that the master plan and the Nusa Dua concept were established without consulting the provincial and local authorities. Although the Nusa Dua concept of controlled development has been deficient in many ways (Wall, 1996), it is being used by the government as a model for tourism development in other provinces. It is in resort development that the government has invested much effort through the years. In doing so, it is hoped that "quality tourism" (i.e., the "upmarket tourism customer") will be encouraged (Sammeng, 1995).

The responsibility for managing tourism is distributed over two main levels of government: the national and the provincial levels. The national government is not willing to transfer authority for programs that produce large financial benefits to provincial and local levels. This concerns the accommodation sector and associated travel agencies rated in the four- and five-star category, generating the government-targeted "quality tourism." Government agencies and offices have been established in the provinces to service the tourism industry and increase the number of tourist arrivals, particularly in the "quality" category. The revenues generated by the four- and five-star category hotels, that add a 21% service and government tax to their bills, flow directly to Jakarta. The star-rated tour and travel agencies and the accommodation sector are organized in centralized associations, ASITA (Association of Indonesian Tour & Travel Agencies) and the BPHN (*Badan Pusat Hotel Negara*), the national hotel association. These associations are Jakarta based with branches in those provinces that participate in tourism development. Airlines and travel agents, hotels, and tour operators based in Jakarta or overseas control much of the tourist sector. As a consequence, a large percentage of the profits from tourist traffic does not benefit the local people in the provinces. Procedures regarding land acquisition, tenure, and utilization, and the management of star-rated hotels and resorts do not fall under the authority of the provincial government (Kumorotomo, n.d.). And, as the analysis of the tourism planning process has shown, tourist flows are strictly controlled through the identification of tourism development areas by the national development plans. At the local level opportunities for tourism development are in those sectors that for a long time have been regarded "inferior" by the national government: on the one hand the domestic market, on the other hand the unorganized international tourism or backpackers tourism that is inappropriately called "low-cost" tourism and that is focusing on the non-star-rated accommodations, local facilities, and the small-scale tourism industry. This is the domain of local government regulations that will be described for the cases of Bali and Yogyakarta in the next chapters.

Critics point to large resort developments, particularly resort enclaves, as being major contributors to the negative impacts of tourism (Brohman, 1986). They are often out of scale with the indigenous landscape and ways of life, it is argued, and they consume large quantities of capital that could be more usefully applied in other ways. The involvement of outside investors is necessary because of the large capital requirements that inhibit the participation of local people. The result is that profits are channeled out of the community. Management positions often go to outsiders, for few local people have the appropriate skills. Local residents are often denied access to resources, such as beaches, which they previously used, and reap few benefits from the developments. Besides the economic costs, large-scale resorts entail environmental and social costs that can be detrimental to a country's development. In contrast, it is suggested that smaller developments are less disruptive, have more modest capital requirements that permit local participation, are associated with higher multipliers and smaller leakages, leave control in local hands, are more likely to fit in with indigenous activities and land uses, and generate greater local benefits (Brohman, 1996; Wall & Long, 1996). Central governments are not generally successful in organizing tourism in developing countries. The market is differentiated and only partly coincides with the objectives of the state-controlled tourism industry. The needs and tastes of Western visitors are different from those of Asian tourists from Japan and the Newly Industrializing Countries in Asia, not to mention the domestic markets that emerge in many developing countries with growing prosperity and political stability. Moreover, there are indications that the Western market becomes fragmented because of changing consumer tastes for highly specialized and individualized programs and accommodations that resort tourism cannot offer (Urry, 1995).Where the large-scale state-controlled sector fails, the ever-present small-scale enterprises get in, offering a vast array of consumer goods (souvenirs, food and drinks) and services (accommodation, transport, excursions, information, and guiding).This small-scale sector cross-cuts the boundaries between the formal, licensed, state-controlled market and the unlicensed, uncontrolled, partially "illegal" economic activities of local tourism industries.

The Indonesian government seems to realize that the preferences and tastes of foreign tourists are changing. Only a couple of years ago the government was reluctant to facilitate "low-cost" tourism. First, the type of visitor that is attracted by low-cost tourism is associated with drug-using hippies allegedly having a rather detrimental effect on local communities (McTaggert, 1977). Second, and perhaps most important, low-cost tourism involves local participation at a *kampung* (neighborhood) and village level, which, by most development planners in Indonesia, is viewed as "traditional." Traditional culture, however, is at best no asset to development and at worst a hindrance to it, always posing a problem to the national government because of its alleged backwardness and resistance to change (Dove, 1988).At present the national planners show a different attitude. In a meeting of international tourism experts in Yogyakarta in 1995, the Indonesian Director General of Tourism, Mappi Sammeng, recognized that tourism trends in the 1990s indicate that many travelers are seeking alternatives to large-scale, beach-oriented resort development.The government agreed to encourage small-scale projects, especially in the outer islands, to support tourism developments in still underdeveloped destination areas. Small-scale entrepreneurs, local people, and ethnic groups are supposed to play key roles in tourism development to accomplish the development objective of the recent national tourism master plan.As a strategy to unify and modernize the country, small-scale entrepreneurs are ascribed prominent positions in the promotion of tourism by the Jakarta government (Wood, 1997). In contrast to the impersonal large-scale resorts, small-scale tourism represents the *couleur locale*, the specific and distinguishing aspects of local culture (Brohman, 1996).

Small and Petty Entrepreneurs in the Indonesian Industry

By the year 2030 Indonesia is expected to have a population of 290 million, 80% of which will be in the cohort of those between 20 and 64 years old, and more than half of this population will live in urban areas (Van Diermen, 1997).The development of large-scale, export-oriented, labor-intensive firms, increasingly reliant on foreign investment, will not absorb all of the anticipated growth in the labor force within the major urban centers.Therefore, the Indonesian government is relying on the development of small-scale enterprises to create additional employment (Berry & Mazumdar, 1991). In contrast to the popular view that small-scale enterprises generally perform badly, Hill (1996) found that employment in small enterprises increased at approximately the same rate as in large- and medium-scale businesses. One of the most important factors that may account for the rapid growth of Indonesia's small-scale industries is government policy.As a starting point for its new industrialization policy, the Suharto government stressed from the outset (in 1966) the need for more liberal economic relations with other countries, the need to encourage the private economic sector, and the need for nationalized enterprise in the industrial sector. In the 1970s, however, the influence of state interventionist policies on the economy as a whole increased (Clapham, 1985). The policy of industrialization has been laid down since 1969 in the Five-Year Plans of the government, establishing major changes in priority with respect to objectives and economic methods (Clapham, 1985). *Repelita* I (1969/70-1973/74) gave a special boost to some sectors of industry with substantial state investments, but relatively low priority to the promotion of small industries and the creation of new jobs. *Repelita* II (1974/75-1978/79) embraced the same industrial aims, but gave top priority to the creation of jobs. Accordingly, greater importance was given to the role of labor-intensive small and medium enterprises. In 1975 a guidance and development project for small industries was launched to provide a coordinated program of assistance to small businesses, providing services, training, common service facilities, and subsidized or bulk purchases of raw materials and machines. A linkage program has been developed between the small industries on the one hand, and the larger industries and exporters on the other hand, the so-called *bapak angkat* policy (Van Diermen, 1997), in order to facilitate marketing as well as to provide technical and managerial assistance, to assist in getting raw materials or intermediate products, to help access to credit, and to facilitate technology transfer (Suhartono, 1995). Against this background a number of special organizations have been set up in collaboration with the national employers' association, *Kamar Dagang dan Industri Nasional* (KADIN), for the promotion of the weak Indonesian sector of the economy and as intermediaries between the government and private enterprises. However, KADIN and these newly established organizations had only limited success in appealing to small entrepreneurs and recruiting them as active members. KADIN failed to act in partnership with the government in helping to formulate and improve economic policy by submitting proposals or comments on economic policy, especially for the small industrial sector (Clapham, 1985). Small and medium entrepreneurs themselves are often very apprehensive about these special institutions because they were not established by individual initiative as self-help organizations, but rather as quasi-state institutions forming an integral part of official industrialization policy (Clapham, 1985). Based on an evaluation of earlier experience, since *Repelita* III assistance for the development of small industries has been given primarily through established groups of small entrepreneurs organized in cooperatives. This approach has been presented as very effective—because no heavy expenditures are required to build a new organization, benefits can be directly shared, and the family-type management can be retained (Suhartono, 1995). At the same time this structure enables the government to exert control on the enterprises involved, as the cooperatives are subject to guidance and assistance from the Ministries of Industry and Manpower.

Discussing the effects of this industrial strategy, Clapham (1985) concludes that this policy unsettled rather than reassured and encouraged small entrepreneurs. "On the one hand, the political emphasis on the importance of the private industrial sector and the principle of protecting financially weak entrepreneurs leads one to expect that small enterprises could, with preferential support in dealing with all adverse factors, follow a course of unhindered development. On the other hand, the principle of 'planned' industrial development is a sign that the government also wanted to control the future structure of the small entrepreneurial sector" (p. 73). Although the creation of employment opportunities figures prominently on the political agenda, preference is given by the Indonesian government to those large-scale industries that are capital intensive and often backed by foreign investors. As Anderson (1990) pointed out, the Suharto government's generally supportive attitude toward large-scale foreign investment, despite what might seem substantial political disadvantages—especially the alienation of a significant component of the independent indigenous entrepreneurial class—have to be understood against the background of the advantages that large-scale foreign investors offer the state. These firms provide the Jakarta government with sizable, easily accessible revenues (taxes, commissions, etc.). As these corporations pursue no political ambitions inside Indonesia, they present no direct political threat to the state, as a powerful indigenous business class might do.

Moreover, analyzing the failure of government measures to support the small-scale industrial sector, one has to note that the government's official target group forms only a small segment of the vast number of "small" entrepreneurs that actually constitute this sector. An important criterion to be eligible for government support is size. Although size may be measured by capital employed, the most commonly used measure is the number of workers in an establishment. In Indonesia, the Central Bureau of Statistics classifies industries according to the number of persons engaged. Enterprises employing up to five persons are classified as household and cottage industries; small industries are called those businesses that employ 6 to 19 workers, and medium- and large-size businesses employ at least 20 workers and more (Van Diermen, 1997). Since 1979 the Ministry of Industry has considered any manufacturing industry to be small if its investment for machinery and equipment does not exceed 70 million *rupiah* (at the time of the research [1995/1996] 1,000 *rupiah* was about US$0.40) and its investment per worker does not exceed 625,000 *rupiah*, whereas Bank Indonesia considers an industry to be small if its net assets do not exceed 100 million *rupiah*. Thus, what is classified as small industry by the Ministry of Industry and the Central Bank may presumably include firms that employ more than 20 workers (Suhartono, 1995). On the other side of the scale, many small enterprises and, in particular, self-employed individuals do not qualify for government support as they are classified as "cottage and household" industries. This category, however, is by far the largest in the Indonesian economy. As N. Sullivan (1989) found in a *kampung* in Yogyakarta, most local people were involved in very small business, owned and operated by *kampung* women. They included street and market peddling; home-based sewing and cooking; *warung* (tiny shops and street stalls); *losmen* (small boarding houses); accommodation agencies (for tenants and property owners); *arisan* organizers (rotating credit organizations); and a wealth of similar informal organizations. The small businesses run by men included: home- or street-based bicycle repairs; tailoring, carpentry; and a range of illicit operations like gaming, home-brewing, *tukang catut* (ticket shark), and organizing and handling cockfights. Most of the other little enterprises were not very profitable, considering the labor invested by their owners. These men worked alone, called on family for help when necessary, and enjoyed little security from their endeavors.

A survey of Indonesian small- and medium-size entrepreneurs conducted in the 1980s (Clapham, 1985), focusing on manufacturing enterprises, shows that the conditions that determine the conduct of the small entrepreneur are the desire for independence and an increase in personal income, a limited formal education, and a small amount of personal and family capital. The weaknesses of Indonesian small entrepreneurs are, in terms of Bourdieu, their lack of economic and cultural capital. Small enterprises in Indonesia are virtually completely dependent on personal and family capital. As Rutten (1997) shows for indigenous (Muslim) entrepreneurs in central Java, their businesses have had little success in establishing forms of economic organization any more complex than the nuclear family firm. As entrepreneurs they have wealth and power and have thus managed to become a local business elite, yet they lack organizational skills and do not have a "capitalist spirit." They seem to be satisfied with the wealth they have attained and do not make use of advanced organizational forms to accumulate capital in order to further develop their businesses.

In Indonesia, small entrepreneurs very often do not have the education, social status, technical ability, and the initiative to make contact with the institutions that could assist them. Many small entrepreneurs keep no written records of expenditures and receipts, do not differentiate between personal and business expenses, and have no accurate conception of their production costs—in other words, they lack basic skills needed to manage an enterprise successfully. Those entrepreneurs who sell a product frequently experience difficulties in all areas of marketing. As a rule, the owner-entrepreneur has no special skills in these matters and does not know where he can obtain reliable information about market developments, advertising opportunities, or better marketing channels. This lack of marketing expertise is an important cause of the widespread inability of enterprises to plan for the medium or longer term.

The strength of smaller producers in Indonesia is their strongly locally based network, or in terms of Bourdieu, their social capital. They operate predominantly in very localized markets and sell their products directly to the consumer (Clapham, 1985). For the producer, this implies a "forward integration process" in trading and transport activities that makes economic sense when small production volumes and fragmented markets are involved. For the consumer, the advantages lie in reduced transport costs and profit margins. Another strength is that many small-scale entrepreneurs benefit from subcontracting relationships with large firms (Van Diermen, 1997). One of the often emphasized advantages of small enterprises is their adaptability in responding to market imperfections (Van Diermen, 1997) or changes in the procurement and sales markets, seeking out market niches uncontested by large firms (Clapham, 1985). One fine example of this adaptability is the clothing industry in Bali (Suhartono, 1995). Here, the large number of tourists provide a wealth of information on current fashions as well as easily accessible test markets for innovation in new products and designs, while the tourist shops can also be used as a convenient channel to sell production overruns. Apparently, small entrepreneurs in Bali can produce labor-intensive products, export efficiently, and compete in higher value markets where shorter product life cycles, rigorous quality control, and tight delivery schedules are standard features.

Small Entrepreneurs in Tourism

Turning to the tourism industry in particular, we are dealing with a sector that is basically service oriented. This implies that the findings regarding management and marketing practices, capital allocation and networking, and the impact of government regulations that have been discussed before are only partially applicable. The bulk of the literature on small entrepreneurship focuses on manufacturing businesses (Clapham, 1985; Upadhya & Rutten, 1997; Van Diermen, 1997). However, a considerable amount of research has been conducted on the travel and hospitality sector, mainly discussing large-scale firms and transnational enterprises (Brent Richie & Goeldner, 1987), whereas small-scale and petty entrepreneurship in tourism is a relatively new area for research. The lack of knowledge on this sector is also reflected in the statistics compiled by the Indonesian Central Bureau for Statistics. In their *Small Scale Manufacturing Industry Statistics 1996* (Biro Pusat Statistik [BPS], 1996b), the only source of data in the small-scale sector, the bias towards tourism is twofold. First, the statistics deal with manufacturing enterprises only, and second, within this category, there is no specification of businesses producing for the tourism industry. Tourism statistics (BPS, 1996a) compiled by the Indonesian Central Bureau for Statistics strongly focus on visitor arrivals and length of stay, they comprise no information about the number of employees in hotels, wages and salaries, investments and turnover, marketing and competition levels. Given this lack of data and the great variations that exist between small enterprises in the tourism sector, explorations into this area should be considered in the context of specific locations and case studies.

In this book, the emphasis is on a number of case studies focusing on family businesses and self-employed individuals, mediating between local tourism businesses and tourists on a commission basis. In terms of Boissevain (1974), we are dealing here with entrepreneurs disposing of first-order resources in the case of the family businesses, and entrepreneurs disposing of second-order resources in the case of the "mediators." In the following chapters their business operations and strategies will be explored in terms of the capital—economic, cultural, social, and symbolic—they invest in their businesses. Here, I want to shed some light on significant aspects of the small-scale tourism sector, by highlighting the most striking strengths and weaknesses of these enterprises.

In the Indonesian tourism industry, we can distinguish patronage and brokerage among the business strategies of most of the petty entrepreneurs. The category that plays a prominent role in the debate on sustainable tourism development is local owners of small-scale and micro tourism businesses. This category controls first-order resources, like land, real estate, money, equipment, or other means of production. We find them in various tourism-related sectors and branches:

- **the accommodation sector**: the owners and staff members of guesthouses, homestay, *losmen*, inns, *penginapan, wisma*, pensions;

- **the tour and travel branch**: the owners of small travel agencies that arrange excursions in the vicinity of their home base;

- **the transport sector:** the owners of local transport and minibuses who rent their vehicles to drivers who in their turn transport tourists;

- **the restaurant sector:** the owners of *warung*, street cafes, and small restaurants offering local and tourist food;

- **the souvenir business:** the owners of small shops and stalls and workplaces producing souvenirs, clothes, cheap jewelery, sunglasses, toys, and other gadgets that tourists buy;

- **the rental companies:** rental agents for bikes, beach umbrellas, diving, snorkeling, and fishing equipment and boats;

- **the beauty service sector:** predominantly self-employed women (and to a lesser degree men) operating as specialists in massage, manicure, hairstyling, and make-up;

- **the entertainment sector:** nonprofessional performers in dance, music, and theater.

Besides these "respectable" enterprises there is a large number of illicit and illegal businesses that demonstrate the sometimes "criminal underlife" (Crang, 1997) of the tourism sector (i.e., the escort services, brothels catering particularly to tourists, gambling halls, and drug dealing).

One of the most striking characteristics of small proprietors of tourism businesses and self-employed individuals in the tourism industry seems their reluctance to organize themselves. There are no indications that they are active members in any of the associations for small and medium enterprises that the Indonesian government has established, or that they are involved in informal organizations. The state-controlled associations fail to benefit the small private enterprises and focus on the industrial sector, which leaves the tourism business without any structural support. Moreover, most small tourism enterprises are not eligible for membership, as the government's definition of small enterprises excludes self-employed and micro businesses. Small establishments find it hard to attract individual tourists and, because of the fragmentation of the industry, they are in a weak bargaining position vis-à-vis the large tour operators. However, these entrepreneurs do cooperate in order to enhance their profits. Although economic considerations are the basis of cooperative efforts, personal networks, family obligations, and friendship are necessary conditions for mutual support. The most important actors in the marketing of the local tourist product are the category of small entrepreneurs known as brokers. There are several occupational groups that fit this category. Tax drivers, pedicab men, lottery sellers, street vendors, and informal guides are the most flexible and mobile people in a tourist area. They usually have access to a large network and up-to-date information. Others are more limited in their freedom because of permanent or part-time jobs, but nevertheless have free access to tourists and connections in the local tourism industry that enable them to operate as brokers. It may be clear that while the position of the "independent patron" can be held by women as well as men, "network specialists," due to the freedom of movement they require, are usually men. In Indonesian society women are, after all, more confined to the home. Brokers are frequently employees of small accommodations and travel agencies, waiters and bartenders, formal guides, shop assistants, and security men. Many brokers combine a number of "informal" jobs to expand their network. On a commission base they frequently work as touts for several shops, restaurants, guesthouses, and bars. Many self-employed people depend for their income on the commissions they receive for taking customers to the small hotels, souvenir shops, bars, and restaurants. The commission is a percentage of the selling price of the products and services purchased by the tourists. In places with a great deal of competition, small business proprietors usually hand over about 10% (but sometimes as much as 50–60%) of the selling price to intermediaries, street guides, and other touts (Soedarso, 1992).

Whereas the "independent patrons" are closer to the formal end of the continuum of employment in the tourism industry, because their enterprises require government licenses and permits, brokers are closer to the informal end. Street guides do not require a license as long as they do not pretend to be proper tourist guides and stay away from the formally guided tourist attractions where they would pose a threat to the professional guides. They therefore prefer to introduce themselves as "friends" or "students" who want to improve their language proficiency. In many tourist places, there is a booming trade in fake student ID and guide licenses. Nevertheless, guides go into hiding when the news of an upcoming police raid is passed by word of mouth. However, these raids, which are incidentally organized by the local police force together with the provincial department of Justice, are not effective in controlling unlicensed guiding. The guides are long gone by the time the police arrive, while their colleagues, the formal guides, are still around, engaged with a group of tourists. If they forgot to bring their ID or extend their licenses, they are fined. Similar raids are held among pedicab men, street vendors, and stall operators. If they fail to produce a valid ID and license, they are fined and have to stop doing business immediately. Goods and pedicabs are confiscated and stall holders have to pack up and move on. Souvenir sellers and masseuses are chased away by security guards and police. Whereas network specialists have to deal with police raids that hinder their mobility and free access to tourists and social contacts, patrons have to cope with increasing regulations regarding the payment of taxes, registration, and licenses. There is a 10% government tax added to all transactions in the restaurant and accommodation sector, and owners have to prove with a certificate that they have paid the tax. Local governments send officials to inspect the accommodations and restaurants and register the number of rooms or tables and the type of facilities. The idea is to establish a classification system. However, as local people point out, the registration is really meant to check whether the owners are evading taxes. As a consequence, many accommodation owners are vague about the number of rooms and the quality of the facilities, and prefer not to be listed in government-issued brochures on local "places to eat" or "places to stay." Officials are bribed to turn a blind eye to an extension to a *losmen*, and only some of the tourists staying in the accommodation are officially registered.

The government's measures do not seem to discourage people from establishing a business. Although we lack official figures, it seems that a growing number of Indonesians are attracted to tourist areas to benefit from tourism developments. Tourism is a catalyst of population movements. As has been observed by several researchers (Cukier, 1996; Kamsma, 1996; Picard, 1993; Wall & Long, 1996), the Javanese often play a leading role in the establishment of businesses in new tourist areas, in the large-scale as well as small-scale sectors. In Java, on the other hand, already established tourist destinations attract people from other, less developed areas in Indonesia (Dahles, 1997b). Young men in particular are attracted by the Western consumption patterns and lifestyles in tourist areas. Tourists enact their dreams of Western consumerism and hold the promise of a better life. Although poverty and the lack of economic opportunity are reasons to leave one's community, the promise of quick money and a better future pulls people to tourist areas.

Conclusions

In the beginning of this chapter the issue was raised whether the small-scale tourism enterprises actually constitute a vital force in the Indonesian tourism sector or whether these enterprises just absorb a labor force that would otherwise be unemployed. It may be clear that small-scale businesses are: a reservoir of hidden unemployment as well as overt innovative and enterprising forces. Small entrepreneurs are operating neither in the margin of the tourism industry nor in the centralized state bureaucracy. They form an integral part of the industry and are becoming more and more important to the Indonesian government in its search for new forms of tourism and a product that is competitive in the global market. Small-scale entrepreneurs are neither representatives of a traditional, informal, bazaar-style economy, nor do they fit definitions of the completely modern, formal, capitalist sector. They participate in both economies. Depending on the kind of resources, some (the patrons who rely predominantly on private property) operate more in the formal sector, others (the brokers who rely predominantly on personal networks) participate more in the informal sector. The relationship between the formal and informal spheres is complex. Patrons depend on brokers for the advertising and marketing of their accommodation, restaurant, or shop. Brokers, in turn, depend on patrons for their commission and access to tourists. Patronage and brokerage actually constitute a safety belt that allows small entrepreneurs to operate in a rather flexible manner. For these reasons small entrepreneurs seem to be more successful and small enterprises seem to be more sustainable than the large-scale resorts that have recently experienced severe setbacks due to a collapse in major tourist markets.

Small entrepreneurs, patrons as well as brokers, depend heavily on networks based on personal friendships, business transactions, family relations, marriage, ethnic, and religious bonds. These networks constitute more meaningful units than formal organizations and state-controlled associations. Though increasing government intervention forces entrepreneurs into formal organizations, these are either ineffective or function according to network principles. The most effective forms of cooperation are those that meet the need for income security, insurance and protection, marketing, advertising, and information. However, this does not mean that small entrepreneurs react passively to changing markets and to attempts of the bureaucracy to regulate economic life from above. They are enterprising, inventive, innovative, and creative in the exploitation of new niches in the market as well as in the law. This book contains an abundance of examples of the flexibility of small entrepreneurs in using changing consumer preferences and government regulations to their advantage. Pedicab men benefit from the tourist quest for authenticity, homestay owners from the budget travelers' need for an inexpensive place to sleep, masseuses from Western beauty standards, and street guides from the disorientation of the unorganized tourists.

Small-scale entrepreneurs, patrons and brokers, are innovative and risk taking in the exploitation of information. They are less so in the product they offer. The products sold by the small-scale tourist industry in Indonesia are surprisingly uniform. Once a product or formula has proven successful, everyone is willing to share in the success. As a consequence, every entrepreneur copies the product or formula. This is the principle of *ikut-ikutan* (imitation), which is well established in all sectors of the Indonesian economy, whether it is furnishing a homestay, arranging a menu, presenting food, organizing an excursion, or selecting souvenirs to be sold, even addressing tourists. There is only limited variation between and among small-scale entrepreneurs and enterprises. Although they do not react passively to external forces, they are not independent and self-sufficient actors either. They act within certain parameters defined by the entrepreneurial culture they depend on.

Chapter 3

Massage, Miss? Women Entrepreneurs and Beach Tourism in Bali

Karin Bras and Heidi Dahles

Introduction

In the literature there is overwhelming evidence that the majority of jobs in the tourism industry, especially those of low skill and wages, are occupied by women (Sinclair, 1997). Access to tourism-related employment is overtly gender biased. However, it is important to emphasize that prevailing social norms regarding "women's work" have underpinned and allowed this to take place (Kinnaird, Kothari, & Hall, 1994). Increased incomes among tourism service workers have led to a redistribution of authority within the family, often resulting in tensions in gender relations (Kinnaird et al., 1994). Women and men are involved differently in the construction and consumption of tourism. Gendered "realities" shape tourism marketing, guests' motivations, and hosts' actions (Swain, 1995). Tourism activity is characterized as "modern" and bound up with major transformations of paid work. Host populations have gendered employment opportunities and control of paid work. As tourism employment is overtly gender biased, reflecting local norms of "women's work," one has to ask questions about the effects of tourism on gender relations: reinforcing the division of labor along sex-segregated lines, or perhaps transforming it by developing new work and income opportunities (Swain, 1995).

As we discussed elsewhere (Bras & Dahles, 1998), very little is known about the impact of tourism and tourism policy on the employment opportunities of women in the informal sector. Recently, Balinese petty traders have become the scapegoat for disappointing developments in Bali's tourism. The government imposed an organization (*Persatuan Pedagang Suvenir Kuta*) and a registration and licensing system on the Kuta street vendors. Raids were held to reduce the number of unlicensed vendors. Although all small-scale entrepreneurs feel the pressing government regulations, the effects of these regulations differ along gender lines. Government measures, taken to curtail small-scale economic activities, will be hard on women who depend on the informal economic activities. There is evidence from developing countries that men and women are affected differently by the developmental process (Momsen, 1991). Tourism being a significant development strategy of the Indonesian government, both at the national and provincial levels, this chapter investigates the ways in which women entrepreneurs in a Balinese beach destination benefit and suffer from tourism in general and government interventions in tourism development in particular. The emphasis is on those women whose working area is the beach of Sanur, a village and upmarket tourist place in the Southeast of Bali, where they sell souvenirs and clothes and offer massage and beauty care. It may be clear that these women belong to the lower echelons of labor in the tourism industry. Street and beach vending is low in the hierarchy of economic involvement in tourism, so low that Balinese male adults would not get involved in that kind of activity. The majority of vendors in both Kuta and Sanur are single men, either teenagers or young adults, from Java with limited formal education (Cukier, 1996). The women, however, are Balinese. Whereas the young men view their job as a means to acquire the skills necessary for securing higher status jobs, even in the formal tourism sector, the women have no such ambitions. The ways in which many women operate in the tourism-related informal sector are favorable to the provision of child care and domestic and ritual responsibilities (Cukier, 1996; Norris, 1994). It is precisely the integration of home and business that enables so many women to take part in the tourism sector, women's productive role being accompanied by numerous responsibilities as mothers, fosterers, and housekeepers (Operations Review Unit, 1988).

The multitude of roles and tasks that women have to fulfill raises questions on the effects of gender on the entrepreneurial activities of women in Bali. To what extent does tourism affect the business opportunities for women in the small-scale tourism sector? What opportunities and what restrictions does tourism development offer to the women? What are the characteristics of the female-run enterprises? To what extent do women move in and out of formal and informal entrepreneurship? What is the impact of government policy, both national and local, on the entrepreneurial activities of the beach women in Sanur? After a brief description of tourism development in Bali in general and Sanur in particular, this chapter focuses first on the business practices of the beach women, and second on the ways in which these practices are affected by gender relations and government measures.

Tourism in Sanur

Sanur stretches for about 3 kilometers along an eastern coastline, with the landscaped grounds and restaurants of expensive hotels fronting the beach. The conspicuous, 1960s-style Hotel Bali Beach is at the northern end of the strip, and the newer Surya Beach Hotel, invisible behind its walls and gardens, is at the southern end. West of these hotels the main avenue, Jalan Danau Tamblingan, runs parallel to the beach, with the hotel entrances on one side and wall-to-wall tourist shops and restaurants down the other side. Sanur was Bali's first beach resort and is famous throughout the island for its religious festivities. Not far from Sanur's beach resorts lie ancient temples and, even though the main economic sector for Sanur is tourism, its cultural heritage seems to remain intact. Sanur was one of the places in Bali favored by Western artists during their prewar discovery of the island. Not long after Indonesia proclaimed Independence in 1945, Sanur witnessed the beginnings of a building boom by expatriates led by the Belgian painter Le Mayeur, whose former studio home on the beach north of the Grand Bali Beach is now a museum (Turner, Delahunty, Greenway, Lyon, McAsey, & Willett, 1995).

When Indonesia started focusing on socioeconomic development in the late 1960s, the tourism industry in Bali was chosen for its potential to attract investment and international attention. A tourism master plan for Bali was written by a consortium of French consultants, and sponsored by the UNDP. This plan proposed that tourism development be concentrated in enclaves in the south with excursion routes into the interior of the island. The approach was designed to protect the Balinese culture from potentially harmful impact of tourism and maintain its attraction as an exotic, unspoiled paradise (Long & Kindon, 1997). In 1988, the Balinese government changed its approach of concentration in tourism planning and adopted a policy designed to diffuse economic benefits throughout the island. This approach allowed for a more equitable distribution of tourism development and represented a more realistic approach to the spontaneous development already taking place (Long & Kindon, 1997).

Today, Bali's tourist industry encompasses two broad categories of facilities and services, catering to quite distinct groups of visitors: package tour tourists with high spending power on the one hand, and individual low-budget tourists on the other (Picard, 1993; Vickers, 1989). Although the national government encourages large-scale *and* small-scale tourism projects, depending on the specific character of a destination area (Sammeng, 1995), tourism development in Bali is dominated by resort tourism. Star-rated hotels are to be spread evenly throughout the island, so as to permit the active involvement of the Balinese population in the tourist trade and to allow for the equitable distribution of its economic benefits (Picard, 1993; Wall, 1996). Resorts attract visitors who leave their hotel only on guided tours and, in their consumption of a constructed paradise, do not want to be disturbed by the hustle and bustle of everyday life. The idea is that resort tourism is less encouraging towards the informal sector as resort tourists interact less with locals (including vendors) than unorganized, low-budget tourists (Cukier, 1996).

Resorts like the exclusive and isolated Nusa Dua, a luxury tourist enclave in the southern tip of Bali that was proposed as the tourism enclave by the first master plan, employ local staff—though mostly of the low-skilled type. They constitute capital-intensive enclaves, with only limited links to domestic Balinese economy (Picard, 1993; Vickers, 1989). In contrast to Nusa Dua, where informal sector vendors are not allowed to operate (Cukier, 1996), Kuta caters largely to the lower budget mass tourists, particularly from Australia, and is a lively and relatively unplanned collection of small hotels, *losmen*, restaurants, and numerous small shops. Most of the owners and employees of tourist accommodations and services are Balinese, and the links with the local economy are close and numerous (Mabbett, 1987, 1989). Here informal economic activities flourish, as the local population responded to the influx of young, low-budget backpacker tourists. Tourism in Sanur represents a compromise between the isolated upmarket resort of Nusa Dua and the mass-tourist destination of Kuta.

The traditional employment of Sanur residents was farming, followed by fishing, animal husbandry, and artisan activity. In the late 1960s there were only a few hundred accommodation rooms in Sanur. By the early 1980s this number had increased to about 2,000 and to more than 3,000 in the 1990s. The resort now consists of a wide range of accommodation from small *losmen* to a number of five-star hotels. Thus, the area caters to a diverse group of clients (Cukier, 1996). The bigger hotels are run by professional managers and the workers are on wages. The money spent in these hotels goes into corporate coffers and probably leaves Bali (Mabbett, 1989). However, Sanur has also witnessed the emergence of a village-run cooperative that was established by the village council as early as 1963. Led by forward-looking village leaders the council initiated a local development program of impressive proportions. Over the next 20 years a substantial network of publicly owned village industries was established to increase local employment opportunities and fund schools, health facilities, and other local needs (Warren, 1989). This approach provided a friendly environment for the establishment of many Sanur-based tourist businesses in a successful attempt to profit directly from the rise in tourism in order to finance social and cultural activities. Presently, the cooperative operates a beach market, art shops, a restaurant, a car wash, and a service station, and owns land in Kuta and Denpasar. Since the 1960s thousands of jobs have been created in the tourism sector in Sanur, but many of these jobs were taken by people from outside Sanur. Over the past 10 to 20 years there has been a trend for village residents to migrate to the main resort areas of Kuta, Sanur, and Nusa Dua in order to seek employment in the tourism industry, primarily due the potential higher wages offered in the tourism sector than in the traditional sectors of the economy (Cukier, 1996).

Upgrading Sanur Beach

Only a couple of years ago tourists visiting Sanur beach were ploughing their way through the soft sand, evading fishing boats and garbage, hassled by persistent beach vendors, and running from the surf that flooded the whole beach at high tide. Tourists seldom walked along the beach. Instead they stayed by the pool in the hotel garden or stretched out on their towels in the sand, only to be harassed by many vendors. Women dressed in *sarong* (wrap-around skirt) knelt beside them to give them a massage or manicure, to braid their hair, or to offer the merchandise they carried around. These women were always on the move, walking the beach in search of customers.

In 1995 the scene changed. The local government in cooperation with a village cooperative and big hotels built a red brick beachwalk stretching along the whole Sanur coastline. This path is above the surf and allows for a relaxed stroll along the beach during high as well as low tide. Bordering the beachwalk restaurants and cafes were opened where tourists can take a rest, looking out over the sea with Nusa Lembongan at a distance and Mount Agung to the northeast. Many new shops and another beach market have been established. Chairs and beds are inviting tourists to sit down and relax. The equipment belongs to hotels and restaurants, but in most cases tourists can use them for free as long as they order a drink. Early in the morning a group of men and women dressed in yellow t-shirts sweep the beach and the path. They are employed by the village cooperative.

With the new beachwalk the interaction between tourists and local entrepreneurs changed. Vendors still offer their merchandise and women still urge tourists to take a massage or come to their shops, but at present most of them are either organized in a cooperative or associated with a hotel. Massage, manicure, and other beauty activities are performed in front of the hotels on the beds. Security men in uniform are patrolling the territory in front of the hotel gardens bordering the beach, keeping an eye on the hotel employees and "wild" beach vendors who keep off the beachwalk and try to attract the tourists' attention from a distance. Besides the uniformed "securities" the big hotels employ "silent" security personnel who cannot be identified as hotel employees by the guests. However, their identity is known among the vendors and masseuses roaming the beach. Their task is to make sure that vendors do not bother the guests, either in the beautifully designed gardens or on the beach. There are regular meetings between the hotel management and representatives of the cooperatives to enforce the rules and to make appointments regarding the number of vendors or boat letters who are allowed to enter the hotel territory to sell their goods or services. The female vendors and "wild" masseuses are not invited to attend these meetings as they are not organized. They flock together in small groups on the border of the hotel territories and the public beach to approach guests who leave the hotel garden.

The beachwalk is one of many initiatives of the Sanur Village Promotion Board that was established in 1986 by an enterprising man who—in 1994—became General Manager of the Bali Hyatt Hotel situated on Sanur beach. He still is the chairman of the Promotion Board. This Promotion Board is an informal organization supported by about 30 Sanur people, all of them owners or employees of hotels, shops, and restaurants and many of them expatriates. Their objective is to "fresh up Sanur" and to "lift up the standards," as a spokesperson from the Bali Hyatt told us. Among the innovations the Promotion Board has accomplished is a festival to promote the local tourist product and the publication of an informative map of Sanur with a short history of the village written by Made Wijaya, the author of *Bali—the Island of the Gods*.

The local initiatives to regulate tourism development have to be understood against the background of the promotion of tourism by the New Order government in Jakarta as a strategy to unify and modernize the country. All over Indonesia small-scale economic activities get more organized, formalized, and regulated, as has been discussed in the previous chapter. The informal sector is seen as a major obstacle to create proper employment, economic growth, and, thus, modernization (Schoch, 1985). The central government established agencies and offices in Bali as early as the 1960s to service the tourism industry and increase the number of tourist arrivals, as the island constituted Indonesia's first and foremost tourism destination area. As a consequence, a large percentage of the profits of tourist traffic does not accrue to Balinese people, as Jakarta overseas-based airlines and travel agents, hotels, and tour operators control much of the tourist sector (Guinness, 1994). The national government lacks the willingness to transfer the authority for managing programs that produce large financial resources to the provincial level, although officially the responsibilities for managing tourism development have been delegated down to the provincial level. Procedures relating to land acquisition, tenure, and utilization and the management of star-rated hotels and resorts do not fall under the authority of the provincial government. Moreover, the budget of the provincial government in Bali comes from the central government as a subsidy, and only 20% comes from the province. This discrepancy has a detrimental effect on local employment and does not encourage the local government to take responsibility (Kumorotomo, n.d.). However, Bali's own response to government intervention has flourished, as the case of village accommodation and entertainment at Sanur illustrates. Rice fields have been converted into areas for guesthouses and farm workers have become artists and souvenir sellers. Despite central government intentions, large amounts of tourist dollars earned by Balinese villagers go unrecorded and untaxed, and most of the creative energy of Balinese people remains outside government control (Guinness, 1994).

Sanur Beach Business

Entrepreneurs in Beauty Care

About 15 years ago, when Sanur was still a relatively quiet beach resort with only four or five hotels, only a few masseuses found their way to the beach. Nowadays everywhere along the coastline hotels have been built and these hotels occupy a part of the public beach. The outdoor cafes with their chairs and parasols have become an integral part of beach life. There are few places where tourists can lie down on a towel in the sand. Approximately 100 women try to find their income on the beaches of Sanur nowadays. They sell clothes or souvenirs on the beach market or in small shops along the beachwalk. Or they offer beauty services like massage, pedicure/manicure, or hair braiding. These services are often combined with the sale of small souvenirs like colorful decorated wooden pencils, napkin rings, or postcards. Some of the women walk around carrying their merchandise with them, others sit in between the tourists and try to make conversation in broken English. At times they are chased away by the security man of the hotel: *jangan menggangu tamu* (do not disturb the guests). The tourists can be quite rude as well, telling them that they are fed up with the constant hassle. Often enough, though, tourist and beach seller come to an understanding. After some bargaining, souvenirs and services find their way to the customer and the women continue their walk along the beach or turn to a newly arrived tourist on the beach terrace. When there are not so many tourists, groups of women sit together in the shade along the beachwalk. They gossip, play with the tourists' children, eat together, or play dominoes. Never do they lose eye of the tourists who stroll past them. The familiar "hello Miss, where you come from" and "where you go *turis*" constantly echo over the beach.

The majority of the women on the beach originally come from Sanur and still live in the direct vicinity of the beach. If they originated from another part of the island, the reason for moving to Sanur was marriage. As the family structure in Bali is patrilineal and the settlement pattern patrilocal, women are expected to move in with their husband's family after marriage. The older women have years of experience in working on the beach and in a lot of cases their own daughters or other relatives follow their example. Because of their long experience and the familiarity local people have with the characteristics of beach tourism, their family and neighbors in the *kampung* are accustomed to the activities they perform on the beach. The women emphasize that the status of their job is not particularly high, but that they are not confronted with prejudices about the type of work. Women coming from other parts of Bali without a tradition of working on the beach will probably have more difficulties in getting their job as a masseuse accepted.

The acceptance of making a living off beach tourism also springs from the fact that giving massage is not a service that started with the arrival of tourists. Although nowadays they practice the profession in another context, it is not necessarily judged as negative. People who can perform massages can be found in every village. Most of the women giving massages are older, somewhere between 40 and 60 years old. It has to be emphasized that giving massage has to be learned by practice. Through years of experience a certain degree of skill can be obtained. The older masseuses learned their skills from their parents or grandparents and will consequently pass on their knowledge to their own children. The other beauty care activities, like manicure and hair braiding, are normally practiced by the younger women. Occasionally they give a massage and in due time they will be experienced enough and have the strength needed to do the job full-time.

For most of these women, though, the acceptance of their work is not an issue. In most cases they are breadwinners who support not only their own husbands and children but also other members of their own family and their in-laws. Often their husbands are unemployed or work only occasionally. Unemployment is in some cases compensated by income through other channels like betting at cockfights. That the irregularity of the income and the risks connected to these activities are not always welcomed by the women is expressed by one of our informants who described her husband's activities as "sleeping with the chicken." If the men have jobs, it is quite often in tourism, like laundry man in a hotel, or artisan working in the souvenir industry. These are low-paid jobs; therefore, their salaries are only sufficient to pay for the daily needs. Giving massage and practicing other beauty services seems to yield a reasonable amount of money. The women use the money to buy clothes and other more expensive consumer goods or to pay for the education of their children. What is emphasized by all women is the importance of earning money to finance religious ceremonies. A cremation ceremony costs more than 1 million *rupiah*, and this is only one of the many religious events for which they are responsible. Because of the unstructured nature of the job and the influences of high and low seasons, it is difficult to get a clear picture of their income. On a busy day in the high season it can vary from 15,000 *rupiah* to an absolute maximum of 40,000 *rupiah*, but this is an exception. Cukier (1996) points out that the modal income earned by the male street and beach sellers in Sanur is between 200,000 and 250,000 *rupiah* per month. In comparison with the minimum wage in Bali in 1992 of 3,000 *rupiah* per day or 84,000 *rupiah* per month (Cukier-Snow & Wall, 1993), this is a substantial amount of money. But the seasonal fluctuations have to be taken into account, although the tourism season seems to become longer every year, mostly because of an increasing number of Western tourists that hibernate in Bali.

Over the last few years the more expensive hotels turned to engaging permanent masseuses in order to regulate the enormous supply of these services and to prevent complaints from their guests. This system enables them to keep an eye on who gets access to their premises and also to control the quality of the services. As a result, two groups of women can be distinguished on Sanur beach. First, the group of women who are employed by the hotels and therefore no longer roam the beach in search for customers. Second, the women who still carry their merchandise with them, walk along the beach, and offer their services whenever and wherever possible. After a description of both groups, the social position of the women making a living from beach tourism in Sanur will be discussed.

Up and Down: Mobile Beach Vendors

Her name is Wayan and she has worked on the beach for 7 years. When her work at home is done, she comes to the beach, sometimes alone and sometimes with one of her children. Her daughter is also working on the beach, walking "up and down" just like her, trying to earn her own school fee. Wayan is lucky she can count on the support of her children. This is, however, not always the case. Not every daughter is that eager to follow in her mother's footsteps. As one of the other mobile masseuses, Nyoman, explained: "My children are too shy to work on the beach. They are afraid that their friends will know that they do a low status job." Before becoming a masseuse, Wayan used to work as a maid with a Chinese family. Although she still does not earn a lot of money, the work on the beach is better. Sometimes she gets some extras, like the time when an American couple asked her to do a massage and paid her more than $20. Every day she walks up and down the beach. In the basket on her head she carries souvenirs, but also a file and nail polish in case someone wants a manicure and, of course, massage oil. "Want look my postcard? No buy, no problem" is her slogan when she approaches tourists. Selling a whole-body massage is her goal. However, tourists can be very offensive, shouting "go away, you no good" without even looking at her. "I have to be flexible, whatever the tourists want I try to deliver." Her prices are not fixed, especially not when she has a slow day. Services and prices are adapted to the tourist's needs. There is always room for a student rate and a whole-body massage can easily become a "*comme çi, comme ça* massage" (i.e., just rubbing the neck and shoulders) (Figure 3.1). As she is not allowed to work in front of the hotels, she has to be careful in finding the right spot for doing the massage. The hotel-employed masseuses will be angry with her. "They already speak badly about me." She tries to persuade her guest to follow her to Werdha Pura, the beach in front of a government resort, which is the only part that is not occupied by the hotels. When she gets the chance to talk with the tourists, she is happy. She speaks highly of some of the tourists she met in the past. They gave her presents like the skirt and sweater she is wearing and even her bra, a white one with lace, which she proudly shows us.

Through the years, the area where these women are allowed to work has become smaller and smaller. Although there are still customers available, the hotel guests in the

Figure 3.1. Negotiating the price of a *comme çi comme ça* massage. (Photo by J. Vissering)

hotel gardens are difficult to approach. From a distance the hotel guests are addressed in a polite way:"Good morning, how are you." When there is eye contact and the tourist seems to be interested, he or she has to get up from the chair and walk to the open beach area because the masseuse is not supposed to enter the hotel premises. Once on the beach, the bargaining can start. Selling small souvenirs can be arranged on the spot, but finding a place to do a massage has become a problem. Not every tourist likes to lie down on a towel in the sand. In front of hotel Tanjung Sari it is possible to hire a chair for 2,000 *rupiah* an hour. But because of the low price the women ask for their services, they cannot afford to take their customers to the hotel. To enhance their economic opportunities, these women offer as many products and services as possible. When they do not carry their manicure set with them, they still try to sell this service, because there will always be a possibility to borrow the things needed or to pass on the job to another colleague or to one of their family members. Building a good relationship with tourists is also a way to increase their opportunities. Maybe a generous tourist will pay the school fee for their children or will buy a new manicure set for them. Maybe tourists who want to enjoy the nightlife need a baby-sitter for their infant. The beach ladies are constantly looking for market niches. In their search for an additional income the mobile masseuses developed the ability to react flexibly on requests from the tourists.

Watching People: Masseuses With a Permanent Job

Almost every star-rated hotel on Sanur beach has its own beauty care team consisting of five or six women. However, the hotels do not pay them a salary. They are free to come and go whenever they want. This provides the women with opportunities to develop other activities, like establishing a small souvenir shop on the beach market. In exchange for a small amount of money per customer (between 1,500 and 5,000 *rupiah*, depending on the hotel) they are allowed to approach the hotel guests. The women sit in between the chairs, chat with the tourists, rearrange their manicure equipment, and watch the beachwalk. It is easy to recognize them, as every hotel makes them wear a special outfit complete with name tag. They are not restricted to the hotel when looking for customers: everyone who passes by is a potential client. The women have a pretty good idea about what is happening on Sanur beach. Whenever possible they ask the tourists questions in order to get more information: "What is your name?" (to address tourists by their name every time they pass by); "How long you stay in Sanur?" (to find out whether a tourist is a potential customer and whether it is worthwhile spending time talking with her or him). Information about the tourist's spending power is obtained by asking "Where you stay?" Meeting a guest of a five-star hotel will certainly make them raise their prices. With all the answers in mind they will decide their strategy and their price. One of the women described her work as "doing massage and watching people." From their strategic position every tourist is closely observed. Whenever a tourist passes by, the women discuss the business opportunities and restrictions of this potential client.

That their position was not always that comfortable is remembered by Made, an older woman who started her career on the beach as a "mobile" masseuse. Every time she sees one of the younger women passing by carrying a basket, Made remembers her early career. Every day she went "up and down," with her children, even when she was pregnant. At that time there were no chairs, so she had to massage the tourists on a towel in the sand. It used to be quite a distance to walk from one hotel to the other when Sanur only had three hotels. Nowadays, the situation is a lot better. She does not have to walk in the hot sun any longer and there is no risk of being sent away by the security guards. In July and August, the peak tourist season, Made has about 10 clients a day, especially when groups visit the hotel. "When one of them wants a massage, all the others follow." But there are also low periods when she has to be satisfied with only one client a day. Although they form a team, the women at the hotels work for themselves. Therefore, they all try to build up their own clientele. When a tourist does not show any interest in having a massage, the woman repeats her name: "My name is Made, come back this afternoon or tomorrow and remember me, I am here every day, Made, don't forget." After being addressed like this it will be difficult for the tourist in question to remain unrecognized when strolling along the beachwalk. Made will remember the tourist's face and his or her name will echo over the beach every time he or she passes by. "There is much competition now, everyone is doing massage, even the younger women, so it is hard to get a customer," Made emphasizes. "Not all of the women are professional, they say they are, but they do everything to earn money. I only work as a masseuse and it takes years to become a skilled one."

The women who work at the hotels are satisfied with their new position, which they consider as a rise on the social ladder. The hotels provide a continuous flow of customers and therefore a more regular income than in earlier times. They are happy to have direct access to the clientele of the star-rated hotels, the "quality" tourists. The fact that they travel in groups and do not know how to bargain makes these tourists easy targets. The women worry about the increased competition, because it influences the quality of their work. The permanently employed women consider themselves as professionals as they acquired their skills through the years and specialized in one activity. Although they feel sympathy for the mobile masseuses, they regard them as outsiders and argue that this group brings discredit to their profession.

Comparing the business practices of both the permanent and the mobile beach women, it is obvious that they dispose of different amounts and sorts of "capital." Both categories basically share the same socioeconomic position in the village. They all live in a *kampung* and their household depends on their income as they either are without a husband or their husband does not have a regular and sufficient income to support their families. To run their business both categories do not need any substantial economic capital. Some massage oil, nail polish, and some other utensils is all that it takes to be in business. The mobile women, who besides offering beauty services also sell some goods, often receive these goods in commission from family members who are the producers. There are indications that the women working under hotel protection make more money and have a more regular income than the mobile women. However, to succeed in the beach business cultural, social and symbolic capital seem to be much more significant than economic capital. First, they need cultural capital, in contravention to the Bourdieuan use of this term not referring to any formal training, but to experience on the job. This accounts especially for the older masseuses working under hotel protection. They distinguish themselves from other women offering the same services by their knowledge, technique, strength, and experience in giving full-body massage; in other words, they distinguish themselves through their professionality, which can be interpreted as a form of "cultural" capital. Other women acknowledge this difference by labeling their service as a *comme çi comme ça* massage. Second, both categories of beach women need social capital to enter and to maintain their job. For the women working under hotel protection it is obvious that they have to be well connected to be admitted by a hotel to its premises. Family members working in a hotel, people from the same village or neighborhood are used as vehicles to get such a job. However, this does not mean that the beach area outside of the hotel premises is free for everybody to enter. The mobile women—although they are not organized in any formal sense—jealously guard their working area. Only family members (in particular daughters) are welcome to offer their merchandise and services—nonrelated newcomers would be chased away. There seems to be little overlap in the social networks of the two categories of beach women. Being connected with a hotel is a distinguishing feature, suggesting that the social capital of the permanently employed women is of higher symbolic value than the kin-based network of the mobile women. Third, it is predominantly symbolic capital that distinguishes the two categories of beach women. Working under hotel protection, wearing a uniform and a name tag, using the hotel beds and towels adds considerably to the women's symbolic capital in terms of professionality and reliability. Tourists feel more comfortable with these women as they seem to be employed by and operate under control of the hotel. The mobile women, on the other hand, lack this symbolic capital; they rather seem to carry a "symbolic burden." They are easily associated with the hordes of street vendors and unlicensed guides that harass tourists and spoil their holidays.

The Politics of Gender

Research in Southeast Asia seems to support the argument that the formal and informal sectors do not necessarily compete. The informal sector, growing at a faster rate than the formal sector, fills a niche left empty by the formal sector (McGee, 1982). In contrast to traditional employment theory, which stated that the informal sector would "disappear" as a country achieved "development," emerging opinion asserts that this dynamic sector should not be simplistically viewed as an economic activity that will vanish with the process of modernization and urbanization (Hull & Jones, 1994). Within tourism, as in other industries in developing countries, the informal sector is a vigorous and notable element (Cukier, 1996). Although much of the employment generated by tourism is in the form of self-employed, small-scale entrepreneurs such as vendors, tourism can provide an opportunity for the native population to increase their income and improve their standard of living, and can also positively affect quality of life through increases in social status, empowerment, and the creation of new occupational opportunities for youth and women. However, in tourism employment can have an impact on traditional lifestyles through competition for workers who would otherwise be available for more traditional sources of employment (Cukier, 1996). This accounts especially for the role of women. To understand why many Balinese women are working in petty enterprises in the service industry at all, one needs to analyze their position within the family and in Balinese society, and to investigate social attitudes towards women involved in economic activities (Long & Kindon, 1997).

Women constitute almost half of the labor force in Bali; however, the majority of them have no formal schooling (Norris, 1994). In Bali women work everywhere: in rice fields, on roads, in markets, in banks, in shops. Although not noticeable at first, a distinguishable sexual division of labor exists in all kinds of work. As for Balinese women, the autonomy that they experience in the economic realm is constrained by ritual and political practices. The functioning and maintenance of the Balinese family is the primary responsibility of the housewife regardless of how many hours she may spend per day at work outside of the family compound. A woman's dignity is associated with family prosperity. Responsibilities of women include: child socialization, food preparation, care for the household environment, and performance of religious activities according to Balinese Hindu custom. Besides all domestic responsibilities— women cook, nurture, groom, sweep, wash, and clean—they handle all small-scale trade within the market place and carry all kinds of goods: they carry the rice after harvesting, the offerings to the shrines, produce to the market place, and building materials with which roads are built (Miller & Branson, 1989).

In the hierarchical Hindu society of Bali economically dominant women threaten male control and must be contained. This is accomplished through religious practices:

images of male and female which stress that women are potentially dangerous and destructive unless under male control are internalized by women through their participation in rituals (P.Alexander, 1989; Miller & Branson, 1989). "In Bali religious symbolism is of fundamental importance in the ideological construction of gender, an ideology riddled with ambiguities, but oriented overall to the control of women. Women are both the source of life and the source of destructive pollution. The interactions between male and female in the projections of the sacred cosmos stress the controlling role of the male and the need for strict regulations of the female" (Miller & Branson, 1989, p. 103). The Balinese Hindu cosmos is linked directly to the world of experience, to the mountains, the coastal plains, and the sea. The heavenly sphere is the world of the mountain, the realm of the Gods and power. It is the source of the rivers that run down to fertilize the receptive impure female world of the coastal plains. This earthly world is the realm of humankind, of dependence, and threat of disaster (Miller & Branson, 1989). Ironically, tourism is perverting the Balinese hierarchical cosmos: tourism development is strongly focusing on the coastal area, the most expensive and exclusive hotels being built on the beach—which is the most impure and dangerous area in the Balinese cosmological order. However, it may be due to the belief system that working on the beach is low in the perception of the Balinese and, therefore, predominantly the realm of poorer women and non-Balinese young men.

The introduction and institutionalization of tourism to Bali has influenced business and employment opportunities for women. In contemporary Bali where ritual is becoming a tourist product, the economy is being undermined by a national ideology and practice of development that treats women as housewives and men as the sole economic actors. The trade, food, and hotel sectors are growing rapidly. The participation of women is increasing in all these sectors, but the greatest percentage increases are in crafts, followed by the trade, hotels, and restaurant sectors. Eighty-five percent of the female workforce operates in the informal sector (Cukier, 1996). Balinese women working in the formal sector are young and single. The majority of working married women make a living in the informal sector. Norris' (1994) study on women entrepreneurs in Bali showed that women traditionally operate *warung*. With the advent of tourism, women have expanded the traditional *warung* to include items relevant to tourists. Mabbett (1987, 1989) has shown that quite a number of Balinese business women became well established in the 1970s in Kuta. These women successfully started small restaurants and homestays during the years of hippiedom and travelers galore. These self-made women were helped by a Balinese tradition that gives women a great deal of freedom in commercial matters. Though the society is patriarchal, women have carved out clear areas of business enterprise for themselves.

Women's participation in the tourism sector is related to time control, flexibility, and financial stability on the one hand, and on cultural perceptions on "proper" female behavior on the other hand. Jobs such as working as a guide or a driver are perceived as "better for men"—"because men do not work in the kitchen in the home" and "if women are guides or drivers they would always come back at night. This is not good for women" (Norris, 1994, p. 113). The tasks of waitresses, cooks, and chambermaids are perceived as more appropriate for women because they can practice these skills at home. Occupations such as bellboy, gardener, security guard, and driver were perceived as more appropriate for men because men are "stronger" than women and these jobs may require working at night. Working as a guide or a driver was viewed as more appropriate for men because these occupations require going outside of the hotel with tourists and women doing these jobs might get a negative "image." Even though both men and women stated that the image of women working in hotels is changing and that night work for women is becoming more accepted, the female tourism workers are still very much aware of how they may be viewed by their family members and the community (Norris, 1994; Wilkinson & Pratiwi, 1995).

For unmarried women all jobs are appropriate as long as they have the required skills. Their lifestyle changes upon marriage: they have to follow their husband, and there are responsibilities at home. In Bali the position of women in the household is below men. To be the sole provider or breadwinner may also represent an increased status position for men; some men are now able to achieve this by securing a high-paying position in the tourism industry and being able to support a housewife (Norris, 1994). Both men and women need education and skills to "move up" in the tourism sector; however, women have additional factors to consider that relate to marital status, family responsibilities, and social and/or cultural norms. Both males and females regarded women as more "patient" and "flexible" than men, qualities that are important in occupations that have direct contact with tourists as "women smile more with tourists . . . and tourists like to look at sweet and beautiful women . . . and because women are better at being persuasive and seductive than men" (Norris, 1994, pp. 135–136).

These perceptions illustrate how stereotypical imaging of women and men play a part in how employees view tourism work in hotels and how they also affect the management of the employment structure based on a sexual division of labor, in anticipation of the perceived wants and needs of international tourists in the tourist setting. The positioning of women in the household is also perpetuated in the political ideology of the Indonesian government concerning women, women's roles, and women's contributions to economic development. The Indonesian government creates a contradictory position for women. In *Repelita* IV (1984–1989), it is stated that women have the same rights, obligations, and opportunities as men. However, Indonesian State Ideology defines women as loyal companions to the husband, procreators for the nation, educators and guides for children, regulators of the household, and useful members of society (Long & Kindon, 1997; Norris, 1994). The government clearly aligns women's function and status in relation to men as husbands and women as wives and mothers, thus predefining the nature of women's role in Indonesia's economic development. Thus, on the one hand, women are assured the same rights, opportunities, and obligations as men. But on the other hand, in their multiple roles—as wife and mother in the familial context in a developing society and as an active participant in developing efforts—they are responsible for creating and maintaining happy and healthy families in addition to contributing to Indonesia's national economic development by being "active participants in developing efforts." The positioning of women first as wives and then as mothers ignores the important role of women as breadwinners, which is a common responsibility to most women in lower income households. The state ideology largely hampers middle-class women to become involved in business activities.

However, the closer a family is to the poverty line, the less the resistance on cultural grounds (Operations Review Unit, 1988). The ambivalent position of women in state ideology is reflected by the rise of the share of female workers in the Indonesian workforce on the one hand, and the takeover of successful female-run businesses by men on the other hand (Guinness, 1994). A similar positioning of women is apparent in the Balinese Hindu religion and ritual practices. Balinese women's economic independence is countered by their political and religious subordination. On the level of political decision making men are in power and decide whether "women's issues" will be on the agenda or not. Consequently, women are not generally invited to meetings discussing community matters (Long & Kindon, 1997).

Conclusions

In Sanur all kinds of regulations prevent the growth of economic activities on the beach. The initiative of the big hotels in hiring masseuses who only work on their premises is one way of regulating these activities. The construction of the beachwalk, paid by the local government and supported by the hotel sector, is the latest regulatory effort. The increasing regulations are not detrimental to all economic activities. Rather, the impacts are differentiated. The upgrading of beach resorts by local initiatives creates new jobs and contributes to the professionalization of the service sector. This applies particularly to women entrepreneurs. Some women benefit from these changes by finding their activities "upgraded" and "formalized," which often represents mixed blessings for the women involved. At the same time the government measures create new market niches that allow informal activities to continue. In Sanur, many women exploit these new market niches in the margin of the formal sector. However, a striking impact of these regulations is the emergence of a sharp contrast between the women who find permanent employment and mobile masseuses who still walk up and down the beach. This research showed that both groups do not benefit equally from the upgrading of the beach. The permanently employed women occupy a protected working place and their activities are structured and formalized, which supplies them with the symbolic capital that is of distinctive value in their working area. The mobile masseuses lack this symbolic capital. Being associated with beach vendors and unlicensed guides contributes to their marginalization. However, although their work is submitted to many restrictions, they creatively look for opportunities and ways to avoid the regulations.

The women who found employment with a hotel benefit most from the beachwalk. By paying a small contribution to the hotel they have obtained a protected place to perform their activities. They have exclusive access to the hotel guests, and in addition can recruit customers among the other tourists who walk along the beach. The number of potential customers has increased considerably since the construction of the beachwalk. The women normally specialize in one activity, like older women in massage and younger women in manicure or hair braiding. Although they all work for themselves, every hotel has its team and the women who are part of these teams support each other in an informal way. The upgrading of the beach also contributes to the professionalization of their activities. Although most of the hotel-employed women once started their careers as beach vendors, they consider the mobile ladies as "unprofessional" outsiders. Judgements about the quality of each other's work—in terms of experience, knowledge, and technique (i.e., cultural capital)—is part of the competition between the two groups of women. In terms of entrepreneurship, however, one may question whether these women can be classified as independent entrepreneurs. Working under hotel protection is a risk-reducing strategy that represents heightened security in terms of income. Moreover, the need to innovate and to be flexible is diminished due to the relative income security. Though these women are not formally employed by the hotels and do not receive a salary, their position is not equivalent to self-employed women; they hold the middle between employees and entrepreneurs.

The position of the mobile masseuses is getting worse. Every new regulation contributes further to their marginalization. Their working area becomes more and more limited, which exerts increasing pressure on their economic capital. They have to walk further and need more time to find clients in order to make some money. Instead of specializing they tend to offer a whole range of products and services. As the mobile women are prepared to lower their prices to an extremely low level, however, the quality of the services suffers. Their activities are performed individually. They are not organized in any formal way; only members of the same family support each other. Not every daughter, however, will follow her mother's career. Further research has to show whether the young women aspire for a career in one of the hotels over that of a mobile masseuse.

The regulations do not prevent the oversupply of services. In comparison with other tourism-related jobs, the activities of the women on the beach are marginal. Nonetheless, their income is quite reasonable. Almost all of the married masseuses—whether mobile or permanently employed—are the breadwinner of an extended family. Both categories supplement other sources of income, like the revenues from a shop, a plot of land, or their husbands' petty trade. Their attitude towards business is quite conventional. They used to spread their risks over a range of activities and give little thought to breaking new ground in the market. As has been shown for women entrepreneurs in other service industries in Indonesia as well (Operations Review Unit, 1988), the women of Sanur beach are more interested in a secure income than in attaining maximum profits and/or expanding their operations. The main reason for this might be that women have a whole range of duties and responsibilities, especially towards their families. What they need, then, is regular sales and a reasonable level of payment, so that they can offer their children a future. This may explain why the masseuses in Sanur enter hotel jobs. Although these jobs curtail their mobility, they offer them a protected work place and a relatively secure income. Most of the women working on the beach are underprivileged. They do not have an opportunity to find work in other tourism-related activities. The beach, as well as the tasks they perform, is easily accessible; they require no formal education and only limited skills. They need little capital investment; the work can be undertaken in addition to domestic and religious tasks and other occupations; and they do not require government permits and licenses. All these factors make working at the beach popular among lower class women. Therefore, efforts to regulate beach life have not led to the disappearance of the informal sector. For each woman entering a hotel job, another one seems to be taking her place in walking up and down the beach trying to make a living.

As this chapter shows, tourism employment in Sanur is gender biased, reflecting not only local norms of "women's work" but also the hierarchical Balinese belief system in which women hold a low position. New work and income opportunities in tourism do not transform gender relations in Bali. Rather, the existing division of labor seems to be reinforced along sex-segregated lines. In this respect, tourism development reinforces the status quo; it does not threaten cultural values and traditions. Lower class women become involved in the tourism industry because their husbands fail to provide an income for their families, or to pay for their children's school fee and for religious ceremonies—child care and religion being considered as female domains in Balinese life. The economic opportunities in tourism leave the women with double or even triple work responsibilities. Our data do not reveal whether the women of Sanur beach gained more control of their lives and feel "empowered," as it seems to be the case among small female entrepreneurs in other tourist destinations areas in Indonesia (Wilkinson & Pratiwi, 1995). However, the women in Sanur do prefer the involvement with tourism over activities in agriculture or domestic trade, because they make more money.

The upgrading of the beach turned out to be beneficial to tourism development in Sanur. Compared to Kuta, where the extreme competition between the vendors makes it very difficult for the tourists to enjoy their holiday, the ongoing hassle has diminished. In Sanur the government regulations did not destroy opportunities for the unskilled and uneducated Balinese community to profit from tourism. This chapter shows that the government measures still leave enough room for the women to exploit new niches in the tourism market. This is in contrast to the luxury enclave resort Nusa Dua, where links with the local economy are weak. In this respect, small-scale business activities in tourism benefit women, but only to a rather limited degree.

Actually, the tourists are the true beneficiaries of the upgrading measures. The beachwalk contributes to their enjoyment of beach life. The area is neat, conveniently arranged, and all kinds of services are easily available. There is more protection against the constant harassment by the beach vendors and masseuses, as "pushing" the guests is strictly forbidden. The hotel and government regulations changed beach life for the better it seems, at least for the tourists.

Chapter 4

Homestays, *Losmen*, and Guesthouses: Doing Business in the Low-Budget Accommodation Sector in Kuta and Ubud, Bali

Eveline van der Giessen, Marie-Chantal van Loo, and Karin Bras

> Culture is the way we do things. The tourists do things differently. They have a different culture—a very poor one, which is why they are so interested in ours. . . . So, we have to make the tourists feel welcome and comfortable, and provide them with the things they need. Now, what do tourists need? . . . They need to buy things. And after they buy things, they need a cold drink of beer. They need to eat and sleep like we do, but they need to eat in a tourist way and sleep in a tourist way. (Darling, 1994, p. 274)

Introduction

Arriving in Kuta or Ubud, many tourists obediently follow their *Lonely Planet* or *Indonesia Handbook* in search for a place to stay. This is probably the best strategy to find your way in the maze of accommodations. At every street corner, in the back lanes, and at the edge of the rice fields, hotels, *losmen*, guesthouses, homestays, inns, *penginapan*, cottages, bungalows, and of course restaurants and souvenir shops are built. A search for the pleasant *losmen* in the middle of the rice fields near Monkey Forest Road in Ubud where you stayed 10 years ago may be without result. It might still be there, but no longer visible between the numerous other buildings that arose through the years. Business is booming in these villages and at first sight everyone seems to be involved in tourism. In 1957, there were only three hotels on Bali: the Sindhu Beach Hotel in Sanur, the Kuta Beach Hotel in Kuta, and the Bali Hotel in Denpasar, all owned by the government's national tourist agency (Vickers, 1989). In these early years traveling to Bali was still relatively exclusive, the real tourism boom started as early as the 1970s; nowadays Bali is the main gateway to Indonesia (Table 4.1).

Through the years accommodation mushroomed. In 1994 Bali counted close to 17,000 rooms in some 90 star-rated hotels and the rest in more than 1,200 non-star-rated hotels and homestays (Picard, 1996; see Tables 4.2 and 4.3). In 1994 the service sector—which includes hotels and restaurants—contributed 30.5% of Bali's local revenues, up from 17.4% in 1988 ("Balinese Sociocultural Values," 1996). Most of the tourism activity is concentrated in the *kabupaten* (regency) Badung and Gianyar where the popular tourism destinations Nusa Dua, Sanur, Kuta (Badung), and Ubud (Gianyar) are located.

At the national level priority is given to the development of areas like Nusa Dua and Sanur, which are designated as luxury beach resorts with mainly star-rated hotels. This focus on resorts, with an obvious preference for the "quality" tourist, made it difficult for the Balinese to participate in tourism, other than being an employee in the hotels or restaurants. At the beginning of the 1970s, however, Bali was visited by an unexpected flow of low-budget tourists—the "hippies"—"a young and educated clientele with a limited budget, less concerned about comfort than with local color, and keen to mingle with the Balinese" (Picard, 1996, p. 70). These "new" tourists came to Kuta, which quickly earned the "reputation as the cheapest and most alluring stop between India and Australia" (Picard, 1996, p. 78). Or they went to Ubud to escape beach life for a few days and get in touch with local Balinese culture. At both locations locals gradually got involved in tourism by turning into this new group of visitors and offering transport facilities or, most noticeable, exploiting restaurants and lodgings. The successful involvement of the local entrepreneurs resulted from an ability to recognize

Table 4.1. Tourist Arrivals at Ngurah Rai Airport, Bali (1982–1994)

Year	Arrivals Bali	Growth	%
1982	152,953		
1983	167,064	14,111	9.1
1984	187,135	20,071	12.0
1985	202,421	15,296	8.2
1986	233,484	31,063	15.4
1987	296,338	62,854	27.9
1988	351,509	55,171	18.9
1989	425,838	74,329	21.2
1990	476,440	50,602	11.9
1991	567,628	91,288	19.2
1992	740,806	173,178	30.3
1993	885,749	144,943	19.6
1994	1,048,901	163,152	16.0

Source: BPS (1991, 1994).

Table 4.2. Number of Accommodations, Rooms, and Beds in Bali (1991–1995)

Year	Accommodations	Rooms	Beds
1991	988	24,846	45,562
1992	1,093	25,862	45,167
1993	1,203	27,863	48,859
1994	1,215	28,967	51,278
1995	1,214	29,898	47,773

Source: BPS (1995).

changes in tourist demands and the possibilities to manipulate traditional resources such as residence, land, agricultural products, and family social networks. Even in situations in which resources may appear limited, local people used the existing resources effectively if they saw an opportunity to engage in entrepreneurial activities (Wall & Long, 1996). In the beginning locals accommodated guests in their own houses. These houses were composed of an ensemble of pavilions around an interior courtyard (Picard, 1996; Wall & Long, 1996) and proved to be suitable as a homestay. These informal arrangements in people's houses developed into a semiformal system of homestays in which families were permanently visited by a steady flow of foreign tourists (Vickers, 1989). With the arrival of a greater variety of customers these family-run places developed gradually into more commercially run establishments of contrasting size and status like guesthouses and bungalows with better rooms and sometimes even air-conditioning.

Instead of isolating the tourists from the locals in resorts, which was one of the major outcomes of Bali's master plan, these small-scale enterprises created an integration of tourism in the local community. Small-scale accommodations—like homestays—are usually family owned and operated, consisting of a room with two single beds, a bathroom, and offering breakfast. Furthermore, "they afford views of traditional housing compounds and family life, cater to the demand from some tourists for interaction with the Balinese and are viewed as a means of establishing interpersonal

Table 4.3. Distribution of Hotel Rooms Among the Four Main Resorts in Bali and Percentage of Star-Rated and Non-Star-Rated Rooms (1994)

Main Resorts	Hotel Rooms (%)	Number of Hotel Rooms	Star-Rated Rooms (%)	Non-Star-Rated Rooms (%)
Kuta	60%	17,600	63%	37%
Nusa Dua	15%	4,500	100%	—
Sanur	10%	3,200	76%	24%
Ubud	7%	2,200	4%	95%
Other	8%	2,400		

Source: Picard (1996).

relationships" (Wall & Long, 1996, p. 37). Up to now staying at small-scale accommodations was regarded to bring tourists closer to the Balinese: "In general, the smaller, family-run homestays of four to five rooms or bungalows are more of a quality experience than the impersonal larger hotels which are run more like businesses. In the smaller places, you get to mix more with the family and you are under the wing of an *ibu* (lady of the house)" (Dalton, 1991, p. 403). Large resorts are not only out-of-scale with the indigenous landscape and ways of life, but, because of the need of large capital inputs, outsiders step in, who inhibit the participation of locals. The opportunities for the Balinese themselves to participate in tourism have greatly enhanced their tolerance to tourist activities. Their small-scale enterprises are more likely to rely on local resources of supplies and labor, and local ownership implies that economic success for the entrepreneurs results in benefits to the local community. In both Kuta and Ubud locals became involved in tourism as entrepreneurs through the ownership and operation of facilities and not merely as employees in the hotel or restaurant sector, as is the case in a resort like Nusa Dua.

Kuta and Ubud have completely different characters. Kuta is a typical beach destination where tourists spend most of their time on the beach, in the discos, and visiting the numerous shops buying souvenirs. Ubud, on the other hand, is a destination for culture seekers. Balinese dances, handicraft, and the beautiful natural scenery are the major attractions. What they have in common is the presence of low-budget accommodation owned and managed by the local population. After observing Kuta and Ubud in more detail, it will become clear that both destinations are in different stages of tourism development in terms of Butler's (1980) tourist area life cycle. Comparing this stage of development with the actual accommodation will shed light on the nature of the low-budget accommodation at these two locations. The following questions have to be answered: Does the development of low-budget accommodation in Kuta and Ubud give reason to advocate a greater reliance on smaller accommodation? How "local" is local ownership and what type of management can be observed at the different types of low-budget accommodation? To what extent do the small-scale accommodations represent a quality experience close to Balinese culture, and to what extent are they affected by commercialization? What is the government policy towards this sector?

Government Regulations in the Hotel Sector

From 1988 onwards the provincial government adopted a policy in which the economic benefits of tourism had to be spread to all parts of the islands, contrary to the original master plan of 1971 in which the resort model was propagated (for more detailed information about this master plan see Picard, 1993). With this dispersed approach the government anticipated the rapid and uncontrolled development of hotels—mainly in the low-budget sector—that occurred already from the beginning of the 1970s. Sixteen centers (Nusa Dua, Sanur, Kuta, Kedonganan and Jimbaran, Ubud, Kintamani, Nusa Penida, Ujung, Candidasa, Lovina, Teluk Terima, Gilimanuk, Candikusuma, Bedugul, Tanah Lot, and Medewi) spread over the island were designated as Tourism Development Areas (Dibnah, 1992). For every one of these tourist areas planning policies were drawn concentrating on types of land use and including guidelines, building height restriction, proximity to beach, zones for hotel development, proximity to river valleys, proximity to temples, public access to beaches, use of traditional Balinese architectural style, and green wedges. In many cases, however, these guidelines have been ignored. Dibnah (1992) gives examples of Kuta, where the preservation of scenic views (green wedges) was given hardly any priority, and of Ubud, where on some occasion hotels are built in protected valley areas. Another example is Bali's most famous temple, Tanah Lot, where a five-star hotel and an international golf course have been established with the twelfth hole only 150 meters off the temple (Leser, 1997).

In these plans the already occurring uncontrolled growth in some of the destinations was totally ignored. The provincial government had hardly paid any attention to the low-budget sector. Their "laissez-faire" policy resulted in an excessive and unplanned growth of low-budget accommodations. Without getting permits locals started letting rooms, building bungalows on their compounds, and offering additional services as bicycle rentals or laundry services. Many of the less expensive accommodations are not registered, or list less rooms than available, they do not pay taxes, and quite often are not mentioned in the guidebooks. The *Indonesia Handbook* (Dalton, 1991) even prefers not to mention them in order not to "blow the cover" of those beautiful hideaways. For Kuta the planning policy concentrated on a further hotel development—21,000 rooms by the end of 2010—along the coast northwards, primarily consisting of higher quality hotels. In the planning for Ubud the focus was on building more star-rated hotels—9,338 rooms by the end of 2010 (Dibnah, 1992). Both examples show that the government is putting more emphasis on quantity rather than quality of the tourism product. The concentration of development already caused "congestion, regional imbalance, in-migration and environmental degradation" ("Bali's Economic Success," 1996; Wall & Long, 1996, p. 32). Without concentrating on the existing problems in both areas, a simple increase in the number of hotels was advocated. The quality is expected to come from the upmarket segment of the industry. This part of the sector—the star-rated or classified hotels—is under the authority of the national government in Jakarta, that is, the provincial office of the Ministry of Tourism, *Kanwil Departemen Pariwisata, Pos dan Telekomunikasi (Kanwil Parpostel)*, responsible for the national tourism policy at a provincial level. The licensing and registration of the non-star-rated or nonclassified hotels, on the other hand, is at the discretion of the Bali Government Tourism Office (*Diparda*, i.e., *Dinas Pariwisata Daerah*), which is an executive organ of the provincial government, financed by the provincial government and under the direct responsibility of the governor.

Major decisions about the tourism development on the island are taken in Jakarta and are focused on large-scale planning initiatives. Bali's own tourism department has limited financial and administrative means to control the island's tourism development. The absence of communication and coordination between the different government departments involved in the planning, and the overall bureaucratic system that lacks clearly defined roles for planning, implementation, and control of development (Dibnah, 1992), have led to an uncontrolled growth of tourist facilities, specifically in the *kabupaten* Gianyar and Badung where Ubud and Kuta are located. According to Picard (1996), numerous Balinese officials and academics have argued that the mandates for *Diparda* and *Kanwil Parpostel* are not clearly defined, with undesirable overlaps and gaps existing between these two institutions as a result. It would be better to "give *Diparda* jurisdiction over the classified hotels and restaurants, protesting the arbitrary nature of the classification criteria applied in the hotel and restaurant industry" (Picard, 1996, p. 132). At the end of the 1980s, in order to get more grip on the nonclassified accommodation, the provincial government introduced a separate classification system for *melati* hotels as an effort to formalize the low-budget sector and to monitor the tax revenues. This classification is a follow-up of the general division of the accommodation sector in: *pondok wisata* (accommodation with five rooms or less), Hotel *melati* (accommodation with more than five rooms) and Hotel *bintang* (Bali Tourism Directory, 1995). Up to now, however, there are no clear descriptions on the basis of which facilities are granted a particular classification, and local authorities have some difficulty in maintaining an accurate and updated record of the various accommodations. The idea is to introduce the *melati* system throughout the island, but this is not realized yet. For the accommodation with less than five rooms (*pondok wisata*)—most of the homestays—there is no classification or other control system yet.

Kuta—"the Least Balinese Place in Bali"

Before the arrival of tourism Kuta was a small, traditional, agricultural and fishing village of little economic or cultural importance on Bali. Kuta began to change in the late 1960s with the coming of the hippies who were attracted by the splendid sunsets and the hallucinogenic mushrooms (Picard, 1996). Gradually the informal accommodation that offered locals some additional income transformed into real business. Research done in Kuta in the 1980s (Hussey, 1989; Wall & Long, 1996) showed that Balinese entrepreneurs were able to meet the relatively low standards sought by budget tourists because of the availability of beaches, the proximity of the airport, and, maybe most important, the absence of competition of professional developers in this area. Before 1970 there were two hotels in Kuta; by 1975 the area contained more than 100 locally owned accommodations and 27 restaurants (Hussey, 1989), and the tourist frequentation of Kuta went from less than 1,000 in the 1970s to nearly 15,000 in 1973. Over the years, the hippie traveler "tended to move north, settling around Legian, which was considered less 'touristic'" (Picard, 1996, p. 79) and they made way for the "surfies," mainly Australians, coming to Kuta to experience the waves and the beer. Bali's reputation continued to grow and the restaurant and hotel owners of Kuta perceived the need for better facilities. Luxury hotels grew among the homestays and *losmen* and the place gradually became urbanized. "In 1994 Kuta had 46 star-rated hotels and 380 non-star-rated hotels and homestays, almost 60% of the island's hotel capacity. The master plan for Kuta, which in 1980 forecasted 7,000 rooms on 150 hectares by the year 2000, had become obsolete by the end of the eighties" (Picard, 1996, p. 80).

Tourism development in Kuta has occurred in a relatively short period of time, which has had its effect on the destination. From a quiet fishing village it changed almost overnight into a tourism destination with hundreds of hotels, restaurants, bars, shops, and banks. Streets are narrow, crowded, dirty, and full of cars, buses, motorbikes, and taxis. The often walled streets look like a maze, with buildings of all sizes squeezed on small parcels of land. Land use has become particularly intensive. Although the occupancy rates of the hotels are declining, new hotels are still built on the last available stretches of land. This unplanned growth has serious environmental impacts and causes fierce competition between the accommodation owners, the shopkeepers, and the street and beach hawkers. Even among the star-rated hotels a price war is going on with the result that some of them cut the price of their rooms to below that of the non-star-rated accommodations, which, on their turn, work with different price levels depending on the season. The competition is most clearly visible on the streets and beaches, where an endless stream of vendors have their permanent place or walk up and down chasing tourists. Having a quiet drink in one of the cafes is almost impossible; every few minutes tourists are approached by people who offer carvings, sunglasses, jewelery, transport, or any other service one can imagine. Sometimes tourists even cancel their trip to Kuta because "vendors use rude words and intimidation to make them buy things" ("Balinese Sociocultural Values," 1996; "Bali's Economic Success," 1996). Issues like crime, drug abuse, and sexual misbehavior are automatically connected to tourism in Kuta. The gigolo industry, part of Kuta's beach scene, makes the Balinese worry about their local youngsters who eagerly copy the way young tourists tend to behave on their 2- or 3-week holiday in Kuta (McCarthy, 1994). Concerns like these are related to the ever returning discussion whether Bali's cultural values are at stake—often with a strong reference to Kuta.

All this bad news about the village could lead to the conclusion that Kuta is out of fashion, the peak number of visitors has been reached, and that the "real" Bali did not survive and commercialization has taken over. These characteristics, together with low occupancy rates—in 1994 the occupancy rate for non-star-rated hotels in Bali was only 36.2% (BPS, 1995; see Table 4.4)—and a heavy reliance on repeat visitors put Kuta in the stagnation stage of Butler's model of the tourist area life cycle (Sofield, 1995). The stagnation stage of a tourist destination is described by Butler as follows: "Unless specific steps are taken, tourist destination areas and resources will inevitably become

Table 4.4. Room Occupancy Rate of Hotels and Other Accommodation, Bali (1991–1995)

Year	Classified Hotels (%)	Non-Classified Hotels and Other Accommodation (%)
1991	62.9%	34.4%
1992	56.2%	34.1%
1993	59.1%	34.8%
1994	62.0%	36.2%
1995	60.6%	29.4%

Source: Statistik Indonesia (1995).

overused, unattractive, and eventually experience declining use" (Butler, 1991, p. 203). Strangely enough, although tourists are complaining about Kuta and the guide books write about "what is wrong with Kuta" (Wheeler & Lyon, 1992), the place is always crowded with visitors.

The negative image of Kuta does not stop locals from finding their livelihood in tourism. The Kutanese host community has both adapted to and modified tourism in such a way that tourism has obtained a place in its culture. This has led to what Picard (1996) calls "touristic culture," which he defines as "a state of confusion between the values of the (Balinese) culture and those of tourism" (p. 129). Although most observers agree that Kuta is the "least 'Balinese' place in Bali" (p. 83), the local population is still able to separate their private lives as Kutanese from their public lives as they attend to tourists (Mabbett, 1987). Tourism, in other words, affects their lives only at the surface. The strong presence of the *banjar*—the neighborhood organization concerned with social control, public order, and religious ceremonies—is generally seen as the main reason why the Balinese are able to preserve their way of living, their traditions and customs. Through the years, the *banjar* concerns in Kuta have adapted to the local situation. Besides addressing religious and community issues, also tourism-related issues are nowadays on the agenda; these include small-scale environmental issues and questions related to the opening of local temples to tourism (Scures, 1994).

Ubud: Living up to its Cultural Image

Ubud, situated on the slopes of the central mountains and surrounded by beautiful rice fields, is called the heart of cultural tourism on Bali. From the 1930s onwards famous foreign painters came to live and work in Ubud. At that time the region was known more for its performing arts—dance and music—than for its paintings and sculptures. Through the encouragement of Western artists like Walter Spies and Rudolf Bonnet and the promotion of their work in Western countries, Ubud's craftsmen developed into artists. Gradually they started to sell their work on the tourist market and to give courses in painting, dance, or music to the culture lovers among the visitors (Picard, 1996). When more and more tourists found their way to Ubud, the locals began to build homestays, just as in Kuta but in a slower pace. But only in the 1980s larger number of tourists started to arrive, when the streets were paved and restaurants, galleries, and travel agencies were opened. Nowadays the village has expanded and homestays, guesthouses, and *losmen* can be found extending to the neighboring villages Campuan, Penestanan, Padangtegal, Peliatan, and Pengosekan, which are part of what most people consider as Ubud. "The hotel capacity went from 450 rooms in 1981 to around 2,200 in 1994 (of which 80 were in three star-rated hotels, the rest being distributed among 350 non-star-rated hotels and homestays)" (Picard, 1996, p. 86).

According to most observers and visitors, Ubud has managed to maintain its cultural reputation and intimate atmosphere of former days, although the visitors outnumber the inhabitants in peak periods. One of the main reasons is the provision of smaller, more intimate forms of accommodation—like homestays—where foreigners can feel they are in close contact with the cultural richness of the area. The accommodations are rarely larger than 20 rooms, built in accordance with Balinese architectural traditions, and the construction of star-rated hotels is kept to an absolute minimum. Also the initiatives of *Bina Wisata*, known as Ubud Tourism Information, in the 1980s contributed to the positive image building of Ubud. This foundation, created by two homestay owners, urged to protect the environment and the culture, two of the main assets of the place. Furthermore, they supplied the visitors with information concerning cultural events and proper ways to behave when attending religious ceremonies (Picard, 1996). These efforts resulted in the government's designation of Ubud as the "storehouse of arts . . . as a living emblem of tourism with a cultural vocation" (Picard, 1996, p. 88).

The question is, however, how long Ubud will be able to live up to its reputation. During the 1980s hotels, bungalows, restaurants, and private houses swallowed up the rice fields surrounding Ubud. In general, Bali is said to be losing 1,000 hectares of rice paddy each year (Leser, 1997). Many permanent houses and more expensive hotels were built on the most beautiful sites—like the Four Seasons Hotel along the Ayung river—and some cases have been sharply criticized for building in ravines— which are protected by Indonesian law—and for damaging the environment. The system for disposal of waste from hotels, restaurants, and domestic property (direct disposal of solid waste down ravines and regular burning) is unable to cope with the amount generated at the present time ("Balinese Sociocultural Values," 1996; Dibnah, 1992; Leser, 1997). The rapid growth has also put increasing strain on the transport system. The center of Ubud is coping with frequent traffic jams, pollution, and inadequate parking facilities.

The government does not seem to be able to control the quality and quantity of the development. The only interference that can be observed are obscure regulations like the felling of shade trees along roads frequented by tourists—believing tourists prefer treeless streets—in order to make Ubud more beautiful with multicolored flower gardens ("Balinese Sociocultural Values," 1996; Leser, 1997). Also the customary institutions, like the *banjar*, play practically no role of importance in Ubud's tourism development (Picard, 1996). Tourism in Ubud is developing totally unplanned and up till now it is predominantly a matter of local initiatives (i.e., individual enterprises). According to Butler's destination tourist area life cycle, Ubud is in the development stage characterized by a rapid growth of visitors and, rather a new phenomenon for Ubud, a growing interest from outsiders to invest in Ubud. Some of the local facilities are replaced by larger, more modern and elaborate facilities, like the star-rated hotels. Especially this growing interference from outsiders and the impact of these rapid accommodation developments on the environment are causing the negative reports about tourism in Ubud and its direct vicinity. The tourists are not among those who are worried. For most tourists Ubud is still the center of Balinese culture in which they can find the integration in village life they are looking for and where the locals are the sole beneficiaries from tourism.

Small Entrepreneurs in the Accommodation Sector

Looking back at the low-budget accommodations in both villages, it can be concluded that the way locals got involved in tourism shows some similarities. They gradually got involved when tourism was not yet a major asset and the destination did not yet occupy a place on the "tourist map." However, a big difference between Kuta and Ubud is the pace of development, the nature of the destination, and the present-day image. To compare the types of accommodation and the local participation and management styles in the next section, we take a closer look at the locals behind these businesses.

Figure 4.1. Signboard announcing homestay accommodation in Kuta. (Photo by E. van der Giessen and M. C. van Loo)

Booming Entrepreneurship in Kuta

Through time many of Kuta's homestays and *losmen* evolved into small hotels where the initial ideas about taking in visitors as part of the family moved to the background (Figure 4.1). As Mabbett (1987) describes—in the story of an elderly villager—the locals were, more or less, forced to improve the facilities because the hippies were replaced by other groups of tourists—predominantly Australians—and standards changed rapidly.

> When we started taking in travelers there was a great demand for cheap, simple accommodation—just a place to sleep, a place to bathe, a squat toilet. People did not make demands and we treated them like members of the family. Now even the poorest of them expect a room of their own, a proper bed, a fan, a bathroom with a shower, a sit-down toilet. We used to provide them just one bed covering, to cover the mattress. Travelers always carried their own top sheets or blankets. Now they don't and we must provide them. We used to give people a little breakfast—coffee or tea and some fruit—and that was included in the price. Then they wanted better breakfasts, so now we give them eggs and toast as well. There's been another change too. People used to be relaxed and grateful but now they are more demanding. It seems that the more we do, the more we must do. (Mabbett, 1987, p. 25)

Generally, locals started with a single room to let which they themselves built. In the early 1970s the *losmen* business in particular was booming. Hussey (1986) states that many of the locals preferred to invest in a *losmen* because of the general lack of experience in tourism. Restaurants were more difficult to run because the business required at least some skill in food, services and management, and constant attention by the owner. Whenever they succeeded to attract tourists, they slowly expanded their business. It happened that locals sold their land for astronomical prices. Mabbett (1987) gives an example of a Balinese who in 1969 bought 75 acres on the beach in Seminyak (close to Kuta) for 3,500,000 *rupiah*. In 1985 it was already worth 500,000,000 *rupiah*. Hussey (1989) mentions a price increase from US$17 to US$8,000 for one acre of prime land in the core area of Kuta between 1970 and 1984. However, Mabbett (1987) argues that most Kutanese have resisted the temptation to sell their land.

The entrepreneurs among the Kutanese established small shops, restaurants, bunga-lows, and *losmen*, which they manage themselves, but more often they have other Balinese performing the actual work (Scures, 1994). Or they lease their land at the beach or along the main roads to outsiders and become landlords, which is regarded as more profitable than investing in a tourism enterprise (Picard, 1996). The popularity of Kuta attracted people from all over Indonesia willing to try their luck in tourism and Kuta became a melting pot of ethnic groups and nationalities. They compete for a variety of jobs, working in retail shops, restaurants, handicraft/garment factories, and hotels. In the hotel sector, for instance, "Balinese fill many of the mid and low-level jobs, while many Javanese hold the upper-level management positions" (Scures, 1994, pp. 140-141). "Between 1977 and 1980, non-locals supplied more than 40 per cent of new investments" (Hussey, 1989, p. 319), mainly in the Legian area. Research done in the 1990s showed that 90% of the tourist enterprises in Kuta are owned by persons outside the municipality, whether Balinese from other regions or Indonesians from other provinces (Scures, 1994). For quite a number of years a large number of foreign businessmen have been active in Kuta, in most cases working together with locals. In former days they invested primarily in bars and restaurants because of the Indonesian law prohibiting sale of land to foreigners (Hussey, 1989). Nowadays they have all kinds of businesses and also joint partnerships with Indonesians in the accommodation sector can be observed. The number of foreign businessmen is estimated as "several thousand people of all nationalities" (Picard, 1996, pp. 79–80).

With the years the type of management also changed. Successful accommodation owners moved out of the compound where they had their homestay or *losmen* and they left the management to other family members or they employed youngsters from outside of Kuta, who were, and still are, available in large numbers, looking for experiences, money, and opportunities in the tourism industry. The accommodation developed from an additional source of income into a business (or one of several businesses) managed from a distance. Nowadays Kuta has homestays (that do not any longer deserve that name), *losmen*, and guesthouses with as many as 33 rooms and with prices ranging from 15,000 *rupiah* to a maximum of 45,000 *rupiah* a night; prices that, depending on the season, are negotiable or not. The differences in facilities are small. Accommodations try to distinguish themselves by the location (close to sea or in one of the famous street like Poppies Lane), by the interior decoration of the place, or by offering additional small services. In earlier days it was not necessary to advertise, but with the fierce competition it is more and more difficult to get visitors. Low-budget accommodations seldom have formalized contacts with tour operators or travel agencies abroad. Not offering package deals, they aim at the group of individually traveling tourists. Promotion is organized informally through their own networks consisting of accommodations in other areas, contacts in the transport and guiding sector, and foreign friends or associates. Brochures or leaflets are hardly ever used; normally the accommodation has a signboard in front of the accommodation and name cards are handed out to tourists on several strategic locations. What is regarded as good promotion is getting a positive review in one of the travel guides and, of course, word-of-mouth publicity, mainly by the tourists themselves (van der Giessen & van Loo, 1996).

The result of this standardization and commercialization of the low-budget accommodation in Kuta is a more business-like approach and a less intimate atmosphere. Although there are still accommodations that are called "homestay," homestays in the original meaning of the word no longer exist in Kuta. When arriving in Kuta, tourists may no longer expect the idyllic tableau of a Balinese family living their life in front of the tourist's room. The only Indonesians they will meet are the employees working at the front desk (if there is any), the same ones that will sweep the terrace in the morning and prepare their breakfast. Communication, normally in English, is limited to the exchange of information about facilities as transport or tours. The closest a tourist will get in his or her efforts to integrate in Balinese culture is by having a conversation with one of the employees about his family, hoping he will be a Balinese and not a newcomer from Timor or Flores. Although not planned as a resort, Kuta actually functions as one, isolating the tourists more and more from the local population and from local Balinese life. The initial intimate host–guest relationship has given way to a large service industry in which a tourist is merely a source of income who gets what he paid for, but will be forgotten immediately after he leaves.

Ubud's Family-Oriented Entrepreneurship

Wherever you turn in Ubud and its surrounding villages, you see signboards announcing "homestay." Although there is plenty of bungalow-style accommodation for up to 35,000–40,000 *rupiah* a night, homestays are still the predominant form of accommodation. The more expensive accommodations in Ubud are situated at the outskirts of the village on the edges of the deep river valleys. The bungalow-style accommodations and homestays, both belonging to the low-budget sector, hardly ever surpass 20 rooms. In 1995 *kabupaten* Gianyar had three star-rated hotels with a total of 96 rooms, whereas in 1991 two star-rated hotels had been registered with 44 rooms in total. In 1991 the number of registered non-star-rated hotels was 260, with 1,636 rooms, and in 1995 the number had risen to 372 with 2,344 rooms available (Bali Tourism Directory, 1995). Because many of the smaller accommodations are not registered, the actual number is probably a lot higher.

Although the homestays in Ubud are still close to the early concept, standards are raised and promotion has become a lot more important. Especially when homestays are situated off the main road, tourists will not automatically drop by. Therefore, homestay owners send youngsters out to the most important entry gates of the village, like the Perama office (a tourist transport company) or the public bus station at the market, to get clients. This direct approach is not that common in Kuta, where the streets are dominated by people offering transport services and souvenirs. Making it more attractive to stay, some of the homestay owners offer better prices for longer stays or promise discounts for returning visitors. When the accommodation is started with financial support from foreigners, as is the case with some of the homestays and guesthouses, these contacts will be used to get clients.

For many of the accommodation owners in Kuta operating a homestay, *losmen*, or guesthouse has become their only occupation, sometimes in combination with other tourism-related activities. However, the majority of entrepreneurs in Ubud—especially the ones with a homestay—are occupied outside tourism. Operating a homestay or *losmen* is in most cases not the only source of income. This kind of low-budget accommodation can still survive with small numbers of customers, but the revenues are generally low. It is regarded as an additional source of income. If revenues are promising, the owners usually plan to expand. This is done by simply adding an extra room when the money is available.

Staying in Ubud's low-budget accommodation will in most cases provide the tourist with a possibility to observe daily Balinese life. Most of the day-to-day work—cooking breakfast, cleaning the rooms, providing hot tea all day, doing laundry, and shopping for food—is carried out by the female head of the family (Long & Kindon, 1997). These activities are easy to combine with child care and the women's domestic and ritual responsibilities, but at the same time the development of homestays has led to a growing workload, especially for women. Although their ability to speak English is generally limited, these women, and also other family members, will be the tourist's local guides when taken to the market or to *banjar* ceremonies (Long & Kindon, 1997). This cultural, intimate atmosphere, which made Ubud famous, is still one of the most important trademarks of the place. Having a room with a view over the rice fields, plenty of possibilities to visit dance performances, and spending some days close to Balinese family life still draw a constant flow of tourists.

Conclusions

An analysis of the low-budget accommodations of Kuta and Ubud shows that this sector of the hotel industry developed totally unplanned. Initiatives to start a homestay or *losmen* came from the locals themselves, who anticipated on a sudden demand. At the national government level the priority was given to the development of up-market resorts and no attention was paid to the growing number of low-budget hotels that catered to the needs of budget tourists. This group was not expected to come and was not really welcome, as they were not regarded as beneficial for the economic growth of the island. When they came, tourism planners tended to overlook the positive aspects of their arrival. Local entrepreneurs or would-be entrepreneurs, however, unerringly sensed opportunities.

The number of accommodations in Kuta and Ubud is still growing, absorbing adjacent villages and more and more determining the image of Kuta and Ubud. Excess supplies, declining occupancy rates, and unacceptable pressure on the environment demand effective and efficient planning—planning that has to be initiated and implemented by the provincial government, which seems to be unable to realize a feasible policy for this sector of the industry.

The good news is that low-budget accommodations have enabled the Balinese to participate in the booming tourism industry. But they do so in different ways and with different levels of success, as the examples of Kuta and Ubud show. Differences between the accommodation sector in both villages are related to the divergent phases of tourism development both places experience. In Kuta, being in the stagnation stage, tourism is everywhere. The commercialized and standardized accommodation (together with all the other tourism-related activities) and the large influx of outsiders make it difficult to talk about Kuta as a village. Kuta is a thriving tourist "city" where the economic opportunities that tourism offers made the local entrepreneurs wealthy. Local participation is no longer restricted to the Kutanese. New opportunities for employment attracted people from other parts of Bali, migrants from other provinces (mainly from Java), and foreigners. Kuta's party image does not any longer invite tourists to a quality experience close to Balinese culture. The way tourists were accommodated in the beginning of the 1970s no longer exists in Kuta. It is, however, reasonable to assume that the more commercialized host–guest relationship in Kuta matches perfectly with the expectations of Kuta's budget tourists.

Ubud is still supposed to be in the development stage, enjoying a growing interest from outside investors. For the time being, however, the family-run businesses dominate the place. Locals from Ubud, sometimes in association with foreigners, and their families have found an additional source of income in tourism. Their enterprises are modest and informally managed. Small investments enable most of the local people to enter this sector and start their own business. Furthermore, this form of accommodation fits in well with the village cosmos. In contrast to Kuta, an overall positive image is the result.

As long as there is a demand for low-budget facilities and services local entrepreneurs can benefit from tourism. But as soon as the demand changes and the scale of businesses increases, the locals will be unable to supply the capital and upgrade their accommodation. Their place will be taken immediately by businessmen from Jakarta or by transnational companies that are waiting in line to invest. This is not yet happening in Kuta and Ubud, although plans for more up-market accommodations have already been developed.

Chapter 5

Gili Trawangan: Local Entrepreneurship in Tourism Under Pressure

Theo Kamsma and Karin Bras

Introduction

> The day the people called "a cloudy Tuesday" (18-4-1995) was the moment on which the cleaning team formed by the provincial government started their action. Houses, tourist accommodation, restaurants, souvenir shops were demolished in a short time. . . . The cleaning began at eight o'clock and four hours later 25 houses were broken down. . . . The result of this action was not only felt by the local people themselves, but also by the tourists who were having a holiday on the paradise island. Tourists usually wake up at nine o'clock, but this morning they were woken up earlier because their bungalows were target of the demolishing action. . . . As a result of this many of them shortened their holiday, which normally lasts a week. (translated from "Bara Pariwisata Gili," 1995)

The provincial government proclaimed a 4-day visit prohibition to keep journalists, activists, tourists, and anyone else away from Gili Trawangan. In spite of this prohibition, the Gili Trawangan case has had national as well as international press coverage ("Bara Pariwisata Gili," 1995; Breda, 1997; Kamsma, 1996; "Mengapa Terjadi Tragedi," 1995). The problems concerning this small island located in the province of Nusa Tenggara Barat (NTB) in Indonesia are characteristic of the Indonesian land policy in areas that are regarded as promising tourist destinations. As is often the case, small-scale local initiatives lose ground in favor of a government-controlled larger scale development. In the tourists' search for new idyllic places, as the Gili Trawangan case will show, locals are often pioneers in meeting the newly arisen demand for tourist facilities. They start homestays, *warung*, and transportation, or hire out snorkel gear, motorcycles, or mountain bikes. The initial investments are small, but the local entrepreneurs gradually expand their businesses, like at several locations on Lombok, where the success of small-scale entrepreneurs did not remain unnoticed. In the last 10 years landownership in present and future touristic areas has felt the growing pressure of commercial interests of a new elite. Wealthy enterprises and private entrepreneurs from the Nusa Tenggara Barat region, but also from Bali and Java, have bought large parcels of land. Apart from land speculation it is their goal to develop large-scale touristic resorts, like the planned Putri Nyale resort in the south of Lombok, where an area of 1,250 hectares is to be transformed into a sun–sea–sand destination that will include a marina, golf courses, dozens of hotels, and other attractions. Or like Senggigi in the northwest, the first area being developed for tourism, that already had a history of land speculation and disputes. Tourism development is of course not the only cause for land speculation, but as the Gili Trawangan case will show, tourism development on Lombok is strongly characterized by large disputes about land and the appurtenant right to build tourism facilities. There is a strong local involvement in this potential growth sector. The introduction of tourism led to economic diversification. In former days the people of Trawangan made their living through agriculture, fishing, and herding small livestock. Nowadays you can find shopkeepers, *losmen* and restaurant owners and personnel, souvenir sellers, boatsmen, masseuses, diving instructors, and local tourist guides on Trawangan. But there is also an emerging interest of outside entrepreneurs who are willing to invest in large-scale resorts. It remains to be seen whether these new initiatives will not be at the cost of the locals of Trawangan.

In this chapter we discuss how local participation in tourism is put under pressure through a government orientation on so-called "quality" tourism, which leads to drastic regulations and the involvement of outside investors. The concept of local participation is an important issue in the debate on tourism development in developing countries and mostly discussed in relation with the growth of mass tourism and its negative impacts on local communities. In developing countries the growth of tourism often is not accompanied by the creation of local linkages to spread the benefits of growth in social, sectoral, and regional terms (Brohman, 1996; Harrison, 1992; Murphy, 1985, 1994; Shaw & Williams, 1994; Simmons, 1994). Brohman gives an outline of the shortcomings that are commonly associated with the Third World tourism industry. He states that normally the three most lucrative elements of Third World tourism—marketing and the procurement of customers, international transportation, and food and lodging—are dominated by vertically integrated global networks. "The technical, economic and commercial characteristics of mass tourism sectors tend to favor the development of large-scale, integrated, multinational enterprises" (Brohman, 1996, p. 54). Foreign capital profits from local natural resources, but because of the high rate of foreign ownership the profits made in tourism are not locally enjoyed. Its rather isolated position in a local economy prevents the tourism industry from being linked with other economic sectors. The consequences are low multiplier and minor spread effects outside the tourism enclaves. These discussions have led to a general conclusion that tourism should be seen as a local resource and that in its planning the principal criterion should be the desires of local residents. Essentially, a tourist destination has to be regarded as a community and the local residents as the nucleus of the tourism product. Local support is indispensable for developing a sustainable tourism product (Brohman, 1996). The introduction of the concept of local participation as "the direct involvement of ordinary people in local affairs" (Van Schaardenburgh, 1995, pp. 10–11) is therefore a viable one. As locals are influenced by tourism developments themselves, it is clear that, in order to control changes that affect their lives, they have to participate in plan making, decision making, and implementation. This means empowering people to mobilize their own capacities, be social actors rather than passive subjects, manage the resources, make decisions, and control the activities that affect their lives. Local tolerance of tourist activities is significantly enhanced if opportunities exist for locals to be involved in tourism as entrepreneurs through involvement in the ownership and operation of facilities, and not merely as employees in the hotel or restaurant sector.

The result of discussions on local participation in tourism was a boom in community development strategies and projects (Bras, 1991, 1994; De Kadt, 1979; Saglio, 1979; Schlechten, 1988; Smith & Eadington, 1992) and the introduction of terms like responsible, sustainable, grass root, and rurally integrated tourism. No attention has been paid in these discussions to the already existing, locally based small-scale private enterprises (Shaw & Williams, 1994; Smith, 1994; Wall, 1995). Private initiatives in the accommodation sector or adjoining sectors like the souvenir industry are evident wherever tourists emerge. The literature, however, is uninformative about the contribution of small-scale private enterprises to local communities.

Notions of small-scale entrepreneurship and local participation have to be described against the background of the provincial and national tourism policy in Indonesia. The national government emphasizes the importance of tourism within regional development and has defined new target areas in its *Repelita VI* (1993–1998). The eastern islands, still regarded as poor and backward, is an area that gets more and more attention in tourism promotion campaigns directed by the government. An analysis of the tourism development on Lombok, and more specifically on Gili Trawangan, will introduce the actors who play a role in tourism development and will provide an insight into the different interests that are at stake. One group of actors is the locals of Trawangan who, by operating small-scale private enterprises, try to improve their living conditions and raise their standard of living.

In this chapter the following questions will be answered:

- How did the local population of Gili Trawangan get involved in tourism and how do they operate their small-scale enterprises?

- How does the local population of Trawangan cope with the growing outside interest and competition in their area?

- Will the locals of Trawangan still be able to meet the required quality standards a few years from now, or will they have to make room for star-rated hotels?

- Why are these initiatives left out of the discussions on local participation?

In order to answer these questions it is necessary to analyze Lombok's tourism development and the interests that are at stake in developing Lombok as a new tourist destination.

Lombok, a New Tourist Destination

Although the province Nusa Tenggara Barat (Lombok and Sumbawa) hosts no more than 3% of the international visitors, especially Lombok is becoming an increasingly popular destination. For a long time Lombok was not noticed as a tourist destination of any importance, mostly because of the popularity of its neighbor Bali. In his book *The Island of Bali* Covarrubias described Bali as an island that has the lush and splendid greenery of Asia, whereas Lombok is arid and thorny like Australia (Cederroth, 1981). For many visitors Bali was the only island worth visiting. Travel guides almost immediately state that tourists who visit Lombok should not expect the cultural refinement of Java or the lively dance and music of Bali. However, with the growing demand for new destinations the interest for Lombok began to develop, and nowadays Lombok is described as a new paradise. Referring to the popularity of Bali, the provincial tourism department on Lombok used to promote the island through a motto: *You can see Bali on Lombok, but you can not see Lombok on Bali.* This slogan referring to the Balinese who live on Lombok is abolished, but Lombok still seems to have difficulties in becoming more than only a nearby replacement of its famous neighbor Bali. In the promotional material the island is still linked with Bali. A hotel in one of the tourism areas, for instance, is using a banner with the following text to promote its happy hour: "Lombok as Bali. In Sixties watching the Eastern Bali with cold draught beer Bintang. Buy one and get two." And the Garuda In-flight Magazine starts an article about Lombok with a comparison: "Lombok? Sure, I've heard of it. The Bali of 20 years ago, isn't it? Without all that commercialization. Sounds great!" This is a popular view of Lombok. Images of empty white-sand beaches without jet skis, traditional villages without tourist buses, and simple bungalow-style guest houses without pizza bars. This image is, however, no longer correct. The number of foreign as well as domestic tourists has increased rapidly in the last few years, just like the number of hotel rooms, as is shown by the overview below (Table 5.1).

Agriculture and Landownership

The island has an area of 4,739 km², dominated by the volcano Rinjani, and a population of almost 2.5 million. Approximately 96% of the people are Sasak, the indigenous population; most of them are Muslims. Another important ethnic group is the Balinese; almost all of them live in West Lombok. There are also minority populations of Chinese,

Table 5.1. Number of Visitors and Hotel Rooms in Nusa Tenggara Barat (1988–1995)

Year	Foreign Tourists	Domestic Tourists	Star-Rated Hotel Rooms	Non-Star-Rated Hotel Rooms
1988	44,846	55,475	340	382
1989	56,148	67,146	340	1,037
1990	107,210	76,817	386	1,216
1991	117,988	99,011	549	2,167
1992	129,997	102,040	819	2,278
1993	140,630	106,907	859	2,463
1994	157,801	120,279	1,025	2,682
1995	167,267	140,940	1,183	2,949

Source: Dinas Pariwisata DATI I Prop. NTB (1995b).

Javanese, and Arabs. Nowadays most of the people on Lombok still derive their income from the agricultural sector, which is based on the growth of rice. Other important agricultural products are: soya beans, maize, cassava, groundnuts, onions, tobacco, and several fruits. In 1990 55% of the population was engaged in the agricultural sector; in some areas, like the southern part of Central Lombok and the mountain villages in the northeast, as much as 98% (Lübben, 1995).

Not all parts of Lombok are equally fertile. Central Lombok, south of one of the highest volcanoes in Indonesia, Gunung Rinjani, is similar to Bali with fertile fields irrigated by water flowing from the mountains. More to the south and east it is much drier. These areas get little rain and often have droughts that last for months. Another problem on Lombok is the shortage of land and the concentration of landownership in the hands of a small group of landowners. As a result, the majority of the local population are landless farmers and share-croppers. In 1990 the average size of farmland was 0.36 hectares and about 50% of the population was landless farmers. In the last 10 years landownership was dominated by the commercial interests of a new elite. Wealthy enterprises and private entrepreneurs from the region, but also from Bali and Java, have bought large parcels of land. Especially the development of tourism reinforces this process (Kamsma, 1996; Lübben, 1995; McCarthy, 1994; Mucipto, 1994).

The main source of income on Lombok is still agriculture. Fifty percent of the gross regional domestic product (GRDP) comes from agriculture (Lübben, 1995). Although the provincial government succeeded in an annual average rise of GRDP of 8.54%, Nusa Tenggara Barat still is the province with the lowest income (Dinas Pariwisata Prop. DATI I NTB, 1995b). The development of larger industries on Lombok is negligible, but the growth of home industry, on the other hand, is considerable. Especially in the handicraft home industry there is a growth in output within the country, but also internationally (Lübben, 1995). The contribution of the industrial sector to the GRDP, however, is only 3%, and that of trade and tourism 16%. The growing importance of tourism and handicraft within regional development is evident. The great number of unemployed, estimated at 35%, urges the creation of work outside the agricultural sector. Jobs in the hotel and restaurant sector, in transport, and in the travel business are regarded as a solution.

Resort Development

In spite of the relatively rapid tourism development Lombok is still predominantly an island of farmers. Almost all accommodation and most of the tourism activities are located in three main areas, namely Senggigi, a beach resort on the west coast; the Gili Islands, three small islands on the northwest coast; and Kuta, a small beach resort in the south. Outside these areas tourists are still rare enough to attract a great deal of attention. The tourism master plan is characterized primarily by large-scale projects launched by Javanese or foreign entrepreneurs, like the Putri Nyale resort, which is planned in the south of Lombok. In the UNDP, which studied Lombok's tourism potential in 1987, the three beaches in South Lombok (Putri Nyale, Seger, and Aan) were designated as an area suitable for the development of an integrated tourism resort. Altogether 1,031 luxury rooms and 953 middle-class rooms were planned. The project area is about 6 km long, from Kuta village in the west to the

end of Aan Beach in the east (World Tourism Organization [WTO], 1987). The
Lombok Tourism Development Cooperation (LTDC) has bought this 1,250-hectare
area and is going to turn it into a sun–sea–sand destination that will include a
marina, golf courses, dozens of hotels, and other attractions. LTDC is a joint venture
of the private organization PT Rajawali Wira Bhakti Utama, which holds 65% in the
LTDC and *Pemda (Pemerintah Daerah)*, the provincial government of Nusa
Tenggara Barat with 35%. The prediction is that "LTDC will create approximately
15,000 jobs during a 10-20 year period. . . . In addition to the 15,000 jobs directly
involved in tourism, an estimated 6,000 to 10,000 additional jobs will be generated
by the new activities (administration, health, education, commercial, handicrafts,
etc.)" (McCarthy, 1994, p. 60). It remains to be seen whether the local population
will profit from this new resort. McCarthy states that luxury hotels require sophisticated staff and that even in Bali the majority of hotel workers are not local. Lübben
(1995) concludes for Kuta that already in the present situation the locals have a very
limited share in the tourism development. What is operational in Kuta at the moment
are mainly *melati* hotels, bungalow-style accommodation, and small restaurants. The
initiatives come from people out of Praya, Mataram, or Bali and hardly from people
out of the Kuta area. Therefore, it remains to be seen whether the local people are
prepared for tourism that is dominated by the international tourist industry. Until
now, the planning of the Putri Nyale Resort already had its influence in this area.
Through the years big parcels of land have been purchased by the LTDC and the
local owners only received low compensation, often not enough to buy a new plot
of land in another area. LTDC bought the land in this area from the local farmers at a
price of 200,000 *rupiah* per acre. The same land is now sold to Indonesian and
foreign investors for the amount of 10-15 million *rupiah* per acre, almost fifty times
the amount of money the locals received (Kamsma, 1996). The latest developments
are land evictions, in order to build the newly planned international airport to make
the Putri Nyale Resort more accessible in the near future. The airport is planned to
come into operation in the year 2000.

Gili Trawangan

Together with Gili Air and Gili Meno, Gili Trawangan is one of the so-called Gilis, three
tropical islands on the northwest coast of Lombok. Until 1976 Gili Trawangan was
uninhabited. The island, covered with dense mangrove woods, was considered to be
impenetrable. In 1976 the former provincial governor of NTB, Wasita Kusuma, gave his
four children the right of customary use (*HGU, Hak Guna Usaha*) of a part of the island
to start a coconut plantation. Also companies like PT Generasi Jaya and PT Rinta obtained
these rights. Officially, the land remained state property. The Sasak, the local inhabitants
of Lombok, were recruited to work on these plantations. Due to difficult circumstances,
the lack of infrastructure, and diseases the harvests failed. The companies withdrew from
the island but some workers stayed. They obtained one or two hectares of land and built
themselves a livelihood with fishing, agriculture, and cattle breeding. Nowadays about
150 families or 350 people live on the island, a number that doubles in the high tourist
season in June, July, and August. In 1995 there were 31 low-budget hotels with an average
number of six rooms each (Dinas Pariwisata Prop. DATI I NTB, 1996).

The story goes that in 1981 the first tourist, a German, spent a night on the island (Mucipto, 1994). He wrote about his experiences to the publishers of a German travel guide. Like other travel guide publishers (i.e., Lonely Planet) their concept relies heavily on contributions of fellow travelers. The author of the travel guide used the information and mentioned the island as a new unspoiled paradise. Since then thousands of tourists visited the island. At first it was quite a project to get to the island by public transport. Nowadays most of the tourists go straight from Bali to Gili Trawangan. They buy a ticket from Perama, a local transport company, which includes a ride from their accommodation to the eastern harbor of Bali, Padangbai, the crossing by ferry (6 hours) to Lembar, transport to the harbor of Bangsal, and a crossing to one of the Gilis (Figure 5.1). As at first there were no accommodations and restaurants on the island; the tourists were invited by the villagers to stay at their homes—board (three meals) and lodging for one price. Later on three or four households built bungalows together. Their relatives were employed in the accommodation; other islanders supplied food, beverages, and transportation to the island. Gradually the standard of living improved as more people came to stay on the island and the locals became more and more absorbed into the tourist industry.

All accommodations, bars, and restaurants are along the east coast beach, from about 500 meters to the left of where the boats land to 1,500 meters to the right. The local residences were also scattered along the east coast beach. Some have their own

Figure 5.1. Outrigger boat to Gili Trawangan. (Photo by T. Kamsma)

dwelling, others occupy a bungalow or live in an extension built next to the restaurant. A sandy path goes around the island and divides the beach from the bungalows. The restaurants are mostly located on the beach, a strip of about 25 meters at its widest. Bamboo is generally used as building material for the dwellings. In recent years, however, many entrepreneurs upgraded their bungalows and restaurants by using bricks for construction. The compact layout gave the area a friendly village atmosphere.

The accommodation and restaurants on the island are no longer strictly run by people from the island or the nearby mainland. Through the years people from other parts of Lombok, but also from other islands and even from other countries, came to Trawangan to work or to operate a business. The majority, however, still originate from the island or the nearby mainland, like Bangsal and Pemenang or the city of Mataram. In spite of this influx of "outsiders" tourism enterprises are identical in form, meaning small scale, locally oriented, and built with relatively small investments. Foreigners are only able to exploit a business in cooperation with an Indonesian partner. In practice these foreigners only show up once or twice a year during their holiday. They consider their enterprise as a nice holiday address rather than an important source of income.

Gili Trawangan's main attractions are the sandy beaches, snorkeling, and the nightlife. The snorkeling is outstanding. It was to be expected that the best place to snorkel is at the same spot where you could find the tourist accommodations. At the beach you can hire masks and flippers. There is a diving school where one can attend classes and go out with a boat to practice. Through the years Gili Trawangan also got the reputation of a party island. Everywhere on the island you can find announcements where to find the next sunset, moonlight, or sunrise party. Young people from all over the world meet, dance, drink, and experiment with sex and drugs (local marihuana and magic mushrooms), and indeed partying goes on till sunrise. Due to that reputation locals often refer to Gili Trawangan as Gili Tralala.

Trouble in Paradise

In 1991 a group of entrepreneurs from the west of Lombok—the Basri Group—demanded that the Trawangan people who occupy the eastern coastal strip, the touristically most lucrative part because of the coral reef in front of the beach, should clear the area. The business group had bought up the rights to use the land (HGU) from PT Generasi Jaya, which had held these rights since 1976 to start a coconut plantation. But the business group was not the only one that claimed these rights. Another group of businessmen associated with Ponco Sutowo (Jakarta Hilton) and Nellie Adam Malik (widow of a former vice-president) are negotiating with two companies that have had government permission since 1986 to develop 200 of Gili Trawangan's 380 hectares for tourism (McCarthy, 1994). A third party is the Bupati from West Lombok. He claims that the former governor of NTB, Wasita Kusuma, had no right to grant the HGUs on Gili Trawangan to his children. These rights should have been given on *kabupaten* level. The children of the former governor Wasita Kusuma are the fourth party. For their part, they of course claim that, although they left the island years ago, their HGUs are still legally valid. The government takes the position that the land is state property and that no claims are legally valid other than those granted by the government. As soon as it became clear that the development of tourism on Gili Trawangan is profitable, the parties that consider themselves involved sought their right. The land in tourism areas is worth 15,000,000 *rupiah* per acre nowadays and is still rising. An investment in tourism promises to be lucrative and selling landownership or user rights in these areas is highly profitable. As a consequence the different parties were and still are entangled in different lawsuits. A party that has not been mentioned yet in these lawsuit entanglements are the local people of Gili Trawangan. They also sought legal aid to protect their interests. The locals consider the claims made by the Basri group as legally invalid. Before selling the land-user rights PT Generasi Jaya, from which the Basri group bought the HGUs, let the land lie fallow for more than 2 years. In that period the people of Trawangan started to use the land for their own benefit. They claim that by law they are now entitled to use the land. Apart from that they consider the plans of the Basri group to build a tourist resort inappropriate, because the land-user rights were granted to exploit a coconut plantation. On the basis of these two matters the Trawangan people started a lawsuit in 1991, which they lost. An appeal against this decision in 1994 was also lost. Paradoxically, the misuse of the land has served as a handle for the provincial government to justify the "slash and burn" actions by the police and army (Mucipto, 1994). After the verdict in 1991 the local police went to the island to confiscate the locally owned bungalows. The locals ignored them, however, and continued to operate their bungalows. The police returned in 1992 to demolish the lodgings. At the same time local activists visited the Minister of the Interior, Rudini, to halt the demolition. The minister sent a radiogram to cancel the action. Nonetheless, in September 1993 all of the bungalows were demolished by force (Mucipto, 1994). As an alternative the provincial government issued a spatial planning concept for Gili Trawangan that allows locals to own and operate lodgings of not more than five rooms, on 1 hectare of land, in a designated area of the island that is the least desirable as it is not near the coral reef. The provincial government and the provincial tourist department claim that local businessmen do not meet spatial management requirements and cannot provide adequate services and accommodations (Mucipto, 1994). The locals for their part claim that if the provincial government treated the local entrepreneurs in the same way as they treat the outsiders in helping them to get the necessary business permits and access to bank credits, there would be no problem meeting the requirements of the provincial government. Some of the islanders accepted the deal with the provincial government and relocated their business to the designated area of the island. Others, partly because they did not possess the necessary documents to claim a new spot, turned their backs on the island embitteredly. A small group persists in its struggle. Even after the last "cleaning action" of the army they rebuilt their businesses on the old spot, albeit on a smaller scale.

Present Day Trawangan

In the summer of 1996 it appeared that the spatial planning concept drawn up by the provincial government had been carried out. Surrounding the area on the east coastal strip, where the new resort is planned, is a barbwire fence. According to the spatial planning concept it is also forbidden nowadays to build any type of construction directly near the beach side. In 1994 the businesses were still built on both sides of the main road. On the seaside there were mainly little shops, travel agencies, and other small businesses. On the land side were the hotels and restaurants. In 1996 all the constructions on the seaside had vanished and flower boxes had been installed instead. On the land side there had been a regrouping of the accommodation setting. Every entrepreneur who accepted the deal with the provincial government was offered a small piece of land on which he could build a five-room *losmen* or homestay.

In the early years the bungalows on the island, and also on Gili Air and Gili Meno, were rather standardized. They were all simple wooden constructions. Prices were also pretty much the same: approximately 5,000 to 10,000 *rupiah* a night. As there were no independent restaurants operating on the island, usually three meals were included. Nowadays this is hardly ever done anymore. There is plenty of choice. There is also a small diversification in accommodations. Bricks are used more and more for construction, and nowadays it is even possible to get a fan in your room. To keep the customers in their restaurants and bars they can watch videos, and every night there is a party somewhere—no two parties on the same night, but evenly divided among the hotel owners.

Conclusions and Future Scenario for Gili Trawangan

On Gili Trawangan the local population responded to tourism by offering accommodation and additional services. They started with few investments and slowly developed the infrastructure and the facilities on the island to a point that almost everyone is involved in the local tourist economy. In the absence of a concentrated effort supported by the government or foreign funds to "implant" tourism in the area, the tourist business developed spontaneously and on a small scale by local initiative. The tourists who visit Gili Trawangan are mainly young travelers who are satisfied with a nice beach, good company, and modest accommodation. They do not demand extensive services, which makes it possible for the locals to take advantage of the needs and participate. The locals are successful in their efforts to accommodate these tourists. At the moment Gili Trawangan, together with the other two Gilis, is the best visited site on Lombok.

In the current debate about local participation, existing locally based, small-scale private enterprises in tourism—like the initiatives on Gili Trawangan—are neglected. One reason for this neglect could be the still persistent, romanticized, Western idea that a local community in a developing country is a unity that has to be saved from larger scale disruptive forces and that local private entrepreneurship undermines this idea of homogeneity. Opportunities for local entrepreneurship are not necessarily equally accessible. Apart from the availability of resources like capital, land, and labor, an entrepreneur has to have the ability to recognize niches in the tourism market, to innovate, and to take risks. Furthermore, the income does not necessarily find its way back to the local community. "The successful entrepreneurship of those who had capital or offered good employment, can lead to a widening gap between them and the community members who were less fortunate" (Smith, 1994, p. 166). An important additional question is: how local is local? What is the identity of the "locals" who supposedly benefit from small-scale tourism developments? New opportunities for employment such as offered in the tourist industry often attract migrants who have different characteristics from the local population and who must be accommodated in the community. This can create stress among the community, and problems in the area of land prices, social organization, and cultural values can arise (Cohen, 1982a, 1996; Smith, 1994; Van Schaardenburgh, 1995; Wall, 1995).

It is inevitable that opportunities for local entrepreneurship are not equally accessible. Every destination is essentially a community (Brohman, 1996), but what is often overlooked in community development programs is that every community is also essentially heterogeneous and dynamic in the sense that there is a constant coming and going of residents. It is an illusion to think that every member of a community should be and can be involved in tourism development equally. Among local residents tourism creates winners as well as losers (Brohman, 1996; Smith & Eadington, 1992; Vickers, 1989).

Without centrally planned community development tourism projects the locals of Trawangan were very well capable of launching a local tourism industry. Although not every inhabitant is equally involved in tourism and although not all of them benefit in the same way, it is evident that the standard of living improved considerably throughout the years. The profits made in tourism are locally spent. The few outsiders who exploit their tourism business on the island make no difference in this respect. Their businesses are small scale, they employ locals, and the leakages are of little importance. In the Trawangan case all the objectives defined within local participation strategies are achieved. The locals participated in planning, as well as decision making and implementation. They are in the center of the development of their tourism product, a product that matches their present possibilities. In areas where tourism is developing rapidly and where new requirements determine the direction and pace of the developments, local entrepreneurs should be given the opportunity to zero in on the new market. Government or NGO support in the area of credit facilities, education, and management is then a prerequisite.

The success of Gili Trawangan attracted outside investors who find the island attractive for tourism development. They put considerable effort into penetrating the area and dislocating the locals. At the same time the Gilis became incorporated in provincial development plans. These plans do not provide for support to small-scale entrepreneurs. The focus of the provincial government is on the development of "quality" tourism. Therefore, priority is given to building resorts with star-rated hotels, swimming pools, and golf courses, like the planned Putri Nyale resort in the south of Lombok. This emphasis on "quality" tourism will lead to rising land prices and to landowner disputes, as is the case on Trawangan. Efforts to upgrade the area, rising costs, and more regulations will make it very difficult for the small-scale entrepreneurs to continue their businesses as they used to. Their low-budget accommodation and other modest initiatives will no longer meet the standards of services and accommodation as required in the resort type of development.

On a national level it is stated that priority has to be given to entrepreneurship in tourism through training programs, marketing, and management in order to ensure that the small business people can compete in an international environment (Sammeng, 1995). But these plans only seem to exist on paper. The Trawangan case shows that small-scale entrepreneurs are marginalized rather than supported through government measures. The riposte of the local entrepreneurs is that if they are given the same support as foreign investors by means of credit facilities, education, and training, they also would be able to meet the required international standards.

After the regrouping of the accommodation setting some of the owners occupy the least attractive sites on the island and are only allowed to exploit five bungalows. Considering the future upgrading plans it remains to be seen whether these locals will still be able to make a living out of accommodating tourists. Another question is whether their target group, the low-budget tourists, will still find their way to Gili Trawangan when the accommodation and the other facilities and services are upgraded and become more expensive. This has already happened in Senggigi. Because of its luxurious image Senggigi is nowadays infamous among the young, low-budget tourists. The low-budget accommodation is pushed away by the star-rated hotels, and new initiatives to exploit modest guesthouses or *losmen* are impossible because of the exorbitant land prices. Where in Lombok will the low-budget tourists go when the Gilis are no longer affordable? Which new paradise will be created?

Chapter 6

A Home Away From Home?
The Production and Consumption
of Budget Accommodations in
Two Tourist Areas in the City of
Yogyakarta

Saskia Peeters, Jolanda Urru, and Heidi Dahles

Introduction

Offering a multifaceted tourism product, Yogyakarta, a city in the heart of central Java, has the ambition to become the center of Indonesian cultural tourism. Due to the government policy of focused tourism development the city has been the second most important tourist destination in Indonesia after Bali since the 1980s. However, changing government strategies towards tourism development, defining new destination areas all over the Indonesian archipelago, threaten Yogyakarta's position. The formerly protected position of Yogyakarta on the one hand, and the pressure to live up to government-set goals on the other hand, has resulted in a standardization of the tourist product. In the tourist arena, Yogyakarta is presented as the center of Indonesian heritage and Javanese court culture and—particularly for domestic tourists—the city of education, the cradle of political resistance against colonial rule and of national unification (Dahles, 1997b). Although official statistics show a continuous increase in the number of "quality" tourists and of star-rated hotels catering to the alleged needs of Western and Asian tourists, local authorities and the tourism industry are concerned about the future of tourism in the city. The length of stay, the flight frequency to Adisucipto Airport, and the number of visits of foreign tourists to local attractions are decreasing (Dahles, 1997). As international tourism experts argue, Yogyakarta has reached the stagnation phase according to Butler's tourist area life cycle (Sofield, 1995). This stagnation seems to be a symptom of the failure of local tourism policy. Although the cultural heritage in (the vicinity of) the city is a government priority, local actors in tourism policy and the industry fail to innovate the tourist product and to anticipate changing tastes of both domestic and foreign tourists. Cultural tourism is still defined as a pilgrimage to the culture temples of an ancient past. A more conceptual perspective on culture is virtually absent from the strategies of tourist marketing. Due to the "sanitized" formula of "quality" tourism that concentrates tourists in air-conditioned resorts and star-rated hotels, visitors are denied a glimpse on how Yogyanese people actually live their lives: how they dwell, work, and play. Instead the city's street life is met with a policy of deterrence. Pedicab men, street vendors, and informal guides, contributing considerably to the *couleur locale*, are threatened by incidental police raids and frequent pettifoggery by the authorities. More and more, the micro businesses and the urban quarters where these businesses flourish have to give way to star-rated hotels and carefully monitored shopping areas (Dahles, 1997b, 1998b).

Ironically, the tourist areas that the local government would rather erase from the city center are blossoming (i.e., the nonquality, low-budget, nonrated, small-scale tourist sector, operated by local people and catering to mostly young budget travelers). Enterprises operating at this level and catering to this type of tourist are manifold. Most prominent is the small-scale accommodation sector—homestays, *losmen*, inns, and small guesthouses—which this chapter will focus on. Linked to this sector are a vast variety of local tour operators, transport companies, ticket sellers, subcontractors of private telecommunication companies, restaurants, souvenir shops, art galleries, grocery shops, self-employed guides, and masseurs/masseuses. A concentration of these partly competing and partly collaborating small-scale enterprises is found in two different areas in the city of Yogyakarta: in the neighborhoods of Sosrowijayan and Prawirotaman. The first area—a densely populated low-class trading quarter—is situated in the inner city adjacent to the main shopping street, Malioboro street. The second—a middle-class residential area—lies south of the center within a short distance from Yogyakarta's main tourist attractions and the inner city.

This chapter investigates the budget accommodation sector in these two neighborhoods in Yogyakarta. Questions will be asked about the factors contributing to the relative success of the small-scale accommodations vis-à-vis the star-rated hotels:

- How and by whom are the small-scale accommodations operated and managed? Which "capital" is strategically employed in the management of the accommodations? How does this affect the daily routine and entrepreneurial culture that characterizes the accommodations?

- Which aspects of the budget accommodation sector determine its attractiveness for tourists? What do tourists expect to find in these accommodations? How does price relate to social and cultural aspects? What significance can be attached to the proximity to everyday life in a *kampung* and the alleged quest for authenticity?

- To what extent does the small-scale accommodation sector represent a viable perspective for the future development of tourism in the city of Yogyakarta?

After a brief description of Yogyakarta as a tourist destination and the government-controlled organization of the hotel sector, the chapter will proceed with a comparison of the small-scale accommodations in the two Yogyanese neighborhoods and a discussion of tourist typologies in both areas. To generate a better understanding of the opportunities and threats to the budget accommodation sector in Yogyakarta, special attention will be paid to the interaction between owners and staff on the one hand and tourists on the other hand, and on the marketing strategies of the small-scale entrepreneurs.

Tourism in Yogyakarta

Yogyakarta is situated in one of the most productive agricultural areas on earth, with a rural population density that is among the world's highest. The city of Yogyakarta is capital of the sultanate of Yogyakarta that constitutes the "special province" Yogyakarta (*Daerah Istimewa Yogyakarta*). The province's 3.2 million people inhabit just 3,169 km^2, an average density of over 1,000 persons per km^2. However, the city of Yogyakarta is inhabited by fewer than 500,000 people (Sensus, 1995). Many sources characterize the city as an "aggregate of villages" (J. Sullivan, 1992, p. 3), as the majority of people live in *kampung* and village hamlets scattered about the countryside (Periplus, 1991). Yogyakarta is a city of great diversity. Cherishing its Javanese cultural heritage, the city has attracted a large number of painters, dancers, and writers. Besides the arts, a large spectrum of traditional handicrafts like batik painting, silver carving, puppet making, etc., is flourishing. The cultural heritage of Yogyakarta is a multifaceted phenomenon consisting of architectural and archeological remains, prominent persons, philosophies, norms, and values, the arts and crafts, folklore, literature, and ways of life (Smithies, 1986). The city seems almost unaffected by the pressing problems that modern mass tourism brings about. Although the city has been visited by over 1 million tourists (foreign and domestic) in 1995 (Statistik Diparda DIY, 1995), lifestyles are unhurried and relaxed, life is relatively inexpensive and crime free, and the people remain courteous and proudly conscious of their artistic traditions, the wealth of fine arts, and refined behavior. However, the impact of Western culture (related to the adoption of Western lifestyles, which is partly mediated by tourism) cannot be denied.

Malioboro street is the center of commerce, amusement, and tourism. The street forms the major shopping area with numerous shops, supermarkets, department stores, and hotels with foreign names and flashing neon lights, playing Western pop music all day long; restaurants with international tourist menus and fast-food; high-rise five- and four-star hotels; a new shopping mall selling internationally renowned brand names. The neighborhood of Sosrowijayan lies right behind the houses that face Malioboro street. This area is situated directly to the south of the railway, between Pasar Kembang street and Sosrowijayan street. Between these two streets lie the alleys Sosrowijayan I and II, which offer the cheapest accommodations and most popular low-budget eating places in town. It is an extremely busy and lively area. Living quarters, tourist accommodations, restaurants, *warung*, tiny shops, and batik galleries share the cramped space. Around the clock, cars, tourist buses, motorcycles, bicycles, and pedicabs frequent the main traffic ways in this quarter, while everyday life carries on as usual in the narrow alleyways. The residents go about their business; the women bargain for fresh fruit and vegetables sold by traders along the street; water sellers and other mobile vendors walk the neighborhood carrying their merchandise; in a stove in front of their homes, women prepare food for their family; children are playing; people hurry to the mosque; cock-fights are organized; older people squat on the sidewalk and comment on the tourists passing by: "Hello Mister where you go?" Young men walk the streets and alleys looking for newly arrived foreigners to take them to a batik gallery to earn some commission. Tourists are an integrated part of the everyday life in this area and nobody seems to feel alarmed or disturbed by their omnipresence (Figure 6.1).

The other popular tourist area, Prawirotaman, is situated a couple of kilometers to the south of the city center, near the main bus station. The actual tourist area consists of two streets (Prawirotaman I and Prawirotaman II street) to the left of Parangtritis street leading south to the coast. The last few years a third street, across Parangtritis street, shows a modest development of restaurants and a few tourist accommodations. Prawirotaman is a quiet middle-class neighborhood. It is characterized by spacious colonial houses with gardens. Until recently, its inhabitants were predominantly members of the local gentry employed by the Sultan's Palace and engaged in local handicraft production. Many households in Prawirotaman run small and medium-sized factories where batik cloth or jewelery is manufactured. The hassle and bustle of street life so characteristic of the low-class residential areas are absent from Prawirotaman. Local residents live their lives behind the facades of their fenced houses and spontaneous face-to-face conversations between locals and tourists do not happen frequently. Locals who do engage in "tourist talk" are mostly

Figure 6.1. Malioboro street life. (Photo by T. Kamsma)

pedicab drivers, offering their services. In the Prawirotaman area local life is kept separate from tourism.

Offering a multifaceted tourism product, the city is represented as the center of Indonesian cultural tourism. The more so as Yogyakarta is the site of the three main objects of cultural heritage around which the construction of Indonesian national identity pivots: Borobudur, Prambanan, and Kraton. As Table 6.1 shows, the number of foreign visitors has increased steadily during the last few years. As far as domestic tourists are concerned, the numbers have grown again after a drop in 1990.

Whereas national tourism development schemes keep up the image of continuous expansion, there is reason for concern about the future of tourism in Yogyakarta. The increase in foreign visitors lags behind the national objective. The political structure and practice in Indonesia is such that the local and provincial governments are supposed to implement the policy that is designed in Jakarta. This means that towards the end of *Repelita VI* a 10% growth in the tourist arrivals has to be effectuated. According to a representative of *Badan Pembangunan Daerah* (BAPPEDA, Agency for Regional Development) Yogyakarta, the Province will accomplish only 6.9%. As recent research has shown, tourism development in Yogyakarta has entered the phase of consolidation (Sofield, 1995). The city is unable to keep up with national objectives, but these objectives of expansion are not questioned. More efforts are put into the development of "quality" tourism through the construction of an increasing number of large and luxurious hotels in the four- and five-star category. There is no government program supporting small-scale accommodations and other tourism-related businesses owned and managed by local people.

Yogyakarta heavily depends on tourism as a source of income and employment. As the city lacks any substantial industrial infrastructure (Rotge, 1991; Soedarso, 1992), it has become clear that future prosperity will depend on the city's ability to capitalize on its rich cultural heritage as the Sultan of Yogyakarta, Hamengku Buwono X (1992), has pointed out. However, the tourism industry of Yogyakarta is not a vibrating business. It is relying on a product that has been unchanged since tourism development started in the 1980s. Innovations are hampered by stifling government regulations requiring discouraging procedures of obtaining licenses and permits. The star-rated hotel sector

Table 6.1. Number of Visitors to Yogyakarta (1989–1995)

Year	International Tourists	Domestic Tourists
1989	180,896	483,520
1990	188,549	398,636
1991	216,051	492,048
1992	256,192	561,224
1993	299,433	610,818
1994	323,194	640,801
1995	344,265	837,265

Source: Statistik Pariwisata DIY (1995).

is relying on the soothing idea that Yogyakarta has a long-standing tradition as a tourist destination. Hotel managers use to point to local travel agencies accusing them of selling "transit tours," that is, package deals with Jakarta- or Bali-based tour operators to cater to organized tour groups that are flown in to Yogyakarta in the morning, visit Borobudur temple and leave again in the afternoon without spending time and money in the city. The travel agencies indicate that they do not have any choice but to accept these deals as a survival strategy. In fact, travel agents in Yogyakarta are subcontractors of the big Jakarta- and Bali-based tour operators. The decisions about the city's attraction system are not made in Yogyakarta at all, but in Jakarta and Bali. Local agencies do not have the means—in terms of money and human resources—to develop new products. They point out that their counterparts in Jakarta and Bali are big enough to operate as risk-taking and innovating entrepreneurs. However, their bosses in Jakarta and Bali are not interested in taking risks for Yogyakarta; they just sell the city as long as it is profitable for them. And when Yogyakarta is "done," then they turn to another—emerging—destination, of which there are plenty, owing to the policy of expansion advocated by the national government.

The Accommodation Sector in Yogyakarta

From the brief description of tourism in Yogyakarta it may be clear that the accommodation sector—despite the building boom—is in a crisis. The growth in the number of tourist arrivals conceals a more serious problem (i.e., the stagnating length of stay), particularly in the star-rated hotel sector. Official statistics show only a very slight increase in the number of nights that visitors spend in the city (Table 6.2).

Data on the star-rated hotel sector in Yogyakarta indicate that the number of hotel rooms has more than doubled since 1991. The occupancy rate, however, has fallen 12%. Though the occupancy rate in the nonrated sector seems to be lower than in the star-rated hotels, there has been a gradual growth in the occupancy in the nonrated sector until 1994 (Table 6.3). This growth, however, has not been as spectacular as in the star-rated sector. The gap in the occupancy rate in the star-rated and non-star-rated sector may be caused by an insufficient administration of overnight stays due to the fact that many small-scale accommodation owners do not list all their rooms and register only

Table 6.2. Number of Nights Spent in Yogyanese Accommodations by International and Domestic Tourists (1993–1995)

| | 1993 | | 1994 | | 1995 | |
Accommo-dation	Inter-national	Domestic	Inter-national	Domestic	Inter-national	Domestic
Non-star-rated	2.25	1.33	2.31	1.40	2.34	1.49
Star-rated	1.60	1.68	1.69	1.69	1.71	1.79
Average	1.93	1.51	2.00	1.55	2.03	1.64

Source: Statistik Diparda DIY (1995).

Table 6.3. Total Number of Hotel Rooms and Occupancy Rate
(1991–1995)

	Hotel Rooms		Occupancy (%)	
	Star	Non-Star	Star	Non-Star
1991	1,201	4,254	60.5%	29.4%
1992	1,511	4,596	58.4%	35.5%
1993	1,920	4,556	48.9%	35.7%
1994	2,290	4,993	51.2%	45.0%
1995	2,468	5,682	48.3%	36.9%

Source: Statistik Pariwisata DIY (1995).

part of their guests. This is part of their strategies to deal with increasing government control and taxation.

The hotel sector in Yogyakarta offers a great variety of accommodations differing widely in price and quality. There is a choice of large (inter)national luxury hotels as well as small-scale and less luxurious accommodations managed by local people. For the latter a large number of names circulates, such as *losmen*, homestay, *wisma*, *penginapan*, inn, and guesthouse. To create more transparency and define quality standards, the Indonesian government established a classification system for the accommodation sector. Basically, the classification system differentiates between star-rated (*bintang*) and non-star-rated accommodations. The *bintang* classification refers to large hotels and resorts meeting international quality standards regarding food (a choice of oriental or Western dishes) and hygiene, and the availability of facilities like a swimming pool, laundry and room service, air conditioning, private bathroom with hot and cold running water, and a money changer. The star system in Yogyakarta conforms to international standards, consisting of five categories and ranging from one-star (lowest in the rating) accommodation to five-star accommodation (highest in the rating). Hotels in this sector charge 10% government and 11% service tax in addition to the room rates, which usually have to be paid in US dollars.

Small-scale, locally run accommodations are generally not awarded with stars. Many travel guide books (particularly addressing the individual traveler) describe these accommodations as inexpensive but comfortable with a cosy, informal atmosphere and good service (Turner et al., 1995). These guide books distinguish between inexpensive and very cheap accommodations. The category of "*wisma*/guesthouse/pension" is in the upper echelons of the inexpensive accommodations, less expensive than a hotel, comfortable, with a simple breakfast included. Prices in this category differ a lot depending on the facilities and the neighborhood where the accommodation is situated. The average price per night for a double room ranged between 15,000 and 50,000 *rupiah* in 1995. *Losmen, penginapan*, and homestays are the least expensive accommodations. They offer moderate quality and service, often not more than a simple bed with a shared bathroom Indonesian style (squatting toilet and *mandi*). There is no air conditioning, you have to bring your own towel and sleeping bag, and breakfast often is not included.

Prices are very low: the average price per night for a double room ranged from 6,000 to 15,000 *rupiah* in 1995.

Although this basic differentiation may be helpful for tourists, the classification system is much more complex than it seems. Quality standards differ widely even within the subcategories. Accommodations with different names and falling into different subcategories often offer the same facilities. Moreover, there is considerable overlap between the better local accommodations and the lesser star-rated hotels. To credit to the quality of local accommodations, and—perhaps even more important—to get a better grip on the local accommodation sector, the Indonesian government started a campaign to classify all *penginapan, losmen, wisma*, etc., under the name "hotel." Paramount to this campaign was the introduction of the so-called *melati* system. Although this system gives tourists an indication of price and quality, it is not consistent, as has been discussed in Chapter 4. Again the problem of great diversity within one subcategory plays a crucial part. Three *melati* can be given to middle-class guesthouses and homestays where room prices are 20,000 *rupiah* or more and where a number of facilities are offered, like a restaurant, swimming pool, private bathroom, and good service. But the same three *melati* can also be granted to accommodations that cost about 8,000 *rupiah* with minimal facilities. The *pondok wisata* category contains the smallest accommodations for tourists, in which the number of rooms does not exceed five, but which overlaps with the other classification system. All accommodations in the non-star-rated sector are obligated to pay 10% tax to the government. To pay for these taxes many owners charge the tourist in addition to the room rate. However, the smallest and most inexpensive accommodations include the government tax in the room rate.

The *melati* system was introduced much to the dissatisfaction of the owners of these accommodations. Their official argument against this campaign was that the old system gave a clear price indication to the guests, which is not the case any longer with the new classification. However, more important and not outspoken is the resistance against the increased government control that accompanied the new system. Since it has been introduced, the accommodation owners have to submit the number of overnight stays on a monthly basis. They have to keep records of the tourists' country of origin, length of stay, previous and next destination, passport number, and kind of visa. Furthermore, they are supposed to update the local government on the number of beds and rooms and the occupancy rate. It is not only because of the small entrepreneurs' dislike of being controlled by the government, but also because of their fear of being classified into a higher category, which implies a raise of taxes, that many owners of local accommodations refuse to collaborate with the government. As a consequence, they register less rooms than they actually dispose of, list less guests than actually stay in their accommodations, and decline to be mentioned in the official tourist guidebooks published by the local government or tourist board.

Homestays in Sosrowijayan and Prawirotaman: A Comparison

According to official statistics there are 25 hotels with one or more stars, 203 *melati* hotels, and 26 *pondok wisata* in the city of Yogyakarta (Statistik Pariwisata DIY, 1995).

The vast majority of *melati* accommodations are situated in and around Sosrowijayan and Prawirotaman (51 and 29, respectively). In the *pondok wisata* category 22 out of 26 accommodations are in Sosrowijayan, only one in Prawirotaman. The new classification system in terms of "flowers" has not been adopted yet by the owners of the small-scale accommodations. Still, one of the most popular names for these accommodations is "homestay." This name can be found on the sign boards along the streets and alleys in both tourist areas announcing the availability of rooms. At the time of research there were six accommodations with the name of homestay in Sosrowijayan. Most of them are situated in the small alleys between Sosrowijayan and Pasar Kembang street. The average number of rooms per homestay is eight and prices based on a double room vary between 6,000 and 12,000 *rupiah*. The facilities in the homestays are diverse. Some offer practically nothing but a place to sleep, whereas others have room service and organize excursions and batik courses. Generally, the rooms are small and only have basic facilities, like a bed, a table with chairs, and a light bulb; some rooms have a cupboard. Only half of the rooms in the homestays have a private bathroom, and only a few homestays offer a breakfast service. The others do not offer any food at all, or just a few snacks, which are not included in the price. Most of the time there is a communal living room for the tourists, furnished with old sofas and chairs; sometimes there is a refrigerator and a television. The occupation rate is high—even in the low season.

In Sosrowijayan, about half of the small-scale accommodation owners first started a batik gallery and—after earning some money with batik sales—invested their money in a homestay. These businesses are quite successful, and the owners expand the number of rooms and improve their services, or open another homestay. Other local people rented one room the family could spare to young budget travelers as early as the 1970s. In some cases their homes have turned into a *losmen* or guesthouse and the family built a room for themselves in the backyard or adjacent to their former home. In other cases the family still shares its tiny house with visitors. Within these small and cheap accommodations two main categories can be distinguished. First, there are accommodations where the owner and his family live in a separate part of the house they share with tourists. The children of the family often are playing in and around the accommodation, hardly paying any attention to the tourists that arrive and depart from their home. Family members help doing the chores in the accommodation, like the laundry or cleaning the rooms. Although tourists can catch a glimpse of the local family life, the family screens off their private life and maintain their distance. The tourists are left alone and the family does not mix with them a lot. In this type of accommodation the contact between owner/staff and tourist is quite superficial. Only when the tourists take the initiative to enter into a conversation will family members sit down to talk to them. The second category of budget accommodation in Sosrowijayan is owned by local people who do not live in the accommodation themselves. The owner hires staff, mostly adolescent males, who stay in the homestay day and night. Often these young men are relatives of the owner. They sleep on a mattress or a couch in the hallway or the common room and they hang around the homestay with their friends watching television all day long. Their salary is minimal: only 1,000 or 2,000 *rupiah* a day including board and lodging. Infrequently, the owner drops by to check if everything is going well. The young males are very interested in Western life; they want to improve their language proficiency and therefore engage the tourists in conversation as much as possible. The communal room is the favorite place to mingle with the guests. Whereas the term homestay suggests sharing the daily life of the local people, most of the owners do not live in the homestay. The owners as well as the staff of the homestay do not have a high level of education. They learn some English by talking to the tourists; but some staff members do not speak any English at all, only Javanese (among each other) and *bahasa Indonesia*. It seems that there is more frequent local-tourist interaction in accommodations that are run by young adolescent males, as they are very eager to learn about the Western way of life. In accommodations where the owner and his family live, there is less local-tourist contact, as the family maintains their distance.

Prawirotaman developed as a tourist area about a decade later than Sosrowijayan. With tourism booming in the city, a number of residents who ran batik or silver factories started to produce souvenirs and to rent some rooms in their spacious houses to tourists. Eventually, the owners built new houses in other areas of Yogyakarta for their families to live in and turned their former Prawirotaman homes into guesthouses or rebuilt them to become small hotels, often with a swimming pool in the garden. In Prawirotaman at the time of the research there were only five accommodations with the name of homestay; most other accommodations are called guesthouse or even

Figure 6.2. Signboard announcing guesthouse accommodation in Yogyakarta's Prawirotaman area. (Photo by T. Kamsma)

hotel (Figure 6.2). The average number of rooms of the homestays is about 15, and prices range from 20,000 to 30,000 *rupiah*. The rooms are spacious and well maintained. All rooms have a private (European) bathroom, some even with hot and cold running water, and breakfast is included. The diversity in facilities offered by the homestays in Prawirotaman is less than in Sosrowijayan. In general, these accommodations are more luxurious and more expensive than in Sosrowijayan. Every homestay has a reception/lobby and the (well-kept) building has a garden with sometimes even a swimming pool. The owners are often proprietors of a number of tourist accommodations. They hire staff, who work at fixed times and earn a salary that meets the standards of the Indonesian hotel sector. Most of the staff members are well-educated and speak English quite well. They look well-groomed and sometimes wear uniforms and name tags. The staff does not stay in the homestay at night; during night hours night guards or security men protect the accommodation. The owner does not visit the homestay a lot and the staff is in charge. In this type of accommodation the local-tourist interaction has a formal character. The staff treats the tourists with respect and provides them with the information they require in a friendly and professional way. Whereas in the budget accommodations of Sosrowijayan staff and tourist treat each other like friends, in Prawirotaman the contact is a customer-related service, the more so as the staff does not stay in the accommodation around the clock but has fixed shifts. In Prawirotaman, moreover, tourists do not spend much time in their accommodation, and when they are in, they stay in their room to rest. Except for the lobby, the homestays do not provide a common room where staff and guests socialize.

There are striking differences between the homestays in both neighborhoods. In Sosrowijayan we are dealing with very small-scale, family-run accommodations that started without substantial investments. Most businesses are owned and managed by Yogyanese people. The level of professionality is extremely low, as neither the staff nor the owners have any formal training beyond primary school education. The product offered is basic, and they cater predominantly to (young) backpackers. The name homestay turns out to be misleading as there is no participation in the home life of a local family. The owners of the more luxurious homestays in Prawirotaman exert a more professional approach to their businesses. Often, they are proprietors of a number of small-scale accommodations, so that several "hotel chains" exist in Prawirotaman. These accommodations needed considerable investments to be established. The businesses are not family run, but are managed by professional staff that are well-trained as far as their language proficiency and hospitality is concerned. These accommodations target individually traveling middle-class tourists that look for some luxury and good service.

Within the budget accommodation sector of Yogyakarta there are no professional organizations that unite the owners to pursue common targets. However, in Sosrowijayan, a network has been established to provide a common meeting ground for owners of budget accommodations. This network, named *Paguyuban Pengelola Penginapan Sosrowijayan* (Association of Managers of Accommodations Sosrowijayan), was established in the early 1990s by of the local *losmen* owners. The main objective is to make price agreements and establish some quality standards for the accommodations in the neighborhood. The influence of this network is limited as only part of the local accommodation owners participate regularly. According to the founder of this network it is not possible to make far-reaching decisions or settle important agreements, as the fear of formalization is deeply rooted among the local small entrepreneurs. Independence and autonomy being their basic interest, they will be scared off and turn against the members of this network if they suspect that any regulations are to be imposed.

The Homestay Tourist

Generally, the budget accommodation sector is frequented by relatively young tourists, about 20 to 35 years old. Although the tourists come from all over the world, it is striking that some nationalities are better represented than others. The major part of the respondents are from Europe, The Netherlands, Germany, Great Britain, Ireland, the Scandinavian countries, and Switzerland being the largest "tourist suppliers." Large non-European groups are from Australia and Canada. The budget accommodations in Sosrowijayan and Prawirotaman are hardly ever visited by Japanese tourists or even the Indonesian themselves. These people either stay in the more luxurious accommodations (the Japanese figure prominently among the "quality" tourists staying in the star-rated hotels) or frequent the guesthouses outside of these popular tourist areas.

The young international budget tourists are predominantly students. They have often temporarily interrupted their studies, just graduated, or find themselves in between two grades and consequently have more time to spend on a long trip abroad. Tourists with a regular job in their home country often appear to be teachers, artists, engineers, or health workers. Some visit Yogyakarta for business. The homestay guests travel alone or together with their partner or a friend. Groups are quite exceptional, but if they occur they are not organized through a tour operator but constitute personal networks. As far as the single travelers are concerned, more men than women travel alone. All the tourists we talked to travel independently. A difference has to be made, however, between those who arrange their trip completely by themselves and those who book their excursions and trips with local travel agencies. The ones who arrange everything themselves only use local transport. The vast majority nevertheless use local transport as well as organized tourist transport. As far as time and money budgets are concerned, the picture is very diverse. The total length of the trip differs from 3 weeks to a couple of years. All the tourists we spoke to prepared for the trip in one way or another: they read about the habits and culture of Indonesian people and the characteristics of the country. The main sources of information are books and travel guide books, as well as friends and acquaintances who had been to Indonesia before (Peeters & Urru, 1996).

As far as the tourists' interest in the everyday life of the local people is concerned, among the tourists we distinguish three categories in Sosrowijayan and Prawirotaman. These categories roughly cover Cohen's (1979) "modes of tourist experiences." Cohen attempts to establish a tourist classification in terms of the depth and intensity of local–tourist relationship. He diverges from the more common tourist typologies in that he sees tourism as a relational phenomenon, not as an amalgam of predefined tourist types. He establishes a continuum of "modes of tourist experiences" starting from the mode in which tourists look for a change of scenery without being exposed to local culture and culminating in a mode that implies total immersion in local culture. Cohen's approach integrates two extreme positions taken by scholars; one position claiming that tourists find themselves in a "bubble" isolating themselves from exposure to local culture (Boorstin, 1964); the other defining tourists by an alleged "quest for authenticity" (MacCannell, 1976). Our first category exhibits a concentration of characteristics of Cohen's "diversionary" and "recreational" mode (i.e., tourists who keep their distance towards local culture). Our second category corresponds with his "experiential" mode (i.e., tourists who cautiously explore aspects of local culture). Finally, our third category matches his "experimental" mode (i.e., tourists who regard local culture as an alternative to their lives at home). However, we did not encounter tourists that fit Cohen's "existential" mode (i.e., the total immersion in local culture). We will briefly discuss the characteristics of these categories.

The first category is not at all interested in the everyday culture of their hosts and do not attempt to get into contact with the local people. They come to Indonesia to see the temples and other famous buildings, the beautiful nature, or just to relax—and not to be disturbed by the locals. The contact these tourists have with the Indonesians remains limited in most cases and can be called superficial and volatile. This is reflected by their high travel speed. Even if they have months to spend on traveling, they move very fast, as they want to see as much as possible in a short time and stay in one place only for a couple of days. The only locals they encounter are the staff members in their accommodations or shopkeepers and waiters. These tourists only initiate contact with the locals in case they need information. Tourists belonging to this group prefer some forms of luxury, what is manifest in their choice of comfortable transport, more luxurious accommodation, and Western food. Two female tourists we interviewed described their vacation as being a quest for "real orange juice" to avoid the "awful stuff they call orange juice here." In this category it is quite common to violate local dress codes. These tourists walk about the city sparsely dressed, a style that makes them easily visible as tourists. The travel behavior of this category is fed by their negative attitude towards the Indonesian people. They are openly annoyed by the obtrusiveness of the locals. They regard Indonesia as a very chaotic country where nothing happens in time or by the rules, while in their home country everything is organized a lot better, as the following quotations illustrate: "The Indonesians are so unbelievably slow. Except when they can make some money, then they suddenly are not so slow any more" or "Really, they see me here as a walking dollar."

Tourists in the second category are more open to exchanges with local people. The conversations they enter into mainly revolve around the tourist attractions to be visited or stories about the family. These tourists, in contrast to the first group, are interested in the local culture and the everyday life of the Javanese. They claim to have enjoyed the bus trips that led through "nice authentic Indonesian villages" and that they often take a walk through the back streets of the places they visit to see the "real Javanese life." They indulge in the specialties of the Indonesian kitchen and refrain from lengthy complaints about the food. They dress more in accordance with local dress codes, covering their arms, shoulders, and legs, and prefer a functional, leisurely style without going to extremes, neither wearing beach dress nor imitating the locals. The tourists in this category generally appreciate the kindness and cheerfulness of the Indonesian people. Although tourists from this second group were eager to experience the "authentic" Indonesian culture, they indicated that they did not want to live like the Indonesians do. They certainly appreciate the presence of Western people and the availability of Western products. A striking example is a male tourist who visited some Indonesian islands where there were no other Westerners. The local people did not speak English and he had to carry on with the little *bahasa Indonesia* he knew. Although he experienced the visit to these islands as very special, he said, that when he arrived in Bali, he was very relieved to switch to "normal" language (i.e., English) again, converse with other Westerners, and drink "good beer."

Tourists in the third category are very eager to experience the everyday life of the local people. This actually is the most important part of their trip. Generally these tourists are characterized by an extended length of stay. Irrespective of how much time they set aside for their trip, they take their time to explore the city and its neighborhoods. These tourists regard their trip as a success only if they have been able to participate in local life, like staying with an Indonesian family. They explicitly use their experiences to distinguish themselves from other tourists, claiming that they do not regard themselves as tourists, and that the locals share this view and accept them in a way. They like to boast of, for example, being present at *wayang kulit* (leather puppet) performances where foreigners were not supposed to attend, or witnessing a ritual at Mount Bromo that was to be kept "hidden" from tourists. The interest in the local culture makes these tourists quite intrusive towards Indonesians. They like to discuss cultural differences between Indonesia and the Western world and the problems tourism brings about. One tourist girl was deeply touched by a long conversation she had with an Indonesian boy about the problems he had with his being a homosexual in a Muslim culture. Among this category the quest for "authentic" experiences can become an obsession. Everything they do has to have this "local touch": they opt for the discomfort of local transport just to get into contact with Indonesian people, eat only Indonesian food, and wear *sarong* and batik clothes. It is not surprising that these tourists have a rather idealized image of the Indonesian culture. They regard the cheerfulness, hospitality, and relaxed lifestyle of the local population as an alternative to their Western way of life. One woman told us that she had such an appreciation for "the fact that the Indonesians respect each other and that all the religions can peacefully live together here."

Bringing together the contrasts we found among the tourists staying in the two popular tourist areas of Yogyakarta and the differences that exist between these two areas, we get a clearer picture of the opportunities and threats that tourism offers to the owners of small-scale accommodation. Sosrowijayan is favored by young tourists, mostly students, who are long-term travelers. Being young and on the move for months entails that these tourists are on a tight budget. Therefore, these long-termers stay in the cheapest category of accommodations, of which the Sosrowijayan area has a large supply. Moreover, these travelers enjoy the hustle and bustle of street life in Sosrowijayan and the modest night life in the street cafes. In Prawirotaman, on the other hand, the tourists belong to a different category. They are older, have a job in their home country, and a (regular) income, can spend more money on a trip that is of considerable shorter duration than the journey of the long-termers in Sosrowijayan. Tourists in Prawirotaman spend their money in the local tourism economy. They book their trips and excursions with travel agencies and take their meals in tourist restaurants with exotic names like Lotus Garden and Hanoman's Forest Garden Restaurant, which close at 10 o'clock at night. The long-termers in Sosrowijayan—because of the time they have at their disposal and the experience they have acquired during their long trip—spend their money not only in tourism businesses but also directly in local shops, on local transport and local food at the cheap *warung* where the locals get their meals as well. It may be obvious that in Prawirotaman our first tourist category prevails, whereas in Sosrowijayan the third category is well represented. The second category occurs equally in both areas. Not only is the Sosrowijayan area a better place to make contact with locals, but also this low-class neighborhood appeals to young student-travelers who are looking for a change. Prawirotaman, being a quiet middle-class area where local people keep their family life from the public eye, appeals to those tourists who seek comfort and privacy themselves and for whom local encounters do not constitute the essence of their travel experience.

Marketing the Homestay

The question that remains to be answered is how the owners of the homestays in both Sosrowijayan and Prawirotaman manage to attract the category of tourists that fits in with the accommodations they offer. Or, from the tourists' perspective, how do the tourists know where to go upon arrival? Certainly, the widely used travel guide books—*Lonely Planet, Periplus,* and *Indonesia Handbook*—provide the tourists with the basic information about available accommodations, price, facilities, and location. Other travelers they meet en route are regarded as very reliable sources of information as they share common interests and often a common cultural background. They exchange information about the cleanliness of the accommodation, the room rates, and the friendliness of the staff; the category or name of the accommodation—whether it is a homestay, hotel, pension, or *losmen*—is not important. Young backpackers usually take the advice of their peers and proceed to the accommodation as recommended. Other sources of information are the notice boards in restaurants where accommodation owners leave their business cards. Only a few homestays have flyers and brochures, which are distributed in places frequented by tourists or maintain contacts with accommodations in other tourist destinations with big international organizations like the International Student Card (ISC). It is quite common to promote one's homestay by what MacCannell (1976) would call "on-sight markers," that is, conspicuous signboards at the main streets of both tourist areas, not only announcing the name of the accommodation but also the facilities and number of rooms. The price, however, is not indicated as this is settled by individual bargaining.

However, there is another more effective way of marketing one's accommodation that overrules all the other strategies, which is networking with informal (i.e., unlicensed) guides and pedicab men. The relationship between accommodation owners/staff and these mobile "network artists" (Dahles, 1996, 1998b) is very complex and ambivalent. Local owners depend on the informal guides and pedicab men for bringing in tourists, but they loath them for demanding money and harassing their guests. When tourists arrive at the Sosrowijayan bus station or Tugu railway station, local guides are waiting to accompany them to an accommodation. This service is "free" as the informal guides receive a commission from the accommodation owner/staff for every guest they deliver. Some tourists are only too happy to be guided to an accommodation after a long and tiring trip, and they willingly hand over their baggage and follow the guide. Other tourists arrive well prepared and want to proceed to the accommodation of their choice. In that case a confrontation can occur with the intrusive guides who will not take "no" for an answer. Tourists who keep refusing the informal guide's services, even scold and threaten them, are followed by the guide who attempts to receive the commission anyway, claiming at the accommodation that it was he who delivered the tourist. This strategy is not always successful as many accommodation owners cooperate with a limited number of informal guides and refuse to pay others. Some owners—those united in the *Paguyuban Pengelola Penginapan Sosrowijayan*—have made an agreement that they do not pay commissions and do not allow informal guides to enter the accommodation to do business. These owners are proud to inform their guests about this regulation to enhance their reliability and make them feel more protected. However, it has been observed that whenever the owner is not present, the young males who run the accommodation allow their friends to enter and sit with the tourists in the common room. In many cases these friends are informal guides, doing business as usual. Moreover, the owners unwilling to submit to the commission system are shunned by the informal guides who attempt to dissuade tourists to rent a room there. "Fully booked" they would say, urging the tourists to follow them to the next accommodation.

Besides directing tourists to accommodations, informal guides have a variety of businesses at hand. When there are no new arrivals at the bus and train station to attend to, the informal guides hang around the streets, alleys, cheap restaurants and cafes, shops, the post office, and the major tourist attractions. There they make contact with tourists to take them to a batik gallery, a shop, a puppet workshop, or some other place where souvenirs are produced. Often, the guide attempts to sell a tour to one of the attractions in the vicinity of Yogyakarta, or a ticket to the *Ramayana* ballet. Whatever their offer, their final aim is to receive a commission from one of the "clients" for whom they are acting as a "broker" (cf. Chapter 1). Informal guides count among their clients travel agents, batik galleries, transportation companies, handicraft producers, other (formal) guides working at tourist sights, and of course hotels and other accommodations.

In Prawirotaman it is the pedicab man who plays a major role in the marketing of accommodations. Here, informal guides are largely absent from the local scene, as tourists preferably book their excursions with one of the many travel agencies in the neighborhood and local restaurants are too expensive to hang around, while the guesthouses and homestays do not allow informal guides to enter. The area of Prawirotaman is situated near Yogyakarta's main bus station where all major buses servicing the routes to Bali via Mount Bromo and to Jakarta arrive. The exit of this bus station is swarming with pedicab men and taxi drivers offering tourists an inexpensive ride to an accommodation in Prawirotaman. Basically, the same scenes occur as in Sosrowijayan: tourists who willingly get into the pedicab or taxi; and tourists who refuse to be followed by the drivers—grumbling and cursing—all the way to the accommodation to cash the commission.

Being situated south of the center, there is no continuous flow of tourists to Prawirotaman. The tourist businesses depend on pedicab men and taxi drivers to provide them with clientele. This may be the major reason why the accommodations in Prawirotaman pay a much higher commission than their counterparts in Sosrowijayan. Whereas in Sosrowijayan the commission is about 10% of the single room rate, in Prawirotaman it can rise to 30% or even 40% of the room rate for each night the tourist stays. As a consequence, pedicab men are very assertive, even aggressive, in persuading the tourists to hire them. They would walk hundreds of meters with the tourists, talking them into their pedicab. Like in Sosrowijayan, there are Prawirotaman accommodations that refuse to pay commissions. They make this clear by placing a sign at the front door saying: "We do not pay commission." As the sign is in English it is reasonable to suggest that the message is first and foremost meant for the tourists who want to stay in a place unharassed by informal guides and pedicab men. This is a marketing strategy to distinguish one's accommodation from the others. Like the informal guides in Sosrowijayan, the pedicab men react to this loss of income by taking revenge on the accommodation owners. Like their colleagues in the other neighborhood, they tell the tourists that these accommodations are full or even closed. Owners in their turn pay them back by warning the tourist of these pedicab men in their brochures and advise them to take a taxi.

Conclusions

Culture in the conceptual definition does not figure in the tourist representation and marketing of Yogyakarta, whereas "everyday life" is a promising marketing asset, at least for part of the tourist market. As has been shown in this chapter, the local–tourist interaction figures prominently in the travel motivations of tourists in the budget sector. The majority of budget travelers want to experience local life in one way or another and get a glimpse of the "authentic" Javanese culture. Definitions of the "authentic" and the desired intensity and depth of the encounters with local population, of course, differ widely (Berger, 1973). Contacts with local people most generally occur with those who are exposed to tourism: waiters, hotel staff, bus and taxi drivers (i.e., employees in the tourism industry), with a basic knowledge of the English language and often with a taste (or at least curiosity) for Western lifestyles. There are different levels of interaction, ranging from simple conversations ("where you from," "where you go") due to the limited language proficiency of both tourist and local, to profound discussions on the role of tourism in local culture and homosexuality in a Muslim society. One arena where local–tourist encounters take place is in the accommodations, small-scale accommodations being the location par excellence where these encounters occur. However, as our research has shown, tourists do not opt for a small-scale accommodation with the expectation of meeting with local people there. Cheap room rates are a much more important factor to look for a homestay or *losmen* in one of the popular tourist areas. Tourists who regard contacts with local people as the ultimate aim of their trip have more chances to succeed in the budget accommodations in the lower-class neighborhood of Sosrowijayan than in middle-class Prawirotaman. Neither the government-imposed hotel category nor the name determines the accommodation's quality and the character of the local–tourist interaction, but the neighborhood where it is situated. Tourist accommodations do not exist in a vacuum, but are part of the social structure and cultural practice. Therefore, "homestays" in Prawirotaman imply privacy and comfort for a reasonable price, whereas in Sosrowijayan they imply basic facilities and personal interest shown by the young staff for a very cheap price.

The owner and staff of the budget accommodation in Yogyakarta reap the fruits of the current tourism growth in Yogyakarta. Statistics may be deceiving, but there are indications that the number of guests, length of stay, and occupancy rates show a larger and more regular increase than in the star-rated sector. Employment for local people is created through the expansion of small-scale accommodations, and through backward and forward linkages. Other local enterprises also get the opportunity to benefit from tourists staying in small-scale accommodations (e.g., local guides, pedicab men, food sellers, laundry women, and local travel agents). Most small-scale accommodations are family businesses that require low capital investment and show a large extent of flexibility. The budget accommodations of Sosrowijayan have a market advantage in this respect. They employ predominantly low or unpaid family members and combine the management of the accommodation with other economic activities (like a batik gallery), which makes them less vulnerable to market fluctuations and to government measures in the tourism sector. The owners in Prawirotaman, with investments in several accommodations in the area and with salaried and professional staff, run a higher risk of being detrimentally affected by changes in the market and in tourism policy.

In both tourist areas, the accommodation sector is constituted by independent entrepreneurs who safeguard their autonomy. As a consequence, the budget accommodation branch is unorganized and therefore holds a weak position vis-à-vis government interventions. Opposition against government measures is strong and each owner individually finds loopholes in the regulations and manages to dodge taxes and license requirements. However, individual wits cannot battle major government decisions, like destroying a local neighborhood, resettling the people, and building star-rated hotels in the area. The initiative of a few accommodation owners in Sosrowijayan is a cautious first attempt to get organized and play a more active role in local tourism development. Whereas formal organizations fail to emerge, informal cooperative efforts are abundant. There are complex networks extending between accommodation owners and their employees on the one hand, and local brokers on the other hand. These networks contribute significantly to the marketing of the tourist product of the city of Yogyakarta, including small-scale accommodations, manufacturers and vendors of souvenirs like batik and jewelery, transportation companies, travel agencies, pedicab men, and informal guides.

Instead of designing more restrictions and regulations, the local government should develop a program to intensify local participation in the tourism sector by improving the position of the small-scale entrepreneurs who represent the *couleur locale* that accounts for the reputation of Yogyakarta as the most relaxed of Javanese cities and that attracts international and domestic tourists. These local entrepreneurs have no opportunity to play a role in the innovation of the tourism product. They are trapped in their insecure economic position, the lack of credit facilities, low and irregular income, dependence on personal networks, commissions, tips, and gifts. More effort should be put into the development of local culture as a tourist attraction through a perspective on "everyday life," allowing for a more conceptual approach in city marketing.

Chapter 7

Tukang Becak: The Pedicab Men of Yogyakarta

Hanneke van Gemert, Esther van Genugten, and Heidi Dahles

Oh *becak* man, oh *becak* man going down the street

Looking for passengers so that you can eat

Your feet turn the pedals round and round

You go a long way and your sweat falls on the ground

From morning till the sun goes down at least

To south, to north, to the west. Then to the east

The heat and rain try to stop you but they never can

Oh *becak* man, oh *becak* man, oh *becak* man

(Popular Indonesian children's song)

Introduction

Tourists leaving their hotel and entering the busy streets of Yogyakarta's tourist areas experience the constant hassle by pedicab men who either park their vehicle along the road waiting for customers or slowly cycle through the streets in search for clients. "*Becak* Miss," "*Becak becak*," "Transport Miss," "Why walk, take *becak*," "Yes Miss, cheap transport," "*Becak* very cheap," "Good price for you," "500 one hour," are the most common modes of addressing tourists. Most of the pedicab men are very tenacious and do not take no for an answer. They follow the tourists, keep urging them to get into the pedicab, lower the price in the process of the negotiation, offer to take them to a large number of tourist attractions and shops. If tourists stubbornly keep refusing, some pedicab men change their tune and try to touch a sensitive cord: "Oh please take my *becak*, I didn't have a ride for two days and I have two children to look after, please take my becak!" Many tourists cannot withstand this very urgent invitation and surrender (Figure 7.1).

Figure 7.1. *Becak* men attracting the tourists' attention on Malioboro street. (Photo by J. Vissering)

A *becak*, also called pedicab, tricycle, or three-wheeler, looks like a big painted rocking chair on wheels. A *becak* is best described as a man-powered tricycle-taxi, propelled by means of pedals operated by a driver. There is room for two passengers who sit side by side in front of the driver. A canvas or cloth canopy gives some protection from the sun, fumes, and dust. When it rains, passengers are protected by a large flap of transparent plastic. As well as a tourist attraction in many Indonesian tourist areas, the *becak* is still a widespread mode of transportation in the towns and villages. The pedicab is used for many different purposes. The rich use the *becak* to chaperon their children to and from school. Traders use *becak* to transport their merchandise to and from the market. Housewives use the *becak* to ferry themselves to and from the market each day. Office workers use *becak* to take them to work. Even the ill are carted to and from the hospital in *becak*. Beds, tables, and all types of furniture are moved across the city by these vehicles, and so are chicken, sheep, and other animals.

The Indonesian government banned *becak* in the busiest areas of the cities of Java, like Bandung, Semarang, and Surabaya. In Jakarta *becak* were completely banned from the city as early as the 1970s and the vehicles were destroyed to prevent them for reappearing (Jellinek, 1991). According to Kartodirdjo (1981), the government legitimized this measure in terms of rapid urbanization, traffic congestion, and security. The number of motor vehicles (both two-wheeled vehicles and vehicles with four or more wheels) was increasing and the condition of the streets was not suitable to handle this increased motorized traffic. Moreover, accidents were usually caused by nonmotorized vehicles such as *becak*. The low speed of *becak* was often seen as a hindrance for the motorized traffic. In addition, the *becak* drivers' lack of understanding of traffic regulations (e.g., their relatively poor understanding of traffic signs) was a cause of disruption. However, another and perhaps even more important reason was that nonmotorized vehicles are considered to be tokens of the past and unsuited for a modern developing nation. Municipal governments prefer a public transportation system in which city buses and trains offer the main public transportation facility, as the exploitation of human muscular power for transportation is widely regarded as inhuman and backward. The other side of the coin is that *becak* not only offer a relatively cheap, flexible public transportation facility but also job opportunities and an income for a lot of urban families (Koetsier, 1989; Soegijoko, 1986). Recently, the *becak* has turned into a tourist attraction that can become an important asset in the marketing of the *couleur locale* of a major tourist destination like Yogyakarta, though many Western tourists regard taking a *becak* as degrading to the individual (Smithies, 1986).

In contrast with other big cities in Java, in Yogyakarta pedicabs are still an important mode of transportation for many local people. Yogyakarta, with its village-like structure (J. Sullivan, 1992) and relaxed lifestyles (Smithies, 1986), is the city par excellence where transport by *becak* is closely intertwined with everyday life. Almost everywhere there are *becak* peddling or parking, queuing and waiting, and their bell is sounding in the streets and alleys. Street life is determined by large numbers of *becak* drivers sleeping, talking, and waiting for customers in and around their *becak*. As has been demonstrated in the previous chapter, tourism in Yogyakarta is concentrated in two neighborhoods, Sosrowijayan in the inner city and Prawirotamen south of the center. These are the major areas for small-scale and budget tourism. A third major tourist area is Malioboro street where the star-rated hotels are situated. Twenty years ago Malioboro street was a quiet street. Bicycles, an occasional motorcycle, horse carts, and a large number of *becak* provided transport. The market to the east supplied the daily necessities and the shops along the street offered more specialized services. Today Malioboro street has become a very busy street where heavy traffic is flowing slowly in one direction. Because of the heavy traffic, by public and tour buses, private cars and taxis, and motorbikes, Malioboro street was converted into a one-way street a number of years ago. Slow traffic, like bicycles, *becak*, and horse carts are confined to the service road on both sides of the street. Malioboro street constitutes the main business, administrative and tourist district with many shops, a large shopping mall, hotels, and major government buildings. Vendors, beggars, batik sellers, touts, and unlicensed guides compete for the attention of foreign tourists.

In general, there are three different categories of *becak* drivers in Yogyakarta. First, and most common, are the pedicab men who provide transport for local residents. This category operates mainly outside the city center in the *kampung* and the middle-class residential areas at the outskirts of the city. Second, there are *becak* drivers who transport both local residents and tourists. These *becak* drivers usually dispose of a permanent pedicab stand in or near to the city center, the market, the train or bus station. Third, there are *becak* drivers specialized in the transport of tourists. This category positions itself in the popular tourist areas, in front of the hotels, souvenir shops, and tourist attractions. It is obvious that the transport of tourists requires *becak* men to speak at least rudimentary English and to have some talent to act as guide, to know where to change money, and where to find the best craft shops, entertainment districts, and cheapest hotels. For tourists, *becak* are not only a means of transport, but they also have a symbolic function. A *becak* ride is a unique experience for most tourists visiting Indonesia. Because of the slow speed, *becak* are a relaxed way of doing some sightseeing and watching the hustle and bustle of street life. Moreover, *becak* represent the local life, the authentic culture and genuine contact with the local population. In short, *becak* contribute to the attraction of a city in a touristic sense.

In the literature on local participation in tourism developments, the emphasis has been largely on small-scale accommodations (Long & Kindon, 1997: Smith, 1994; Van Schaardenburgh, 1995; Wall & Long, 1996), local manufacturers (Telfer & Wall, 1996), street and beach vendors (Bras & Dahles, 1998; Cukier, 1996; Cukier-Snow & Wall, 1993; Timothy & Wall, 1997), and street guides (Crick, 1992; Dahles, 1996, 1998a). The significance of local modes of transport for local participation in tourism and for the development of small-scale tourism has been neglected. This is rather striking, as one of the major problems in tourism management besides accommodating, feeding, and entertaining the tourists is to relocate them. Tourist transport is more than a logistic phenomenon. As will be demonstrated in this chapter focusing on the third category, the tourism-related *becak* drivers, there are significant economic, social, and cultural aspects to be considered. The central question that will be dealt with is in which ways and to what extent tourism affects the life of pedicab men in the main tourist areas in the city of Yogyakarta. To answer this question, we will discuss how *becak* drivers operate, how they approach tourists, and what determines their success in the tourism market. We will analyze the "capital" (in a Bourdieuan sense) they both invest and acquire while participating in tourism. Furthermore, we will investigate under what conditions these *becak* drivers benefit from tourism and what role networking and organization play in their business strategies.

Becak in Yogyakarta

The *becak* appeared in the streets of many Indonesian cities shortly before World War II, and after the war it came in great numbers and became very popular and widespread. The vehicle originates from Chinese or Singaporean design. The popularity of the *becak* was due to the occupation of Indonesia by the Japanese during the war period. The Japanese used almost all the petrol and iron for themselves, so cars could not be used as a means of local transport due to a shortage of gas and spare parts. Nonmotorized modes, such as the *becak*, replaced the useless cars. Originally, the *becak* was equipped with wooden wheels, but in the 1950s these wheels were replaced by rims with rubber tires (Koetsier, 1989). There was also plenty of manpower to operate the *becak*. In those days, the popularity of the *becak* was soaring because it provided a very convenient and cheap door-to-door service. It has a rather simple construction and is easy to operate; and because *becak* driving does not require special skills or technical know-how, the *becak* transportation system has provided job opportunities for a large number of the unskilled work force that has come as migrants from the rural areas. In most Indonesian towns the *becak* was compatible with the city transportation in general (Kartodirdjo, 1981).

However, since the 1970s there have been several attempts by the local government to limit the number of *becak* and to control their activities. In the 1980s a regulation was issued that only 1,800 *becak* were allowed to operate legally in the city, 60% of which at daytime and 40% at night. The *becak* operating at daytime would be painted red and the *becak* operating at night would be white. This system was short-lived and was abolished shortly after its introduction (Koetsier, 1989). Currently, the local government intends to introduce *becak*-free zones for the inner city. The idea is that the city has to become more attractive for tourism, starting with the extinction of the traffic congestion, which causes pollution and is unsafe. *Diparda* intends to improve the motorized transport system in the future. *Becak* are regarded as the ultimate cause of the traffic chaos and a threat to safety. Therefore, *becak* are to be banned from the center. The role of *becak* for employment and for the cultural identity of the city is not considered in this policy.

In the 1970s, a team of researchers from Gadjah Mada University (Yogyakarta) did a survey among *becak* men in the city to map the economic and social conditions under which those people making a living in urban low-cost transportation lived and worked. This research counters the then prevailing government view that *becak* form an obstacle to the modernization of Indonesian cities. The findings are analyzed in the report *The Pedicab in Yogyakarta* (Kartodirdjo, 1981) from which the subsequent data are derived. As the report points out, the *becak* transport industry forms an essential part of urban employment for the poorer sections of the community. A shift to motorized transport and a ban on pedicabs could deprive 14–40 persons of jobs for every new motorized three-wheeler (like *bemo*) because it can displace 15–40 *becak*. Although motorized vehicle use has grown considerably since the 1970s, it is unclear whether the number of *becak* in Yogyakarta has declined, as accurate data about the number of pedicab drivers are not available and estimates differ widely. In 1975, according to the Police Department of Yogyakarta, there were 5,971 *becak* in Yogyakarta, which probably means that in fact there were more, because a number were bound not to have been registered (Kartodirdjo, 1981). In 1989 there were about 8,000 *becak* in Yogyakarta whereas only 3,416 *becak* were registered officially (Koetsier, 1989). The nongovernmental organization Dian Desa on behalf of a United Nations development program estimated that there were about 2,500 people involved in *becak* riding in the late 1980s. This estimation was based on "observations," not on reliable counting (Soedjarwo, 1991).

According to the Gadjah Mada survey (Kartodirdjo, 1981), *becak* drivers are always males in the age bracket of 20–50 years. Their education is mostly limited to the primary school level, and more than half of them never completed primary education. Most pedicab men come from villages surrounding Yogyakarta, especially the poorest and dry areas at Gunung Kidul to the southeast of the city, where they were unskilled and semiskilled farm workers. Only a part of them can rely on additional income from their home village, through the produce of their small plot of land. Most became *becak* driver because no other job was available. They prefer any other job, because the work is hard and the rewards are few. Occasionally, *becak* drivers are students earning money to help them through school or even university, but this is very rare. Although most of the *becak* drivers have their own houses, living conditions are rather poor and due to various hardships their family faces endless financial problems. Their life aspirations for themselves and for their children are rather low. But not one of the *becak* drivers wants his children to follow in his footsteps and become a *becak* driver.

The income is insufficient for daily needs and the status of a *becak* driver is low. In the 1980s, the average revenue was about 3,000 *rupiah* per day. Deducting the price of their meals, they can bring home about 2,500 *rupiah* per day. This can be increased up to 5,000 *rupiah* either by operating also at night or by transporting tourists (Soedjarwo, 1991). However, the majority of the Yogyanese *becak* drivers do not have a *becak* of their own. They have to rent the vehicle at a rental company for about 1,000 *rupiah* per day, which is a heavy drain on the income. Rental companies often issue contracts that give *becak* drivers the opportunity to save for the purchase of the *becak* they are renting. Some drivers look for "sponsoring" by a shop, hotel, restaurant, or bar. In that case the driver paints the logo of the sponsor on his vehicle. This type of sponsoring has not much significance in terms of additional income, but it can be strategy to ensure the pedicab man of a profitable stand where many potential customers pass by. Another and much more remunerative income-securing strategy is acquiring commissions from shops, restaurants, and hotels. Commission is paid by these establishments for delivering buying or paying customers, as has been shown in previous chapters in this book. In Yogyakarta *becak* men generally receive 5–15% of the customer's expenditures. This percentage varies widely: some accommodations in Prawirotaman pay up to 60% (cf. Chapter 6), whereas others refuse to pay any commission at all, and some hotels and silver shops offer their "regular" *becak* men a t-shirt once a year.

Becak differ from motorized public transport by the absence of fixed routes and fixed fares. The fares are set by bargaining. According to Dalton (1991), there are three kinds of prices. The first one is for local people. In Yogyakarta, the *becak* is frequently used by women to run errands and for children to be taken to school. Local people rarely bargain with a *becak* man as there is a shared opinion what a ride from one location to another is worth. The second is higher than the local tariff and is charged to customers from out-of-town who are not familiar with the local situation. A third and even higher price is applied to Chinese people (generally regarded as rich), *orang besar* (big man), Indonesians from other islands (like domestic tourists), and, of course, foreigners and international tourists. The foreign tourists, being the most ignorant and the richest of all, get overcharged constantly (Turner et al., 1995), and travel guide books, especially those addressing individual travelers, elaborate on the issue of how to deal with pedicab men (Dalton, 1991; Turner et al., 1995).

The Daily Life of *Becak* Drivers

Life of a *becak* man is hard. He starts very early in the morning, makes long days, and earns little money. Most *becak* drivers have to work each day, because they cannot afford to take a day off. Where they cater mainly to the local people, they have to get started at 4 o'clock in the morning to take the housewives to the market and subsequently the richer people's children to school. They work till 4 or 5 o'clock in the afternoon. A few work until late at night, after taking a siesta in the afternoon, as they may charge their clients more at evening hours. *Becak* drivers like to work overtime in the evening if they have an appointment with tourists to bring them to a sight of the city (e.g., to the *Ramayana* ballet). This is a very profitable business, not only because tourists are generally overcharged, but also because they earn a commission from the theater where the performance is held. A threat for the *becak* driver is the increase of other modes of public transport in the city, like the public bus and the taxi, and of organized forms of tourist transport. The growing supply of transport is not only a competitor for the *becak* drivers in terms of decreasing numbers of customers, but also in terms of increasing numbers of people claiming commissions. Tour leaders, guides both licensed and unlicensed, taxi and bus drivers are aware of the opportunity to receive a commission when they bring tourists to shops and accommodations and they do not hesitate to do so.

Most of the *becak* drivers rent their *becak* at a rental company (*juragan becak*). These companies are owned by successful entrepreneurs, mostly Chinese people, who never worked as a *becak* man themselves. Only very few *becak* men succeed in establishing their own company by investing their savings into more *becak*, which will be rented to other drivers. *Becak* men prefer to live in the vicinity of these companies, as the *becak* are kept at the owner's place. They have to pick up the *becak* in the morning and bring it back at night when their job is done. As a consequence, a number of concentrated living areas for *becak* men have emerged in Yogyakarta (Soedjarwo, 1991). The rent that they have to pay is very diverse. Some say that they have to pay 700 *rupiah*, others say that they have to pay 1,500 *rupiah*, to be handed over to the owner at the end of the day. If they did not make enough money to pay, the owner will give them postponement of payment. Other *becak* drivers pay an amount per month (about 45,000 *rupiah*). The rate also differs during day- and nighttime, the rent for the night shift being higher. The happy few who are able to save money for several years to acquire their own *becak* usually buy a second-hand vehicle for 300,000 or 400,000 *rupiah*; a new *becak* costs about 700,000 *rupiah* and is unaffordable for most.

Most *becak* drivers are married with children. Their wives also have jobs to support the family. These jobs differ from working at the market, in the rice fields, being a cook, or doing housework and making pottery. Only a few stay at home to keep house and take care of the children. These are mainly the mothers of young children who do not go to school yet. It is remarkable how many times *becak* drivers start talking about their children during rides with tourists. In particular the cost of education is the object of their constant worries. The expenses for school education are very high, almost unaffordable for a *becak* driver. Pedicab men often make up large amounts of money for school fees and other expenses for the education of their children. For example, one *becak* driver told us that the school fee of his two children was 35,000 *rupiah* a year. A few weeks later we used the *becak* of the same man. In the meantime the amount of money he allegedly needed to pay for his children's education had risen to 150,000 *rupiah* a year. This example is typical for the way in which *becak* drivers attempt to make foreign tourists pay more for a trip. However, it would lead too far to interpret the *becak* men's worries about the school fee for their children purely in terms of a "tourist trap." They do believe that education is very important for the development of their children and that it is necessary for acquiring a position in society that is better than their father's. *Becak* drivers want the best for their children and the last thing they want is for them to become a *becak* driver like themselves. Twenty years ago when the Gadjah Mada survey was held, the majority of men started working as pedicab man after finishing the SMP (*Sekolah Menengah Pertama*, lower secondary school). Still, for being a *becak* driver not many skills are required and the threshold to become a *becak* driver is low due to the ease of renting a *becak*. In spite of the low education some of the *becak* drivers speak English fluently. In particular, those who have their permanent stand in the tourist areas master the English language well. However, some drivers claimed to be well-educated, for example as a teacher or accountant. One *becak* man showed us his ID stating as profession "doctorandus," which is a university grade, not a vocation. As has been observed for other entrepreneurs in the urban arena, fake ID cards are easily available in Yogyakarta and widely used to appear more reliable and professional when dealing with foreign tourists (van Genugten & van Gemert, 1996).

Many *becak* drivers expect to remain a *becak* driver for the rest of their lives. Chances of finding a job in a different profession are small or even absent. The lack of money and education are the major limiting factors. Especially those who have to pay for the school fees of their children are unable to save any money from their daily earnings. Only few are satisfied with being a pedicab man, in particular the ones who claim to earn a lot with the tips and commissions through tourism. Those who want to be a *becak* driver for the rest of their lives often cherish the ambition to buy a *becak* of their own. They dream of receiving a large commission one day, large enough to buy a *becak*. All know of cases for whom the dream came true. Like Idaman, a *becak* man one of the authors hired frequently. Idaman's favorite story is about a pedicab man who was given 750,000 *rupiah* by a tourist out of sympathy, more than enough to buy a shiny new *becak* and pay for the school fee of his children. Owning a *becak* is economically advantageous, because it saves the rent a *becak* man has to pay to the proprietor. Moreover, it is prestigious among *becak* men to operate as one's own boss. However, most *becak* drivers dream of another job in the future. A few are hesitant, they do not know exactly what kind of job, but they think that every other job is a progress compared to the work of a *becak* driver. The reasons for wanting to escape are obvious: their income as a *becak* driver is not sufficient for their daily needs, and, growing older, they feel they will physically not be able to continue their work in the future. The majority, however, know exactly what kind of job they want. They dream of buying a piece of land and becoming a farmer, like their kin and their forefathers. Others aspire to a career in the tourism industry, to become a batik vendor, or trader in silver jewelery or other souvenirs. They are aware of the increasing number of tourists in Yogyakarta and see good prospects in selling to tourists with large profits.

Making money from tourists requires clever strategies. First of all, *becak* drivers are alert to spot tourists, preferably newly arrived ones, as they are disoriented and perhaps naive and need "assistance." Even if *becak* drivers lie drowsing in their vehicles, they scan the street for potential customers. If they have directed the tourists (in)to their *becak*, as they persistently will attempt to do, the bargaining starts. For many Western people bargaining is a technique that has passed into oblivion in their culture, so they feel quite uncomfortable with this situation. Many experienced travelers like to give good advice how to proceed to trick the *becak* man. Dalton (1991) recommends not to bargain with *becak* drivers at popular tourist sites, but to walk a block away in any direction and look for another pedicab. The "walk-away" technique works well with *becak* drivers. There are always lots of others who want to give you a ride if one of their colleagues does not accept your offer. To arrange a price *becak* men use different measures. Sometimes they charge per kilometer. The cost of 1 kilometer differs from 300 to 1,000 *rupiah*, depending on the *becak* driver and location. Others charge per trip. They ask where you want to go and then offer a price. They usually start with a very high price and the tourists are supposed to bargain for a lower price. Sometimes tourists do not know how this works or are too shy to do so, which is the driver's lucky day. The general procedure is that the customer offers half of the rate the driver asked for, and subsequently both parties meet somewhere in the middle. The bargaining process can take a while, as the *becak* driver is reluctant to lower the price, explaining that the proposed price is low and that he needs to earn some money to feed his children. Hilly roads and the weather ("It is so hot") are introduced as arguments to charge more. A rather successful bargaining trick is the "up to you" strategy, asking the tourists to pay him any amount they regard as reasonable at the end of the ride. These are the trips when the *becak* driver tells about the generosity of other tourists, the regular price per kilometer, and the expensive school fees for his children. If the tourists do not pay enough, then the pedicab man's face gets clouded, his eyes look sad, and he exclaims to be *bankrut* (broke). "With this trick I earn more money than with a serious price," one of our informants admitted.

The price for a *becak* ride also differs according to the tourists' destination. If they want to visit a batik gallery, a souvenir shop, or a *Ramayana* performance, *becak* drivers, in anticipation of the commission they hope to receive for the tourists' purchases, offer a very cheap price. They think that tourists always buy upon entering a shop. In case they do not buy anything, the *becak* driver becomes angry, refuses to continue the trip, and asks for more money. "If tourists don't buy when I bring them to the shop than I become real mad. This because, you know, I have to pay the rent of my *becak* and food for my children." Tourists who intend to use the *becak* purely as a means of transport to relocate are less interesting customers, as two of the authors were able to experience themselves. A *becak* driver offered 300 *rupiah* for 1 hour cycling around, but actually he wanted to go to the shops. When we told him that we wanted to go to *kantor pos* (post office) the negotiations stopped. He preferred a ride to the shops, with the uncertainty of not receiving any commission at all, above the certainty to have a ride with a value of 2,000 *rupiah*. For tourists not speaking the local language, it can be hard to arrange for a trip to relocate from one place to another without being delivered at several batik shops on the way. *Becak* drivers charge different prices for tourists and local residents. They even apply different measures for different categories of tourists. Therefore, *becak* men almost always ask at which hotel a tourist is staying. Star-rated hotels guarantee a well-to-do customer who can afford to pay a high price. "Once a man ask me to take him to the

Radisson Hotel. I thought that this must be a rich American, so I ask 25,000 *rupiah* for this trip of 5 kilometers. No bargaining, he accepted this deal."

Sudiman, a *becak* driver who operates in the Malioboro street, is a smart man and has his own special strategy to approach tourists. He is very friendly, open-minded, speaks English well, and always has interesting things to tell. He successfully combines his profession as *becak* driver with being a silversmith. "I use the *becak* to get potential customers to my silver shop." By inviting tourists to visit his "home and family" he cajoles them to his little workshop in *Kota Gede* (which is known as the "Silver Village," as many silver factories are situated there). This happened to the authors. During the trip to his home, we got the impression more and more that it was a commercial trip. First, Sudiman asked if we had to go to a bank, because there were no bank facilities in *Kota Gede*. Secondly, he dropped us at his "sister's" batik shop and he kept urging us to buy. We had a strong feeling that the woman was not his sister at all, because they both did not behave like family, more like business partners. During the visit at his house he showed us a catalogue with jewelery made from silver. Continually he emphasized that if we wanted to order something we had to do it through him. During the conversation he asked us many times how much money we had in our pockets. It is clear that Sudiman is very a business-minded *becak* man. Besides his *becak* and silver smithy, he sends batik paintings to a "friend" in Switzerland for sale. From this man he also received seven new *becak*, each with a value of 700,000 *rupiah*. Sudiman, then, is a patron in the sense of Boissevain (Chapter 1). He rents these vehicles to other drivers. "Now I use the profit from the *becak* to pay the cost of my children's education." He may be regarded as a wealthy and very successful small-scale entrepreneur.

The price elasticity during the bargaining process depends strongly on how desperate the *becak* drivers are. If they have not had a ride that day, they accept a low price easily. If they earned their daily minimum, they accept only rides with a good price. We have noticed that *becak* drivers who earn enough money during a particular day start demanding "impossible" prices, even for small distances. Negotiations are hardly possible in that situation, giving the impression that the drivers actually do not want another ride. From a capitalist point of view, one could argue that pedicab men have a short-term perspective only to survive for 1 day. They do not capitalize on opportunities and accumulate capital. From the pedicab man's point of view, one has to consider whether one additional ride on top of earning a day's minimum renders a profit that covers the additional costs in terms of physical energy and health (Figure 7.2). In the *becak* man's calculation these costs are only covered if the additional ride is extremely well paid.

The income of *becak* drivers in the tourist areas varies widely and depends on a large number of factors. In interviews it is hardly possible to come up with reliable data as *becak* men are rather reluctant to discuss these matters. They prefer to complain about their poor income as they equate Western researchers with tourists, a potential source of income. Some say they earn an average of 1,500 *rupiah* a day, others say they earn about 30,000 *rupiah* on a successful day. In general, *becak* drivers with the highest incomes are the ones that exclusively transport tourists, and have their permanent

Figure 7.2. *Becak* man taking a rest. (Photo by K. Bras)

stand in a busy tourist area. However, as tourism is seasonal, their income shows strong fluctuations. During the low season, they may earn little or nothing. Their average income is then about 2,000 *rupiah* a day. Moreover, in the rainy season they loose it to the taxi drivers, as many tourists prefer a taxi when it is raining. Finally, the income of a *becak* driver depends on his "cultural capital" in the broadest sense. A successful pedicab man is a good performer and has a thorough understanding of the tourists' way of thinking. He has to have a good proficiency in the English language, a lot of interesting things to tell that appeal to the tourists' imagination, and a good feeling for timing to present his case without being too intrusive. In that case, tourists think that he is a nice man and give him an extra tip, pay for his children's school fee, or even buy him a *becak*.

Besides the fare for the trips, *becak* drivers are keen to receive commissions. The way commissions are paid differs and depends on the kind of shop. Some receive the commission in *rupiah*, others in natura (rice, t-shirts, etc.). There are many different stories about the acquisition and the amount of commissions. *Becak* drivers do not receive commissions in every shop. Some shops give only commissions to guides. In other shops *becak* drivers receive some money once a year—a t-shirt or a *sarong* at *Idul Fitri*, the last day of Ramadan when it is the habit to beg forgiveness and to exchange presents. As one of our informants stated: "Normally I get a commission 2.5% at a shop, but during *Idul Fitri* I get 25,000 *rupiah* because I bring so many customers in." Generally, pedicab men are very secretive about the acquisition of commissions. They often get a nervous smile when asked about the commissions, then they deny. They fear that tourists think they pay a higher price for the things they buy when arriving by *becak* as the *becak* man's commission is paid from their purchase. Some *becak* men, however, tell tourists about the commission system and how it works. This is a good way of clarifying the nature of the service and the price they bargained for. Most *becak* drivers admit that receiving commissions is a very lucrative business. Some *becak* drivers see the commissions as an extra bonus above their daily income and keep it apart for the days they do not earn sufficient money. "If I bring tourists to the Prambanan Hotel, I receive 50,000 *rupiah*. Sad to say that happens not often because most of the time such hotel room is already booked." Or: "Last week I brought a Dutchman, from The Hague, to a silver shop. I do not know what he bought but I received 20,000 *rupiah* on commissions" (van Genugten & van Gemert, 1996).

Networks and Organizations

Although *becak* drivers are self-employed individuals that protect their relationships with commission-paying establishments, "sponsors," and customer-generating areas, a considerable number have joined organizations that contribute to their income security and risk avoidance. This means that the *becak* men in Yogyakarta can be distinguished into organized and nonorganized categories. Unorganized are the *tukang becak liar* (i.e., the "wild" *becak* drivers). They are without a license and a permanent stand. These *becak* drivers are always on the move looking for customers or a parking lot. Others, who have a license and a permanent stand, predominantly in quiet nontourist areas, are nevertheless unorganized and work alone. The organized *becak* drivers have a license, a permanent stand, a lot of "regular" clients, and privileged access to tourists. The benefits of being organized will be discussed more in detail below.

There are many different organizations of *becak* drivers in Yogyakarta. Basically, these organizations are related to one specific neighborhood and associated with particular shops, restaurants, bars, or hotels. The members of the organizations are often recognizable by their shirts or advertisements on the *becak*. The organizations claim a territory and establish the permanent stand for their members on profitable locations. Their target group is predominantly tourists, although some also transport local residents. The *becak* organizations own bank accounts with a saving system, which each member has to contribute to. However, the organizations use their bank accounts for different purposes. Some save money as a kind of insurance, some as a form of retirement payment, and others save money just for unforeseen expenses and hardships. All organizations charge a fee for new members.

In the Sosrowijayan area, the organization *Jalan Sosrowijayan* is operative with three subdivisions and about 40 members per unit. The members pay a contribution—5,000 *rupiah* in the most prosperous unit, otherwise less—to a common bank account. Once a year a percentage of the savings is redistributed among the members. The *becak* organization in the adjacent Pasar Kembang area uses the savings for the purchase of additional (second-hand) *becak*. In this case, the organization receives an extra contribution from the local Borobudur Bar, which is the primary beneficiary of *becak* men delivering customers. In Prawirotaman the first organization of *becak* drivers was established 20 years ago, before the tourism boom in Yogyakarta. Some of the members have worked in this area for that long. They witnessed the emergence of tourism and a change of customers. The formerly well-to-do citizens living in the area gave way to tourists who need a ride from the bus station to the accommodations and back. Nowadays these *becak* men have the privileged position of exclusively transporting tourists. Through the years their involvement with tourists has brought about an increase of their daily income. It is not surprising that the Prawirotamen *becak* drivers are quite protective towards their territorium. The organization charges new members about 300,000 *rupiah* entrance fee. This amount of money covers the costs for a second-hand *becak* and only few can afford to pay it. Outsiders are not allowed to pick up customers in this area; exceptions are those who have a close friend among the members. As Prawirotaman is good for business, many *becak* men want to work there, and many do. As a consequence, the *becak* drivers have to wait a long time until it is their turn to take a customer—as this is the rule. Therefore, these *becak* drivers always insist to wait for the customer to take them back home, no matter how long they have to wait. It probably pays better to wait for the customers than to wait at the stand. There, so many *becak* drivers wait for their turn that there is a little chance to transport tourists twice a day. Malioboro street is different from the neighborhoods in terms of *becak* organizations. Most pedicab men who have a permanent stand at Malioboro street are not eager to join an organization; in fact, except for the northern part of the street, the *becak* drivers are unorganized. The reason for staying independent self-employed people may be that Malioboro street is the business center of the town providing an abundance of customers both local and tourist. In this situation of bounty, no need is felt to impose restrictions and rules, as this is what membership in an organization implies besides the privileges. The organizations of Sosrowijayan and Prawirotaman exert social control on the members in exchange for protection.

As may be clear from the brief description of *becak* organizations in three prominent business and tourist areas, the streets and neighborhoods are differently classified into more or less desirable (i.e., profitable) stands for *becak* drivers. Three kinds of locations can be distinguished: top locations, good locations, and inferior locations. Working at a top location means that the *becak* driver has his permanent stand in a street that is characterized by the presence of many hotels, guesthouses, shops, and restaurants. The main streets in the neighborhoods of Sosrowijayan and Prawirotaman fit this picture. It is hardly possible for other *becak* drivers to operate in this street because they are not members of the organization. The organizations of Sosrowijayan and Prawirotaman have in common the policy of refusing *becak* drivers from other locations. These protective measures and the presence of a constant flow of tourists make these areas desirable places to work for *becak* drivers. Organizations on the top locations are more strictly formalized and organized than others. They operate independently from the local tourism industry, in that they do not look for sponsorship or other forms of support by the tourism businesses in their street. The members of the organizations on the top locations profile themselves as a group. They exchange customers, share the commission-paying businesses, help each other with the negotiations with tourists, and have a credit system for emergencies.

A "good" location is a place where many tourists pass by and that offers *becak* drivers opportunities to make lucrative trips. Pasar Kembang, streets adjacent to Prawirotaman, and Malioboro street are examples of this type of location. *Becak* drivers operating on the "good" locations are less protective and more permissive towards other *becak* drivers than their colleagues on the top locations. The organizations of the "good" locations are often connected with a hotel, a bar, a restaurant, or a shop that acts as "sponsor" of the *becak* drivers and gives some financial support to their organization. The prospect of being supported by the local businesses may be the impulse to establish an organization. Inferior locations are characterized by the purely "local" clientele and the absence of tourists. The transport of local residents offers no opportunities for lucrative trips in terms of extra tips or commissions. It has to be kept in mind that the majority of the *becak* drivers in Yogyakarta work on this type of location.

Local Participation

It is obvious that the presence of tourists forms the crucial criterion for the quality of a location. The *becak* drivers who are fortunate to have access to a permanent stand on such a location have organized themselves to protect their position against the competition of other pedicab men in the city. However, the effectiveness of their organizations extends no further than their immediate working area. No influence is exerted by these organizations on local politics and policies. *Becak* drivers are not aware of the government's plans to ban their vehicles from the city center. They do not feel threatened in their future existence, neither by government policies nor by fluctuations in tourist arrivals. They cannot imagine that the tourists could ever stay away from Yogyakarta. *Becak* drivers live in their own small world and are hardly aware of the developments at local, national, or global levels. They resign themselves to their fate. On being asked, they quote the Sultan who is said to have promised once that "there will always be *becak* in Yogyakarta."

Becak drivers benefit from tourism in terms of an increase in income, but they are not empowered through tourism. They strongly depend on tourism once they specialize in the transport of tourists, and they are at the mercy of tourist seasons, foul play of companies, and local government. *Becak* drivers do not have the power to change the situation, and this makes them vulnerable. The members of a *becak* organization emphasize that working together makes them stronger and more powerful in relation to the unorganized *becak* drivers. These organizations share some characteristics with trade unions, like establishing an insurance against sickness and other calamities that prevent pedicab men from working. However, the organizations do not represent the interest of their members in negotiations with *becak* rental companies or in local politics.

Conclusions

This chapter has shown that tourism has affected the lives of at least a fraction of pedicab men in Yogyakarta, specifically those who are so fortunate to find their customers in the major tourist areas. When *becak* men get involved in tourism, their mode of operation, their economic position, and their personal network relations change. The emergence of tourism has created opportunities to earn considerably more money through overcharging tourists, arranging commissions, and support by the local tourism industry. Some become an independent entrepreneur by acquiring a *becak* as private property instead of renting a vehicle. And other *becak* men become the head of a *becak* rental company or a small souvenir workshop. It is safe to say that tourism enhances the economic capital of those pedicab men who actually get involved with tourists. For those who remain in the position of exclusively transporting locals, tourism does not seem to have any impact in terms of a multiplier effect. Further research should investigate whether increasing income rates through tourism among the urban population either improves or worsens the economic position of the pedicab men in the "inferior" locations.

The majority of the *becak* drivers in Yogyakarta work in the "inferior" locations, wholly dependent on local clientele. Their location provides them with regular clients, an almost fixed number of daily rides, and a low but stable income. Working in the tourism sector involves less stability, more spectacular windfalls, and more risks. As we have seen in this chapter, the establishment of *becak* organizations forms important risk-reducing and income-securing strategies. Being eligible for membership, a *becak* man has to dispose of a network that gives him access to such an organization, either by being one of the first to subscribe or by being able to pay for the entrance fee. However, even to be allowed to pay this fee, the introduction by a member is necessary. It has become clear that for the *becak* drivers on a top location, the organization is a way to exclude outsiders and to protect their own position. This is necessary because tourism has made certain locations extremely popular for *becak* drivers. Without the social control and discipline imposed by the organization, the tourist areas would turn into a battlefield with hordes of *becak* drivers competing for customers. Although the expansion of tourism in Yogyakarta created new opportunities for *becak* drivers, further growth represents a threat for the *becak* drivers who already operate in the tourist sector. The ease to enter into the profession of pedicab driver and the windfalls that can be made in the tourism sector will increase the number of competitors. This applies for migrants from rural areas looking for job opportunities in the city. These people may be less inclined towards starting their own tourist business because they lack the economic capital, or becoming an informal guide as they lack the cultural and social capital, but entering into *becak* driving may establish a viable opportunity. This prospect illustrates that concentrated tourism development in one destination area without parallel development of the surrounding rural area will not effect the modernization and development of the country as a whole as desired by the Indonesian government.

The emergence and expansion of tourism has contributed to the process of modernization in the city of Yogyakarta. A number of *becak* men have risen to the challenge. They established themselves in the city's tourism business and their entrepreneurial activities are strongly intertwined with the tourism industry as a whole. The local government should be aware of the consequences of banning the *becak* from the inner city. Not being the solution for the traffic congestion, pollution, and insecurity, the disappearance of *becak*s would be a loss in terms of cultural heritage and authentic local life. With regard to the recent stagnation in tourism development and the need to revitalize the tourist product of the city, it would be foolish to destroy a cheap, distinctive, and easily available asset in tourism marketing.

Chapter 8

Mountain Guides in Lombok: Pathfinders up *Gunung* Rinjani

Karin ter Steege, Sandra Stam, and Karin Bras

Introduction

Gunung Rinjani is the highest mountain in Lombok and the third highest in Indonesia. It is an active volcano that has a huge half-moon-shaped crater with a large green lake, hot springs, and a new volcano—*Gunung* Baru—in the center of the lake. The climb up Rinjani is one of Indonesia's unique experiences. Depending on time and fitness, tourists can make a quick 2-day dash to the crater rim, a 3-day trek to the crater lake, or a 4-day climb to the very summit at 3,726 meters. As Wheeler and Lyon (1992) write:

> You can do the trek from Bayan without a guide, but in some places there's a confusion of trails branching off and you could get lost. The other advantage of guides is that they're informative, good company, and also act as porters, cooks and water collectors. When you're walking with a guide make sure you set your own pace—some guides climb Rinjani as often as 20 or 30 times a year and positively gallop up the slopes. (p. 271)

Every year more and more tourists find their way to the little village of Senaru, at the foothills of the Rinjani, one of the starting points of the climb. Local mountain guides offer their services to the tourists and arrange the trekkings. Next to guiding the tourists to the top, they take care of the most important things tourists need on their trek: a tent, sleeping bags, cooking gear, food, and water. The local mountain guides also arrange porters who will carry the supplies up the mountain. Besides foreign and domestic tourists, Balinese and local Sasak climb the Rinjani, mainly for religious reasons.

The aim of this chapter is to analyze in which way local mountain guides contribute to the construction of *Gunung* Rinjani as a tourist attraction and how their activities fit in with the recent tourism development in this area. Until recently, anyone who had some experience in climbing the Rinjani could become a local guide. However, nowadays guiding is developing more and more into a profession with specific standards and requirements. Governmental efforts of improving the quality of guiding result in measures to get a grip on all the local tourist guides who work without a government license. In government training, for instance, the importance of language skills and guiding techniques is emphasized. Because the local guides from Senaru operate far away from the administrative center Mataram, they seem to be safeguarded from government regulations. But indirectly they are confronted with the standardization and formalization of the guiding sector. Before describing their activities and the area in which mountain guides operate, a brief overview of the different academic approaches on guiding will be given, necessary to understand the guiding business. The following discussion of their activities provides some insight into the way mountain guides make the Rinjani area—a unique but at the same time vulnerable area— accessible to tourists, which resources mountain guides utilize, and what position they hold in local society. Moreover, it gives us a better view of how local mountain guides experience the possibilities and restrictions that they face in their daily activities. Furthermore, the government policy on guiding as well as related initiatives in the area of ecotourism will be discussed in order to understand the conditions under which mountain guides operate in this specific area.

Local Guides: Pathfinders or Small Entrepreneurs?

The "pathfinder" is a geographical guide "who leads the way through an environment in which his followers lack orientation or through a socially defined territory to which they have no access" (Cohen, 1985, p. 7). From way back pathfinders can be found in mountain and other off-the-beaten-track areas where trails are numerous and detailed maps are not available. To find their way around tourists need help from someone who knows the area and who will double as a porter, a cook, and a water collector. The interest of tourists in trekkings and mountaineering has led to a growth in these rudimentary guiding services. Indonesia has several volcanos that are popular destinations for 2- or 3-day trekkings, like the Merapi on Central Java and the volcano discussed in this chapter, *Gunung* Rinjani on Lombok. Also the Himalayas in Nepal (Gurung, Simmons, & Devlin, 1996) and the northern part of Thailand (Cohen, 1996) are well-known trekking destinations where locals are hired to guide tourists. Next to finding the way in an unmarked and rugged territory, local guides—like the jungle guides in North Thailand—are faced with the task of ensuring the goodwill and hospitality of the natives of the area (Cohen, 1982c). Gaining access in a remote social environment and making himself and his party acceptable proves to be a difficult task for the local guide who has to take into account his own "go-between" position, "a position which makes him the only link in the encounter between complete strangers" (Cohen, 1985, p. 13). He has to assure himself of the hospitality of the natives by building a long-term relationship with representatives in the area. But he also has to find ways to transfer this hospitality to his guests (Cohen, 1982c). The pathfinder, in other words, eases access to local culture and no longer only in remote areas. Street guides in crowded cities also geographically guide tourists through an area where they lack orientation. But, more important, they point the way in a practical sense. Providing access to local culture means access to nonpublic territories and to informal services like souvenir shops, art exhibitions, performances, restaurants, and accommodation. Local street guides are small entrepreneurs who mediate between tourists and the local shopkeepers and the local service industry (Dahles, 1996).

The pathfinders or original guides are "marginal natives" (Cohen, 1985), self-employed local people with little formal education who work without the regular licenses. They are not permanently employed in guiding, but make a living from several activities. Normally they focus on the noninstitutionalized tourist: the young backpackers (Cohen's drifters or explores) who travel alone and are in search for direct experiences. They mainly operate in the early stages of tourism development or in the periphery of the tourism system, like in the Rinjani area, which can be classified as a secondary category in the whole range of attractions (Leiper, 1990). Secondary in the sense that the Rinjani is not the major determinant in the tourist choice of destination, but of sufficient interest to tourists to visit it once they have arrived in the area. Therefore, the role of the pathfinder is considered as being productive in the sense that they contribute to the growth and expansion of the tourist attractions, which gives them the name "pathbreakers" (Cohen, 1985, p. 25).

Next to finding the way, also the "go-between" tasks (the local guide as a mediator) are regarded as an essential aspect of the pathfinder type of guiding. This "go-between" role is characteristic of the mediation activities of local tourist guides in general. The mediating role is mentioned by many authors as being an essential part of guiding (Cohen, 1982c, 1985; De Kadt, 1979; Gurung et al., 1996; Holloway, 1981; Pearce, 1984). The local tourist guide is portrayed as someone who builds bridges between the tourists and the locals, through the mediation of money, services, access, and information. His attitude and abilities seem to be of vital importance in safeguarding a certain balance in the destination area. Gurung et al. (1996) argue that

> the main duty of the tourist guide is to create a social climate and environmental understanding under which both the visitor and the visited will benefit in the long term. There is evidence that the tourist guide plays an important role in tourism by enhancing the quality of the experience for visitors and by minimizing undesirable outcomes of tourism for the host-community. (pp. 113–114)

The authors paint an idealized picture of guiding. It cannot be denied that local tourist guides are intermediaries, but the question is whether much emphasis should be put on their mediatory function and, therefore, on keeping all parties satisfied and keeping the development of tourism in a specific area in balance. Is it not more likely that an important part of their activities is centered upon the question of how they themselves derive the greatest benefit from their work? Although local tourist guides usually do not sell products, they can be regarded as small entrepreneurs trading in services and information. Therefore, local guides fit neatly into the picture Boissevain paints of brokers as entrepreneurs. "A broker is a special type of entrepreneur: one who controls and manipulates strategic contacts with other people for his own profit" (Boissevain, 1974, pp. 147–148). This approach is in sharp contrast with the cultural broker described by Gurung et al. (1996), who is considered to be someone with such qualities as "interpretation, knowledge, communication skills, and cross-cultural understandings; essential skills needed to bridge the gap between diverse communities" (p. 113). The qualities mentioned are not necessarily deployed to reach a balance, but to improve the guide's personal situation. Rather than putting too much emphasis on the mediatory function of local guides, their activities can be regarded as mostly entrepreneurial in the sense that the local tourist guides sell images, knowledge, contacts, souvenirs, access, authenticity, ideology, and sometimes even their body and their feelings. The ability to carry out these activities requires an extensive "body of knowledge" about the local culture. Their knowledge of the local culture is not limited to facts, figures, and *couleur locale*, but also includes the art of building a network, monopolizing contacts, exploiting the commission and tipping system, and sensing trends within tourism. Moreover, insight into the culture of the guests is a prerequisite for success. Local tourist guides have to search for convincing ways to address tourists and find out their interests and wishes. To make the encounters as profitable as possible, efforts are made to develop longer lasting relationships with their guests. Important in becoming a successful guide is the ability to turn social relations and narratives into a profitable business asset (Boissevain, 1974). In other words, local tourist guides need to develop their social, cultural, and economic skills in order to maximize their profits and improve their personal situation.

The Rinjani Area and Senaru

Established in 1990, the Rinjani National Park is one of the latest national parks in Indonesia. It covers 41,330 hectares and is located in the north central part of Lombok (Figure 8.1). All the major rivers of the island originate inside the park, and these rivers are an important water source for irrigation and agricultural industry in adjacent lowland areas. For this reason the most important objective of conservation is to maintain the natural forest cover of the Rinjani Complex from where these rivers arise (Beterams, 1996). Another important aspect of the Rinjani area is its scenic beauty. Besides beautiful panoramas from the summit of Rinjani over the lake and the whole mountain complex, the area offers traditional villages and waterfalls. Together with lake Segara Anak, the hot springs, and wildlife the Rinjani area is a worthwhile destination for foreign as well as domestic tourists. The development of tourism is an integral part of this national park. With entrance fees revenues will increase and a contribution to the protection of the national park can be made.

Senaru is the main entrance to the Rinjani National Park, where people start their climb up the Rinjani. Senaru's rich local culture and two impressive waterfalls also attract tourists on a day trip. The traditional *dusun* (hamlet) Senaru (part of the bigger administrative unit *desa* Senaru consisting of 11 hamlets) is perched in the foothills of Rinjani and surrounded by a wooden fence. It comprises 20 wooden huts, some on stilts (for the storage of rice), others low to the ground. The majority of the villagers of *dusun* Senaru are followers of the Islam *Wetu Telu*, a unique religion that is said to be the remains of the first efforts to islamize Lombok. The *Wetu Telu* originated in northern Lombok, in the village of Bayan, where the oldest mosque of the island is located. The number of *Wetu Telu* followers is not known, but is estimated somewhere around 28,000. Although members of the *Wetu Telu* regard themselves as Moslems, the ortho-

Figure 8.1. Mount Rinjani area. (Photo by S. Stam and K. ter Steege)

dox Moslems do not officially accept them as such. The most common interpretation of the Islam *Wetu Telu* is that its followers adhere to only three of the five pillars of Islam. *Wetu Telu* members do not obey the Ramadan, they only fast during a 3-day period. Furthermore, they do not follow a pattern of praying five times a day. The term *Wetu Telu* is contrasted with the *Waktu Lima* or five times referring to orthodox Moslems. *Wetu Telu* followers have integrated Bali-Hinduism and Islam in their indigenous religion. They revere nature and have maintained a belief system that honors the forest as sacred. In *dusun* Senaru the villagers consider the Rinjani as the center of their local universe and believe that the lake inside the crater is the dwelling place of the ancestors and the Supreme God (for more detailed information about the *Wetu Telu*, see Cederroth, 1981; McVey, 1995). The presence of *Wetu Telu* followers in this area and the old mosque in Bayan have contributed to the integration of the Rinjani, Senaru, and the surrounding villages in Lombok's attraction system.

Dusun Senaru has a population of only 80 persons. Their most important daily pursuits are the cultivation of rice, soybeans, shallots, garlic, and coffee. The economy of Senaru is basically a closed and self-sufficient system. Families use their surplus of crops to barter for items that they themselves do not produce (Beterams, 1996). Furthermore, income is obtained by the sale of bamboo or rattan and by providing services to tourists (accommodation, restaurants, guiding). The development of small-scale tourism in the Rinjani area started at the end of the 1980s with the construction of the first homestay in the area. Until then, the few foreigners who visited Senaru could spend the night in the school building. The area around Senaru nowadays counts nine homestays or guesthouses and at least one more is under construction. Most of the homestay owners and managers are originally not from Senaru. They came from other islands or other parts of Lombok to the village when tourism showed the potential to become a lucrative business. All of them offer cheap, basic rooms and charge about 8,000 to 15,000 *rupiah* (low- and high-season prices) for a double room, including a simple breakfast. As additional services there are a modest restaurant, a small shop with food supplies, trekking equipment, luggage storage facilities, guides and porters, and complete tours.

Local Mountain Guides

Most of the local mountain guides and porters are born and reared in Senaru or in the neighboring villages Batu Koq or Bayan. The majority are not permanently employed in the tourism industry. In the wet season (from October until May) it is not safe for tourists to climb the Rinjani, because of the slippery trails and unexpected thunder-storms. Guiding is combined with work in agriculture, renting trekking equipment, and managing homestays. In total there are approximately 200 guides and porters in the Rinjani area of which the majority are porters. Accompanying tourists up the Rinjani is considered as a lucrative job. In the rice fields the men have to work a whole day for 600 *rupiah*, whereas on the mountain they can make 10,000 to 15,000 *rupiah* a day. The skills needed to become a mountain guide are not acquired through formal training. In general, the maximum level of education in this area is primary school, in some cases completed by language courses. Local mountain guides "learn by doing" and distinguish themselves on several points from porters. Mountain guides have better language skills, necessary to communicate with their clients, whereas porters usually only speak the local dialect. Whereas porters carry the tourists' luggage and cook, mountain guides are responsible for their guests' safety and are expected to give information about the environment and the local customs. Because local guides try to spend as much time as possible in the company of tourists, they presume to know exactly why tourists visit the area and how they want to spend their holiday. Their knowledge of the tourists is restricted to the individual traveling tourists who, alone or in a small group, arrive in Senaru where they want to make the arrangements for a trekking. The knowledge mountain guides have of Western culture and their ideas about the tourists' wishes and desires are based on what they learn in practice from associating with these tourists. Attracted by the Western lifestyle, they feel at ease in the company of tourists; this in contrast with porters, who have limited contacts with tourists and do not associate with tourists outside the trekking. Porters, for instance, still climb the Rinjani wearing a *sarong* and slippers, whereas guides make a lot of effort in obtaining the right (Western) outfit, preferably jeans and hiking shoes.

Acquisition and Networks

Most of the guides from Senaru are, one way or another, connected to one of the homestays or guesthouses; their main job being hustling tourists and organizing trekkings. Hustling tourists is not restricted to Senaru; local guides hang around at the bus stations in Bayan and Sweta (central bus terminal of the island) or at the harbors of Lembar (where the hydrofoil from Bali docks) and Bangsal (the departure point to the Gili islands). These are the places where the individual traveling tourists catch a minibus, bus, or taxi to other parts of the island. Guides try to convince tourists to follow them to the homestay in Senaru for which they work and their main goal is, of course, to interest them in a trekking. For every tourist that is brought in local guides receive commission in *rupiah*, cigarettes, or a free meal. The amount depends on how much money the tourist will spend; just spending the night will not yield as much as a combination with an arrangement for a trekking. Mountain guides use each other's resources and contacts, pass on jobs to each other, and share each other's income. Guides from other locations, like Senggigi or one of the Gili islands, receive commission from their colleagues in Senaru when they bring in guests: 1,000 *rupiah* for tourists who look for accommodation in Senaru and 5,000 *rupiah* for trekking clients. In this preparatory stage, mountain guides can, without having made a trekking, make money "selling" services. Getting enough customers for a trekking depends a great deal on the size and shape of a guide's network. Loose contacts in the tourism sector—in hotels, *losmen*, restaurants, at car rental services, boat services, and souvenir shops—are necessary to get access to tourists in another way than only by chasing them in public areas. Making friends or having relatives working dispersed over these places will help the guide to obtain clients and regular trekkings. Their access to resources as transport and accommodation are generally informal; mountain guides rarely know their way around in the formal ranks of the tourism sector. Occasionally Senaru guides are hired by one of the local tour operators, but normally these offices only employ porters and hire equipment in Senaru and prefer to have the job done by their own guides, even if these are not specialized in trekkings.

A Guide Association

Since April 1995 *dusun* Senaru has an organization for guides and porters, called *Sukur Hati*, established with the help of the Rinjani Eco-Development Project (RED project). In order to protect the Rinjani National Park against increasing economic activities in the area—mainly logging and tourism—four Indonesian nongovernmental organizations (NGOs) initiated the RED project; *Wahana Lingkungan Hidup* (WALHI), a national Indonesian environmental network advocating environmentally sustainable development in Indonesia; *Forum Sumberdaya Rakyat* (FSDR), a network of 38 NGOs in Bali, Lombok, and Sumbawa focusing on alternative development; the Center for Indonesian Studies on Eco-development (CISED), which offers cross-cultural study programs in Bali and Lombok oriented towards eco-development; and *Yayasan Mitra Nusa* (YMN), a small NGO in Lombok responsible for environmental sanitation (Beterams, 1996; Center for Indonesian Studies on Eco-Development [CISED], 1995). The RED project includes three interrelated components: eco-cultural tourism, sustainable park management, and eco-village development. Each component includes training for community groups: mountain guides, women, farmers, and water management groups (CISED, 1995). In 1995, as part of the sustainable park management program, an eco-guide training was developed for which more than 30 villagers signed in. With this training the initiators hoped to educate guides who are:

- valuable to conservation in the region,

- capable of offering search and rescue assistance and first aid to travelers,

- instrumental in establishing park standards and travelers' guidelines, and

- involved in a community co-operative collaborating with WALHI's National Eco-tourism Network and the CISED's eco-cultural tourism program, as well as independent travel agencies and tourists, to ensure tourism that is sustainable, culturally sensitive, and economically viable for local people (CISED, 1995).

The course included English language lessons, business skills, lessons in environmental conservation, first aid, and general guiding techniques. Only a few participants have finished the course and obtained an eco-guide certificate (Beterams, 1996).

Besides education, efforts are made to develop a rotation/donation system among the members of *Sukur Hati*—5,000 *rupiah* for every trekking—to enable the association to buy additional trekking and camping equipment and finance an information center in the near future. For several reasons—"limited participation and competition from several of the homestays" (Beterams, 1996, pp. 94-95)—*Sukur Hati* is not living up to its expectations. A few years earlier, there already was an attempt to establish a guide association in the neighboring hamlet Batu Koq. This association was not granted a long life, mainly because of the reluctant attitude of many of the local guides to become members of an organization. Unwilling to share their contacts and to work in a rotating system, the more experienced local guides preferred to work outside of the association, mainly because they expected to earn more through their own networks (Beterams, 1996).

On the Slopes of the Rinjani

The following account of a trekking—a compilation of several trekkings made by two of the authors in the summer of 1996 (Stam & ter Steege, 1997)—will give an impression of the activities of local mountain guides in the Rinjani area (Figure 8.2).

Day 1

Early in the morning, at about 6 a.m., tourists depart for their first day of the trekking. Guide and porter are waiting for them in their homestay or in the village of Senaru. The porter takes over most of the supplies, which he ties to both sides of a bamboo stick and will carry this load all the way. The first 1.5 hours to POS I (920 meters) are rather relaxed, no climbing yet. The tourists arrive fresh at POS 1. At this post is a hut where the tourists rest and guides and porters prepare something to eat or drink for their guests. Most tourists are, however, eager to continue climbing and only want a short break and a piece of chocolate. From POS I the trekking is getting steeper and more difficult; the real climbing can begin. It is another 2.5 hours to POS II (1,850 meters). Generally, guides keep up the pace and not all tourists can keep up with them. Some guides, however, adjust their pace to that of their guests, they practice their English, and occasionally tell something about the natural environment. Often, however, they limit themselves to some pep talk. At POS II is another hut and a water supply, which is not easy to locate. Guides and porters collect water, which they use for cooking a hot meal with noodles and sometimes chicken. It takes another 2 hours to POS III (2,100 meters) where some people spend the night. According to the guide

Figure 8.2. Local mountain guide. (Photo by S. Stam
and K. ter Steege)

book the climb to POS III is: ". . . relatively easy going through dappled forest, with the
quiet only broken by the occasional bird, animal, bell or woodchopper" (Wheeler &
Lyon, 1992, p. 272).The guidebook forgets to mention the transistor radios of some
guides, which break the silence playing popular Indonesian songs, helpful in keeping
tourists and guides going. Most tourists are eager to see sunset and for that experience
they are willing to climb another 2 hours to the rim of the crater (2,600 meters).The
view from the rim is stunning. Besides the crater, it is possible to see the whole north
coast of Lombok.While the tourists enjoy this view, the guide and the porter pitch the
tents and prepare another meal.After 6 p.m. it is getting rather cold on the rim and the
tourists put on all the warm clothes they brought.After a pleasant but short evening

near the campfire with guides, porters, and other tourists, everyone tries to get some sleep in the cold night (about 5 degrees Celsius).

Day 2

The next morning the guides wake their guests for sunrise and show them the best spot. After breakfast guides and porters take the tourists down to the lake. According to the information of the provincial tourism board "a trip down into the caldera is only recommended for those who have a sense of bravado, as it is another six hours' descent with numerous patches of scree." Although quite dangerous, many tourists are looking forward to a bath in the hot springs to soak their weary bodies. A walk around the lake—also a narrow and very slippery track—takes the tourists to *Kokok Putih*, a number of natural hot springs. The temperature of the water of each spring differs, ranging from 40 degrees to a vaporous 60 degrees. These springs are said to have remarkable healing powers, particularly for skin diseases. At high season (July-September) this place is crowded with domestic tourists who pitch their tents on this side of the lake. After a quick lunch at the lake—again prepared by guides and porters—it is time to climb back to the rim, where the second night is spent.

Day 3

After breakfast the whole group tries to clean up the camping site. Most of the time guides and porters burn the rubbish in the campfire. It is all downhill to Senaru, which takes 5 to 8 hours, depending on the guide. After arriving in Senaru, the tourists—true to tradition—buy drinks for the guide and porters to celebrate the safe arrival.

Having a "good catch," at the bus station or one of the homestays in Senaru, means that the most difficult part of the guide's job is done. Developing a strategic acquisition technique is a prerequisite to becoming a successful guide. Without a network and reasonable language proficiency, the mountain guide will not be able to get enough clients and it is through these abilities that the mountain guide distinguishes himself from porters. Guiding, therefore, does not begin the moment the trekking starts. The efforts of mountain guides to bring in guests shows us interesting elements of their work that cannot be related to activities in the field of organization or information, but more to their entrepreneurial talents. The first contact made with the guests is the opportunity par excellence for the local guide to find out who the tourist is and what he or she wants. These potential clients are considered as assets; valuable as long as they yield the expected income. In their contacts with tourists, mountain guides can be rather money oriented. In general, tourists are associated with money. Remarks like: "Of course, I like tourists! When there are no tourists, I am not able to smoke and drink" or "Tourists are very nice. A month ago I climbed with an Australian guest and I charged her 150,000 *rupiah*, that was very nice," are often heard. Also tourists can be rather suspicious and believe that guides are only trying to extort money from them. Whenever there are problems between tourist and guide it concerns money: the price of a trekking, advanced payments, or preparatory costs (food and water). One of the guides told about his experiences with male French tourists. "I am sure there was enough food for three days, but the tourists just ate too much, I even gave them my own food." His warnings were not heard and in the end there was not enough food left. The tourists blamed the guide and, after arriving back in Senaru, refused to pay the prearranged sum of money.

Climbing and guiding the newly obtained clients to the top is not considered as difficult. Mountain guides are more than familiar with the area, as some of them claim to have climbed the Rinjani more than 100 times, this in contrast with the guides from other parts of the island. However, on the slopes mountain guides predominantly play the traditional pathfinder's role. They lead the way from one post to the other, make sure that the tourists see the obligatory sunset and sunrise, organize the campsite, and prepare food and drinks. The conversation with tourists, if any, is restricted to practicing their English and answering questions. The mountain guides provide the tourists with practical information—where to look and walk and how long all of this will take—and do not dispose of a narrative about the Rinjani area. Although they are born and raised in this area, they have difficulties in understanding what a trekking is really about. Mediating information by composing a narrative of the environment and, for example, the spiritual relation locals have with the Rinjani is scarce.

Guiding in Lombok

The rapid growth of tourism in the province Nusa Tenggara Barat (NTB), and especially on Lombok, has led to an enormous increase in the number of tourist guides. In 1988 NTB had about 32 licensed guides working for travel agencies (Dinas Pariwisata Prop. DATI I NTB, 1995a). The most recent figures (Dinas Pariwisata Prop. DATI I NTB, 1995a) point out that officially NTB has 392 licensed guides (360 junior guides and 32 senior guides). The guide association HPI (*Himpunan Pramuwisata Indonesia*) of NTB claims to have 327 members of which 70% are active as a tourist guide. The provincial government of NTB defines a local tourist guide as someone who takes control, clarifies and explains the tourist objects, and helps the tourists with everything they possibly need. In more detail their major tasks are described as:

1. Organizing safe transport for groups or individual tourists.

2. Explaining the itinerary and everything there is to know about the travel documents, the accommodation, transport, and other tourism facilities.

3. Giving information about the tourism objects.

4. Arranging the luggage of the tourists.

5. Helping tourists who are sick, who have had an accident, or who have things missing (Dinas Pariwisata Prop. DATI I NTB, 1995a).

The enormous growth of the number of tourist arrivals over the last decade (see Chapter 5) has not only put great pressure on these tasks and on the quality of services local tourist guides are expected to offer, but also on the importance of their role in the process of image making. The governor of NTB indicates that tourist guides are considered as a vital link in the development of the image of the province. For this reason the provincial government, following the national policy, has decided to give more attention to the work of tourist guides.

One of the results has been the government's interest in getting an overview of what they call "illegal guiding activities." Unlicensed guides are regarded as an obstacle in the development of tourism on the island and through rules and regulations their activities are discouraged. In the latest report from *Diparda* on guiding the most urgent problems are summarized as follows:

1. There are still too many guides who operate without wearing a badge and without the required decent outfit.

2. There are still travel agencies, tour operators, and other tourist organizations that use the services of unlicensed guides.

3. Some of the guides of Nusa Tenggara Barat are too money minded.

4. At the tourist objects several incidents of swindle, violence, and drunkenness occurred due to guide *liar* ("wild" guide) or unlicensed guides.

5. The guide association still does not operate optimally as coordinator of the licenses and as representative of local guides in general.

6. There is not yet an optimal evaluation of the organizational and educational needs of the licensed and unlicensed guides while working in the field (Dinas Pariwisata Prop. DATI I NTB, 1995a).

Diparda is the governmental organization entitled to set out a policy on guiding. In their latest report (1995a) on guiding they mention the most pressing actions. Through precautionary measures (sweepings) they hope to detect in an early stage the guides who violate the rules. Licensed guides who work for an official tourist organization are obliged to wear an identifying mark (a badge) so they can be distinguished from unlicensed guides. Actions have to be taken against travel agencies and tour operators who employ people who do not fulfill the necessary conditions (who in other words employ unlicensed guides). By controlling the so-called untrained and unprofessional wild guides, the provincial government hopes to undermine activities that are not in line with the general policy on guiding.

Government's Guiding Courses

Another way of controlling the quality of guiding is through education. To become a licensed tourist guide it is obligatory to follow a government training organized by the provincial tourism office in cooperation with HPI. The tourism office has an "Education & Training" division (*DIKLAT—Dinas Pendidikan dan Latihan*), which organizes courses at three levels.

1. Junior guide (*pramuwisata muda*), qualified to work on regency (kabupaten) level (*Wilayah Daerah Tingkat II NTB*).

2. Senior guide (*pramuwisata madya*), qualified to work in the whole province (*Wilayah Daerah Tingkat I NTB*).

3. Special guide (*pramuwisata khusus*), qualified to work at one specific tourist object, like, for instance Narmada, Lingsar, or the traditional village Sade.

For both junior and senior guides the minimum education requirements are senior high school (SMA, *Sekolah Menengah Atas*) or secondary tourism education (SMIP, *Sekolah Menengah Industri Pariwisata*). For all levels a preparatory selection is standard, consisting of an interview in which the ability to speak proper English is tested and a written test about the State Ideology. Senior guides are also expected to have at least 3 years of experience in guiding. To enable guides (although not licensed yet, the majority of the junior guides already work as guides) to participate fully, the courses are organized in the low season. Every course has place for around 30 participants. Every year the provincial government decides which courses are held and financed. The strong growth of tourism and the resulting lack of licensed guides in the province implies a guaranteed yearly junior guide course. In March 1996 the first senior guide course was held in Mataram. Of the 57 people who signed up for the course, 30 passed the selection and could follow the 12-day course, which was predominantly focused on guiding techniques. The provincial tourism office regarded the course as a possibility to cultivate a greater awareness and interest in guiding and to improve the image of the profession.

Next to language abilities the most essential elements of the government's courses are performance, attitude, and guiding techniques. Guides are taught to be sensitive towards the tourists and their needs and to address them in the right way. Good manners with reference to appearance (hair, dress, hands, complexion, body odor, voice, and speech), shaking hands, eating, and, most important, conversation are give much emphasis (Balai Pendidikan & Latihan Pariwisata Bali, n.d.). Cultural knowledge of the area where the guides will operate and more specific facts and figures about the tourist objects are taught at the course and are elaborated and translated by the local guides themselves into accessible narratives in the field.

From the perspective of the provincial government a visit to the local community is part of the tourist gaze and an important ingredient in the image-making process of the island. But within the composed narratives and also in other elements of the course—performance, attitude, and guiding techniques—this very local community is ignored or portrayed in a standardized way. Being a "bridge actor" between the local community and the tourists is not regarded as important in the government courses (for a more detailed discussion about Lombok's policy on guiding and guiding government courses see Bras, forthcoming).

Ecotourism Education

A new initiative for guide education came from the CISED. Acting as spokesmen of the local community they emphasize the effects of development on local communities and the environment. Experience with training local guides and a mutual interest of HPI as well as CISED in the conservation of Lombok's natural attractions resulted in a 5-day ecotourism course—mainly focusing on the Rinjani area—for senior guides organized in April 1996. Three mountain guides from the guide association *Sukur Hati*, who finished the eco-guide course in Senaru, also participated in this course.

Instead of focusing entirely on the natural environment, a holistic view on ecotourism was propagated in the course. Respect for and an understanding of the relationship between the local community and its immediate natural surroundings were considered vital for the development of ecotourism. The local guides were defined as stakeholders—next to the government, tourism businesses and the local community—who not only have to sell the natural environment, but also have to manage it. Being in the field most of the time and being a member of the local community and therefore well informed about local rules and regulations regarding the natural environment, local guides were granted a large task in environmental conservation and the education of tourists.

Becoming an active and concerned stakeholder was the message of CISED to the participants. Bridging the gap between tourists and locals, educating tourists as well as locals, and involving the locals who become part of the tourist gaze are elements of the host–guest relationship that local guides can try to control as suppliers of information. Providing adequate information can diminish the culture shock both tourists and locals experience when they are confronted with each other. Also the money-minded mentality expressed by locals—called the "money shock" by one of the local guides—which is characterized by a short-term urge for direct profit and the inability to reflect over the future, can be overcome by education. Local guides have to convey the message that "economically poor doesn't mean culturally poor" and explain what will happen to a locality when tourists no longer are interested in visiting the area. Many of the participants struggled with these difficult tasks and regarded their own role in the tourism industry as too marginal. Examples were submitted to illustrate their inability to become an active participant in the tourism development, simply because they had no voice. Where to go with problems and irregularities and who to turn to in the villages where the arrival of tourists caused tension were questions that returned in every session.

During the ecotourism course a lot of topics were discussed and the participants were stimulated to discuss their own role in the tourism development. For many of them it was the first time they were motivated to take on a broader perspective, which included not only their clients' wishes and demands but also the interests of their fellow community members. The course material and lectures were not limited to the eco-aspects of tourism in the Rinjani area. A whole range of problems was raised and efforts were made to define the modest role a local guide could play in this process. Too occupied composing a positive image of the area and satisfying the tourists, the government courses fail to raise any of the issues discussed in this course. As one guide concluded: "The knowledge of the HPI-members is insufficient. Indirectly we destroy nature and culture. Guidance in upgrading our knowledge and changing our attitude has to become a continuous process."

Conclusion

Lombok, being included in the government's *Beyond Bali* campaign, is experiencing a rapid growth. As a consequence, there is a serious shortage of skilled and low-skilled labor for tourism jobs, especially in the high season. Although guiding, on Lombok, is more and more regarded as a real profession, this sector is still open for anyone to enter. The government's regulating and standardizing efforts have not yet led to the disappearance of unlicensed guides. On the contrary, the boundaries between unlicensed and licensed guides are blurred. Unlicensed guides still have opportunities to undertake temporary activities in the formal tourism sector or to move on to permanent jobs. When all their regular staff is busy, local tour operators recruit unlicensed guides so their guests will not have to travel unescorted around the island. The work of many of the unlicensed guides—for instance the mountain guides in Senaru—is, however, marginalized. Although Senaru is not yet the target of recurring sweepings, the activities of mountain guides are submitted to a growing number of restrictions. Their educational background and language abilities are insufficient to join in with the formal tourism sector. Local tour operators from Mataram and Senggigi, who mainly cater to the star-rated hotels, rather work with their own licensed and specialized trekking guides instead of hiring mountain guides from Senaru. They consider the Senaru guides as not educated and responsible enough to accompany regular trekkings. The result is that the working area of mountain guides is limited to the unorganized tourists who make no use of the services of the local tour operators. Having to rely predominantly on their own networks in Senaru and its direct vicinity, local mountain guides experience that these networks are not far-reaching enough to establish a better position in the tourism sector. Also access to formal education is limited, because mountain guides lack the requested preparatory education.

Recently, however, efforts are made to provide local (Senaru) guides with specific training. The provision of this education is an effort to formalize the guiding sector. On the one hand, the government guide courses' main emphasis is training local guides to become a perfect host. No guidelines are provided about communication with the local community and about the interpretation of their task as cultural broker or bridge actor—the mediating role that is mentioned as an essential part of guiding in much of the literature about this topic. The initiative for an ecotourism course, on the other hand, stems from a general concern about the effects of tourism on the Rinjani area and its inhabitants. Although the local guides are motivated to bridge the gap between tourists and locals, the main attention is focused on the interests of the local population and the environment in which they live.

Both these efforts, however, do not match with the interests of the mountain guides, who are basically small entrepreneurs selling trekkings up the Rinjani. Their final aim is not mediation between the different parties and the transfer of information, but developing an entrepreneurial strategy to attain their own private goals. During the trekking mountain guides predominantly play the role of traditional pathfinder. But also the periods before and after the trekking prove to be important, when they are looking for newly arrived tourists or trying to hold on to economically interesting relationships. If their guests are worth the effort, mountain guides will take great pains in offering them additional trips—to a Sasak wedding, to one of the waterfalls, or to a meeting with friends to drink rice wine. Tourists are important assets in improving their personal situation. Also of vital importance are their networks, which require a lot of time and energy to be maintained. Whereas a personal network is expected to facilitate the guide's work, a membership of an association (like *Sukur Hati*) is limiting to them in their freedom. Within the margins defined by their network, they can freely decide how to operate. An association is considered as another effort to formalize their activities, which does not fit in with their daily mode of operation. Instead of focusing on education, these guides rely on their contacts and their familiarity with the area. They are Rinjani "experts" who have difficulties developing a long-term orientation on their profession and making the area—which is so extremely familiar for them—into a tourist attraction. The question is if the Senaru guides will be able to anticipate on the future—government initiated—requirements in the guiding sector. Will they gradually lose their autonomous position as a guide in this area and be downgraded from guide to porter because of the growing competition from guides outside of Senaru? Instead of marginalizing their position, the provincial government should try to benefit from the local expertise of mountain guides by not focusing entirely on formal education, but finding ways to integrate their local body of knowledge into the tour programs.

Chapter 9

Pathfinder, Gigolo, and Friend: Diverging Entrepreneurial Strategies of Tourist Guides on Two Indonesian Islands

Karin Bras and Heidi Dahles

Introduction

> Hello Miss, you look happy today!
>
> I like your shoes, Miss, where you go?
>
> Want transport Miss? Give you special price.
>
> Excuse me Miss, where you stay? Are you married? Have boy friend? Want boy friend? Me your boy friend. Have many girl friends from Europe, America, all very happy.
>
> Want banana, Miss? Indonesia banana small but hot!
>
> Are we going out tonight? You remember me?

These and other related modes of address are typical for the way young men, hanging out in the bars and restaurants at Indonesian beach resorts and in the streets of popular urban tourist destinations, approach individually traveling female tourists. It is the mode of behavior that is typical for self-employed tourist guides—street guides and beach boys—to attract the tourists' attention. As Crick (1992) observed in Sri Lanka, and as the authors were able to experience in Lombok, Bali, and Yogyakarta, street guides and beach boys are skilled in catching the eye of tourists and engaging in tactics talks. Their purpose is to make tourists buy souvenirs, book a tour, or make use of their services, as they largely depend on a commissioned income. However, there is another dimension to approaching tourists:

the sexual dimension, which is omnipresent wherever female tourists appear without male company.

As we have shown elsewhere (Dahles & Bras, 1999), those males have been denominated as gigolos—men living on the money paid by women for their sexual services; in other words, male prostitutes. In many cultures, men supported by women are regarded as deviant as their behavior violates "traditional" gender relations (Firat, 1994). Instead of looking at the sexual overtures of local males toward female tourists in terms of prostitution and the supposed detrimental impacts on social life, this chapter analyzes this behavior from the perspective of the everyday life of these men. To understand why young local males desire sexual relationships with female tourists, it is argued that these sexual advances have to be understood within the context of small-scale entrepreneurship in the informal sector that is characteristic among street guides and beach boys. They can be defined in terms of petty producers of cheap goods and services, making a living on their wits from day to day and creating new opportunities in an already crowded environment (Guinness, 1994). Public space being their domain, street guides and beach boys grasp occasions for gain as they fitfully and spontaneously arise, benefiting in every possible way from the diffuse flow of individual tourists passing by. With tourists around, the chances of making a quick windfall are bigger, but the stakes are higher—not only economically speaking. Doing business with tourists involves selling goods and (sexual) services and strategically exploiting personal networks—as is characteristic of small-scale entrepreneurs in the informal sector.

This chapter addresses the extent to which romantic entrepreneurship poses a challenge to the vast number of young men on a marginal or near-marginal level of living in two Indonesian tourist areas: the new beach resort of Senggigi (Lombok) and in the downtown area of Yogyakarta with a long-standing tourism industry. Whereas Senggigi is a beach resort offering sand, sea, and sun as major attractions, Yogyakarta constitutes a center of cultural tourism. As research has shown, both areas differ in terms of Butler's tourist area life cycle. The model describes the life cycle of a tourist destination starting with an exploration phase that eventually merges into, subsequently, an involvement, development, and consolidation phase. When a tourist destination has passed through this life cycle its continued existence depends on its ability to renew itself. A group of Indonesian researchers has applied Butler's model to Indonesian tourist destination areas, situating Bali and Jakarta in this renewal phase, Yogyakarta in the consolidation phase, and Lombok in the development phase (Sofield, 1995). Yogyakarta has been participating in international tourism for about 20 years. Strongly relying on its history and heritage, it has become a mass tourist destination, being sixth on the list in terms of foreign visitor arrivals after Bali, Jakarta, North Sumatra, Riau, and West Java (Sofield, 1995). Lombok is a newcomer in the market, a shooting star, having gained the eighth position in the national list within only a few years. Yogyakarta is a densely populated but economically weak area (Rotge, 1991). The city accommodates a large number of small-scale and micro businesses in the service sector, particularly catering to students and the administrative staff of the numerous provincial government offices. Except for a small but growing number of four- and five-star hotels and related tour operators, the tourism sector is characterized by small-scale and micro businesses catering to young budget travelers in the cheap downtown tourist areas. In these areas, the demand for souvenir shops, excursions, transport, accommodations, restaurants, and cultural performances seems to be saturated. There is fierce competition between small producers; established businesses suffer from a decreasing turnover, and new businesses often go bank-rupt within a short period of time. The major concern of the tourist industry is the short and slightly declining length of stay. The average length of stay is only two nights, whereas foreign tourists in star-rated hotels stay a considerably shorter period than the backpackers in cheap accommodations (Diparda, 1995). In Lombok, the situation is different. The island offers a more differentiated tourist product, combining cultural tourism with nature tourism, adventurous mountain climbing with vivacious street life and almost empty beaches. Statistics are unreli-able: estimates of the average length of stay of foreign tourists vary from 2.1 to 5.0 nights on the island (Dinas Pariwisata Prop. DATI I NTB, 1995b; Statistik Indonesia, 1995). The focus of tourism development is mainly on the establishment of large-scale resorts. However, as few areas are developed for tourism yet, there is plenty of opportunity to establish businesses, opportunities that are not only grasped by large-scale investors but also by local people. In contrast to Yogyakarta, it still pays to initiate new enterprises and to invest in tourism development in Lombok. As will be shown in this chapter, this position affects the opportunities and restric-tions that self-employed young males experience in their participation in the informal tourism sector and, as a consequence, their prospects regarding their relationships with female tourists.

Small-Scale Entrepreneurs in Tourism

The categories of small entrepreneurs we are dealing with here distinguish them-selves by strategically operating networks instead of land, equipment, or funds. The beach boys and street guides of Lombok and Yogyakarta dispose of none of those "first-order resources" (Boissevain, 1974). They rather operate by their wits and act as intermediaries by managing sources and flows of information. They put people in touch with each other directly or indirectly for profit, and bridge gaps in com-munication between people. Following Boissevain, we define these network specialists as brokers. A broker's capital consists of his personal network of rela-tions, his communication channels, his role relations, which are governed by notions of reciprocity and transaction; he is dealing in expectations and possible future services. The following section describes the strategies that beach boys in Lombok and street guides in Yogyakarta apply to make a living in the tourism sector. Guiding or escorting tourists is an important, but not exclusive, activity of these men. Tourists are resources to deploy strategically for making money and improving one's network.

Senggigi's Beach Boys

The village of Senggigi, located 10 kilometers north of the Lombok's capital city Mataram, used to be a fishing area. When tourism forced its way into village life, most of the fishermen disappeared. Only at sunset, when a few small boats sail to sea, can some evidence of the earlier fishing activities be observed. In 1984 the first mid-range accommodation was built, Pondok Senggigi, until now a popular hangout for young travelers. In 1987 the first star-rated hotel, Senggigi Beach Hotel, financed by the government-owned Aerowisata, was opened and gradually more star-rated hotels determined the upmarket appearance of Senggigi. At present the whole beach site is taken by hotels, restaurants, and souvenir shops, and tourism is no longer integrated into village life, which takes place further inland. During the daytime, Senggigi looks quite deserted when the tourists are on the beach, in the hotel gardens, or on a tour. Nightlife, however, can be vivacious. In several locations local rock bands perform before an audience of tourists and locals. The cafes are the domain of male youths operating as tour guides and looking for potential customers. When a guide has earned money, his friends will help him spend it on drinking beer in one of the bars. If there is no money to spend they take strategic positions along the main street where they can keep an eye on everyone who passes by. These males, who are called beach boys, are not allowed to hustle tourists on the premises of the star-rated hotels and therefore roam the streets, the beaches, bars, and discotheques.

Beach boys seek their livelihood directly from tourists. They have a whole range of activities that can be related to tourism. Guiding is combined with being a waiter, a driver, a musician, or with being jobless. Usually beach boys only appear in the beach areas during high season when the chances to meet tourists are highest and considerable windfalls can be made. During off-season they take other jobs or simply rely on the support of family members. Because of their limited education and insufficient proficiency in the English language, chances to obtain a job in a hotel or at a travel agency are small. However, this is not of any disturbing concern to them, as being *bebas* (free) is of crucial importance to their image. Working in a tourist environment where there is no direct supervision, or working independently, corresponds with this desire for freedom. It is therefore doubtful whether they aspire to a job in the formal tourism sector. Instead, they seem rather reluctant to give up their independent position and join an organization where they have to sit and wait, risking that no work will come their way. They call themselves *orang jalan*—people from the street—who prefer to work for themselves. This gives them the opportunity to decide when and where to operate. After making a good deal of money out of their guests, they can withdraw for a while, relax, or change to another activity.

The only organization the beach boys tend to associate with is the transport organization *Kotasi* (*Koperasi Taksi Senggigi*). In 1992 *Kotasi* gained official status. This cooperative mediates transport and services for the star-rated hotels and travel agencies in the area. Guides have to pay a once-only entrance fee, which gives them access to the *Kotasi* network. However, the beach boys do not necessarily join this organization by payment, they rather gain access through friends or only pretend to be a member by using the name of *Kotasi* to appear more reliable in front of tourists. In practice, almost everybody who works in the Senggigi area claims to be part of *Kotasi*, whether this is true or not.

The success of the beach boys depends on their network. On Lombok the tourist attractions lie scattered around the island, which demands mobility of the local guides. Most of the attractions are visited during day trips in which considerable distances are covered. A prerequisite for working as a guide is access to motorized transport in order to make a tour to the most popular attractions. Beach boys working as a guide have to establish contacts with an organization like *Kotasi*, or with individuals with access to cars and minibuses. To do so, beach boys cooperate on an ad-hoc basis; they use each other's resources, pass on jobs to each other, and share each other's income. In this way they establish ties of reciprocity. To get access to tourists in ways other than approaching them in public areas, they maintain friendly relations with the personnel of hotels, *losmen*, restaurants, at the car rental services, the boat services, and the souvenir shops, and with close and distant kin. To please the tourists, they do whatever small jobs and favors the guests require. These jobs vary from arranging a ride to the airport or to town, going to the repair shop with a broken camera, looking for that one particular souvenir, or assisting in making collect calls.

Beach boys offer day trips that are comparable with the programs of local tour operators. The famous tour to the south of Lombok is the first thing they try to sell to newly arrived tourists. But, different from the travel agents' program, the route can easily be adapted to the tourists' wishes when traveling with a beach boy. Beach boys claim to be flexible in their time and route management. As one group of beach boys stated: "We never tell the tourists that they only have twenty minutes at Narmada or Tanjung Aan, like the guides of the travel agencies. We stay as long as they want to stay. The result is that our tours take a lot longer than the average eight hours. But we do not mind, the tip will also be higher when our guests are satisfied." The services of the beach boys are cheaper than those of the travel agencies, and it is always possible to bargain for an even better price. Sometimes they do not ask for money but offer to accompany the tourist to the market or invite him for a ride on the back seat of their motorbike. They speculate on a tip and on a longer cooperation. Another way to top up their daily income is by obtaining commissions. The weaving village Sukarara is the most popular stop among all of the local guides of Lombok. The beautiful *sarong* and *ikat* do very well as a souvenir and the commission is generally up to 50% of the purchase price. Whenever possible, efforts to include this village in the day trip will be made, even though it means making a detour. Beach boys often bring in their own personal environment in the tours they offer. A visit to the house of a relative where Chinese cemetery decoration is made, a stop at their own house for a cup of tea, an afternoon at the cockfight organized by a neighbor, or drinking rice wine with some old friends can be part of the program. These strategies serve two aims. The first is to enhance the tourists' satisfaction, which pays in terms of money; the other is to maintain their personal network, which pays in terms of resources.

Yogyakarta's Street Guides

Malioboro street and the streets in the Kraton area are swarming with young men offering their services to passing tourists. They call themselves friends; but the authorities and representatives of the tourism industry call them unlicensed guides, informal guides, wild guides, or, simply, a nuisance to be removed from the tourist area by occasional police raids. Along the streets there are a number of hangouts from where street guides approach passing tourists. Popular hangouts are the major meeting points of tourists: the doorstep of shops, cafes, and restaurants; the street corners of Malioboro street; the low walls surrounding the flower beds on the shopping street; the *wartel* (the telecommunication office visited by tourists who want to phone or fax home); the main post office; the market; the lounges of many budget accommodations; the central station; and the *alun alun* (the big square) in front of the Sultan's palace.

In Yogyakarta some street guides operate in small, loosely structured groups of friends sharing and controlling a hangout, but many operate on their own, only sharing the hangout with colleagues. The hangouts may be organized according to a shared ethnical and/or geographical background: the men having visited the same school or university, or being relatives. The best hangouts—the ones along Malioboro street—are controlled by men from Yogyakarta families, their relatives, or in-laws. Being engaged or married to a girl working as a shop assistant or being related with the security or parking lot man enhances one's opportunities to be tolerated at the doorstep. A newcomer requires the introduction of an already established friend or relative, otherwise he will not be accepted at a hangout. Being born and raised in Yogyakarta facilitates the access to these hangouts; men from outside of town find it difficult to be admitted into such a group.

Within a group there is a loosely structured division of tasks. Success in the "tourist hunt" largely depends on communicative abilities, outward appearance, and mastery of foreign languages. Group members scoring high on these criteria usually take the initiative of approaching tourists. If they are successful, they receive the biggest share of the profit. If they fail, other group members try to take over. Although the tourist experiences a series of approaches by different young men during his city walk, these men often belong to the same group. If one of the group "has a bite," the others follow him and his guest at a distance, observing which restaurants or shops are visited, what souvenirs are bought, and how much money is spent. After the tourists and their "guide" have left, group members enter the shop or restaurant to collect the commission, which will be divided among the group. The smart and handsome guides break away from the group when they turn out to be successful. In that case they prefer working for themselves.

Accompanying tourists, the most evident aspect of the street guides' work, is only a strategy to earn money. The guiding as such does not provide a substantial income. They have to be satisfied with a tip that tourists give them voluntarily, a meal, a drink, or cigarettes. If they are lucky they receive gifts of some value: Western consumer goods like wrist watches, walkmans, radios, leather jackets. Street guides do not ask for money straight away. If a tourist is reluctant to buy souvenirs, the guide starts talking about "problems": his poor family being unable to pay for his expensive education; his old mother requiring medical treatment; his young children going hungry; him being an orphan. If the tourist does not or pretends not to understand, then the street guide has no other choice than turn and walk away, as he has no right to ask for a fee. The street guides' income consists substantially of the commission they receive for taking customers to the small hotels, the souvenir shops, and restaurants that the city has in abundance.

The street guides want to make tourists *senang* (happy). If the tourist is happy, then he or she is in the mood for spending money, which makes the guide happy. To bring the tourists into a happy mood, the guide takes a rather flexible and sympathetic position. Never would he take the lead; he rather tries to find out what the tourist wants. Seeing a specific attraction? The guide shows the way. Peeping into backyards? The guide takes tourists to a *kampung*. Buying batik paintings or silverware or puppets? The guide knows where to find a shop or local factory. Finding an inexpensive place to eat where the locals meet? Drinking excessively? Buying joints? A prostitute? The guide knows the right place and the right person.

Street guides have to attend to several jobs all the time. They usually combine the guiding of tourists with different kinds of economic activities. Some of them do odd jobs for a (souvenir) shop, a boutique, a small workshop where batik, masks, *wayang* puppets, or other souvenirs are manufactured. They always work as touts on a commission basis for several shops. Some sell toys, ice cream, or cold drinks on the street; others work occasionally as a barkeeper, waiter, security man, or bellboy in a hotel. Sometimes they invest money in bulk buying goods to sell with a profit. At other times they walk the streets with samples of fake Rolex watches or perfume, trying to sell these products on a commission basis. Most of the time they do all these things.

Young men from Yogyakarta families who enjoy the privilege of living in the Kraton area combine a job in the Sultan's palace—being a gamelan player, dancer, singer, security man, cleaning man, or formal guide—with incidental street guiding. Working for the sultan is not paid in money but in kind, and the employees can walk away from their task whenever required by other obligations. Other street guides are migrants from less prosperous and less touristic areas of Java and even from other islands of the archipelago. Attracted by the city as an economic and cultural center, these men try to find a niche in petty trade. They make a living as street vendor, pedicab man, taxi driver, and street guide. Due to their ethnic background, they belong to the marginal people in Yogyakarta, where being of Javanese origin still is a precondition for access to networks that provide a successful business career. This also applies to a "career" in petty trade, as even the access to small-scale peddling is controlled by Javanese people. Among the marginals one can find young men with an excellent education, with diplomas from polytechnics and universities, who cannot succeed in finding appropriate work. To make a living, they collaborate with other young men of a similar ethnic background to benefit from tourism.

Working as a street guide is popular with schoolboys, students, truants, and drop-outs. In the afternoon, after the lectures and lessons in the countless institutions for vocational and professional training are finished, the number of street guides increases significantly in the streets of Yogyakarta. Many students (and those who claim to be students) try to make some extra money by taking tourists to shops and restaurants. Some are so attracted by the money and glamour associated with tourism that they discontinue their studies to focus completely on petty jobs in the tourism sector. Vice versa, identifying oneself as a student who wants to practice his English is a strategy of the less-educated street guides to appear more reliable to tourists. It is quite easy in Yogyakarta to purchase fake student ID cards; numerous copy shops produce them made to order.

Basically, the dealings and strategies of Senggigi beach boys and Yogyakarta street guides are similar. They position themselves in public places to approach tourists and they mobilize their networks to take as much advantage as possible (in money or kind) from tourists. However, the areas differ in geographical layout and tourism development and, thus, constitute different conditions for guiding. Tour guiding in Lombok forces the beach boys to mobilize their network and deploy their resources each and every time they have a customer. There is no other way to make money from tourists than to take them on a day trip, as the tourist attractions are scattered all over the island. The acquisition and management of such a trip represent a considerable investment in terms of wits, time, and contacts. Although there is growing competition among beach boys, they are quite successful in the tourism business. Lacking a public transport system that is easily accessible for tourists, transport is a scarce resource in Lombok. The beach boys, *Kotasi*, and the travel agencies control this resource either directly or indirectly through their networks. By operating independently and relating flexibly to the market, the beach boys are a serious competitor in the local tourism industry (Dahles & Bras, 1999).

In Yogyakarta most tourist amenities and attractions are situated in the city center within walking distance from the tourist accommodations. The compactness of the urban attraction system causes a concentration of tourists and street guides. The competition among the street guides is fierce, the profits are marginal, but the costs are low: street guides need not invest much time and effort to find customers. They do not even need to cooperate with others. There is an endless stream of tourists walking the streets and it is obvious where they go. All the street guide has to do is to walk along with the tourists, involve them in small talk, and maneuver them to the shops, either straight away or with a small "cultural" detour. The accessibility of the tourists, however, is seriously hampered by the large number of local people competing for this resource. In contrast to their colleagues in Lombok, the street guides of Yogyakarta do not offer any scarce good, specialized knowledge, or exclusive contacts. Everybody familiar with the local situation can take tourists to a shop or accommodation and receive some money in return—and everybody does. Waiters, shop assistants, receptionists, taxi drivers, *becak* men, schoolboys, students, and even policemen make the most of their opportunities to earn a little money from tourists. Instead of using their network to provide better services to the tourists, street guides need their contacts to find jobs that compensate for the decreasing revenues from tourism (Dahles & Bras, 1999).

Romancing the Tourist

The literature suggests that tourism and prostitution are closely related. In many exotic destination areas female prostitution is common (Graburn, 1983; Hall, 1992; Kruhse-Mount Burton, 1995; Shaw & Williams, 1994). It has been reported in Africa (Crush & Wellings, 1983), Latin America (Roebuck & McNamara, 1973), and Asia (Cohen, 1982b, 1986, 1993; Hall, 1992; Kruhse-Mount Burton, 1995; Lee, 1991; Leheny, 1995; O'Malley, 1988; Truong, 1983, 1990). Knowledge of tourism-related male prostitution, however, is still limited (Harrell-Bond, 1978; Lea, 1988; Wagner, 1977; Wagner & Yamba, 1986). One of the first documented cases is the tiny West African country of The Gambia, which has successfully been marketed in Scandinavia causing middle-aged Scandinavian women to openly solicit. Cohen (1971) examined the motives of Arab boys making sexual overtures to female tourists as early as the 1960s. Other evidence of local males taking a sexual interest in female tourists is from Barbados (Karch & Dann, 1981) and other Caribbean islands (Momsen, 1994), Ecuador (Meisch, 1995), Israel (Bowman, 1989, 1996), Sri Lanka (Crick, 1992), Bali (Mabbett, 1987; McCarthy, 1994; Vickers, 1989), Java (Dahles, 1996, 1998a), and Lombok (Bras, forthcoming). More recently, our attention has been drawn to the phenomenon of rastamen as a major attraction for white female tourists not only in the Caribbean (Hellingwerf, 1996; Pruitt, 1993; Pruitt & LaFont, 1995; Sutherland, 1986; Van Schaardenburgh, 1995), but also in other tourist areas such as Southeast Asia (Dahles, 1997a; Dahles & Bras, 1999; Mabbett, 1987; Wolf, 1993).

Cohen's research (1982b, 1986, 1993) on the prostitutes of Bangkok indicates that their dealings fit in with established Thai *and* Western cultural norms: weak young woman depends on older and more powerful man. As far as the sexual involvement of local males with Western female tourists is concerned, the Thai model simply seems to be reversed: poor local young men "prostitute" themselves to rich white women who often are considerably older. Referring to the Gambian case, Wagner noted that this "inversion" is perverting the norms ruling gender relations in many societies, including ours. Wagner (1977) detects a destructive potential in these relationships: ". . . what to the tourist is a pleasant and refreshing interlude where the disregard of norms in no way threatens the structures pervading in their home society, could result in the destruction of one of the very foundations of local social structure, that of ordering social life according to age and generation differences" (p. 50). As may become clear in this chapter, their sexual overtures have to be understood within the context of their subsistence strategies.

In Kuta, the infamous beach resort in the south of Bali, male youth, the so-called "bad boys," "Kuta cowboys," "gigolos" (by other people), or "guides" (their own term), hang around the tourist places—the beach, bars, restaurants, and accommodations—and live, eat, and breathe tourists (McCarthy, 1994). Their "trademark" is their *gondrong* (i.e., "cool and dreadly") appearance: they usually wear tight black jeans, loose shirts that are unbuttoned to the belly, long black hair, and dark sunglasses that recast beach life. They play guitar like Hendrix, sing Marley's songs, and dance like Michael Jackson. "You look happy" is their favorite mode of addressing tourist women while exhibiting the "don't-worry-be-happy-attitude." Their self-image is intertwined with outspoken ideas about masculinity. In a series of articles in an Indonesian news magazine, Kuta beach boys expressed their conviction that Western women come to Bali to conceive a child from a local man as they dispose of "better seed" than Western males (Suardika, 1996a, 1996b). They achieve status among their male friends through sleeping with as many female tourists as possible. In the short term their aim is to pick up an endless stream of white girlfriends, but in the long run most of them strive for a steady relationship with a woman who will take them off to her country for a better life in the West (or Japan) (McCarthy, 1994; Vickers, 1989). Their romantic and sexual behavior has to be understood as part of their entrepreneurial strategies to make a living as well as to secure their future. As romancing the tourist seems to be the major economic strategy of these boys, we suggest to label them as romantic entrepreneurs.

The lifestyle of the Kuta cowboys seems to have spread to other tourist areas in Indonesia. Commenting on the subculture of young males in Bali, an Australian journalist contrasted the life of a rice-cultivating peasant, a factory worker, and the head of a large family in a situation of dire poverty with the world of the Kuta cowboys, "whose peripheral yet lasting flirtation with the West has left them with a taste for drugs, alcohol, and one night/one month relationships with tourist girls. . . . Maybe a life of shallow, temporary relationships, on the fringes of the tourists' largesse is better than the alternatives" (Wolf, 1993, p. 17). Young men, from Bali but to an increasing degree from other Indonesian islands, come to Kuta to make money accepting casual work in the tourism industry, collecting commissions by selling jewelery, carvings, or paintings, and picking up tourist girls "who would pay for everything" (Mabbett, 1987, p. 15).

It seems that a lifestyle copied from the Kuta cowboys exerts an enormous attraction on the male youth in other tourist areas as well. At night, the pubs in the downtown areas of Yogyakarta and the restaurants and discotheques of Senggigi are crowded with the guides, drinking beer, smoking weed, and flirting with female tourists. Their lifestyle is an imitation—not of Western tourists—but of the Kuta cowboys, who lead the fashion in the world of guides. Many street guides and beach boys boast of having visited Kuta in Bali to see the "bare breasts" on the beach as well as the Kuta cowboys. Young men inspired by their Bali counterparts aspire to a career as musician in a local (reggae) band, which supposedly is a life of sex, drugs, and rock'n roll. Apparently, the ever-present chance to enter into a sexual relationship with a tourist adds glamour to this lifestyle. Regarding the strict cultural codes for the public behavior of women—Indonesia is a Muslim country after all—females offering their services as guides or friends are immediately associated with prostitution. Only a small number of the (street) guides are females, and most of the women working as street guides actually are prostitutes. On the other hand, offering sexual services to female (and male) travelers is quite common among male guides.

It is mostly in cafes, restaurants, and hotel lounges that the first romantic overtures are made, but these overtures do not originate exclusively from street guides. Waiters, receptionists, bellboys, and other personnel actually hold the best position to approach female tourists, and they do take advantage of this privileged position. However, many beach boys and street guides hang around in these places, cultivating friendly relations with the staff to share their access to the constant flow of newly arrived tourists. Introducing oneself as a guide, a promise for a ride on the motorbike, or a trip to a remote beach have proven to be successful strategies of getting into contact with the ladies. The Lombok beach boys take advantage of excellent opportunities to flirt during the long day trips with tourists and to continue the contact during the days following the trip; an opportunity that is definitely absent in Yogyakarta, forcing the street guides to be rather explicit about their intentions. Telling lies about their activities, their names, and marital status is part of their tactics to secure the attention and lasting interest of the female tourists. Many beach boys and street guides like to adopt popular English names and prefer pseudonyms that sound more familiar in the tourists' ear. To establish even more familiarity, they show business cards or letters they received from tourists originating from the same country as the woman they are approaching. They usually claim to have many friends in her country to make her feel more comfortable. Others introduce themselves as local (village) boys who never have

Figure 9.1. Guide *liar* in Lombok. (Photo by T. Kamsma)

left Lombok or Yogyakarta and who never had an affair with a Western woman before. Some women are totally taken by this "authentic" and "exotic" image. Although the boys often have the well-known Kuta-style *gondrong* look, they easily manage to keep up the image of the "exotic other" (Figure 9.1).

When a street guide in Yogyakarta is becoming friendly with a female tourist, he will take her to "romantic" places, like the Watercastle, the remains of the pleasure mansion of the royal family, to tell stories about the virility of previous sultans (who kept 40 wives and made love with two of them each night—so the story goes), and to praise the virility of Yogyakarta men in general. He will try to take her to the tombs of Imogiri or to Parangtritis beach: both well-known but quiet attractions, as they are situated away from the main tourist routes, allowing for a romantic interlude. As Budi (22 years), one of the informants, recalls:

> My most beautiful experience with a woman happened when I met this Italian girl. Her name was Carmen. If I think of her, I see her body, as beautiful as a Spanish guitar. She had white skin and her hands and legs were covered with soft hair. We went to Parangtritis and on the beach we made love like husband and wife. . . .

If such a romantic interlude leads to a relationship, the street guide might leave his various jobs for a while, make travel arrangements for the remaining days or weeks the tourist will spend in Indonesia, and accompany her on her trip. The tourist is supposed to pay for all his expenses. A similar strategy is pursued by the beach boys in Lombok. The lovers spend time (and her money) together in one of the bars of Senggigi or on trips on the island or further away. Usually the beach boy suggests to go to one of the romantic Gilis and to other tourist hangouts in Kuta (Lombok) in the south. The guide becomes the woman's personal broker, someone who will provide her with access to the local culture. Normally they will spend a great deal of time with his own peer group—his friends who hang out together in the beach areas and in the bars and discotheques.

The boys know exactly how to entertain, amuse, and attract Westerners. They even cultivate different styles to cater to specific target groups. Some play up to the younger tourists with calculated cuteness, dance, and sway seductively to the reggae and disco tunes, sing, giggle, and flirt outrageously. They affect a particular style of dress. Most prefer "cool and dreadly," with their long black hair as their most important attribute. Only a few boys wear dreadlocks and other symbols of the rastaman. They all, however, adhere to reggae music. This presentation of self seems to be the most successful of presentations on the dating scene. Other guides who are also interested in having an affair with a female tourist in general lose to the *gondrong* type of guide. They do not hang out at the bars in Senggigi but meet their guests only during the tours. They do not seem to be in great demand and rarely succeed in making a romantic overture. Rizal, one of the less successful guides, explained his failure as follows:

> Maybe I look too decent and too serious. I wear my shirt in my trousers, my hair is neatly cut and I am clean. Maybe women think I am not interested in having a relationship, that I am too serious, with my religion for instance.

However, there seems to be a niche in the "romance" market for non-*gondrong*
type of men. In Yogyakarta, there is a "sophisticated" type of street guide, targeting
middle-aged and middle-class "quality" tourists. As can be observed on Malioboro
street and especially in the shopping mall, the Malioboro Plaza, these guides prefer
short and neatly cut hair, pinstripe trouser, white shirt, "pilot-style" sunglasses,
ballpoint in breast pocket, and some papers in their hand, apparently on their way
to some very important business or sipping coffee in an expensive cafe and only
by coincidence bumping into some lost tourists. They do not visit the pubs downtown, but prefer to associate with the more stylish places of entertainment—
although the expenses often exceed their possibilities and each drink they have to
pay for themselves lasts an hour. They imitate a Western lifestyle and like to display
consumer goods they received as a gift from their tourist friends (Figure 9.2).

Ticket to a Better Life?

Although a relationship emerging from these arrangements is of a transitory and
instrumental nature, it can acquire other than purely financial characteristics. The
relationship can become intense, as tourists can become an entry to the guides'
good life. Tourists give gifts of both money and kind to their young friends, and
take them along on excursions, visits to night clubs, and other leisure activities. It
is understandable that the chances of acquiring money and gifts, of having a good

Figure 9.2. Guide *liar* in Yogyakarta. (Photo by H. Dahles)

time, and, for the very lucky ones, a free ticket and an invitation to stay in Europe, America, Australia, or Japan, are an enormous attraction. But because it is never sure whether a relationship will turn out that way, guides tend to spread the risk of an eventual break-up by being engaged in several relationships at the same time, which can lead to complicated situations whenever those female "true loves" plan their holidays in the same period (Cohen, 1986).

The guides tell their prospective partners that, unlike all the other boys, they are after a one and only "true love." Though the boys prefer girls of their own age, they do understand that older women often find themselves in a more secure economic position with better purchasing power, which makes them highly attractive as sexual partners promising a ticket to a better life in the West. Female tourists in their thirties, forties, and older find themselves "courted" by boys in their teens and early twenties. "I do prefer older women," one of our informants (24 years old) used to say, "they are more mature and patient, they understand how my heart feels." Izul, who was interviewed by a local Lombok newspaper about his experiences with an older female tourist during a 3-day trek up Mount Rinjani, looks for female tourist companionship for the money and the sex. It is not that he prefers older women, but they usually have more money than young ones who still go to school or college. He, however, does not like to be called a gigolo because he never received any money after having sex. His female clients gave him some pocket money or paid him for his services as a guide ("Penuturan Seorang 'Guide'," 1996).

Whatever role model a street guide in Yogyakarta is associating with, there is one desire all of them are cherishing. They all share the dream of acquiring a ticket to one of the "promised lands" where their ever-changing "true loves" come from. A lot of time is invested in that one love that promises to take them on a trip to her homeland. This is basically the guides' future perspective. Meeting individually traveling female tourists they do not beat about the bush: they offer their services as a lover, servant, housekeeper, cook, and they want to fulfill these tasks without any payment, just for board and lodging in the tourist's home country. Some street guides succeed in obtaining an invitation to follow their tourist friends to their home country. About 10% (in Yogyakarta more than in Lombok) of the authors' informants visited Europe or Australia; in most cases they were invited by their girlfriends. However, for many, life in the West turns out to be disappointing. Whereas they expect to lead a prosperous and leisurely life, they soon experience that working life is exhausting and boring, jobs are hard to find, and lifestyles are different. Their relationship breaks up and they get incurably homesick. Provided with some savings, they finally return to Yogyakarta, to play the big spender for a short while, buying drinks all round and throwing parties. When the money is spent, they are back on the street again.

> The experience of Sugyo is illustrative of the disillusion a local male may encounter. Five years ago, Sugyo went to Austria to live with a young woman he had met in Yogyakarta. They got a child, a little boy, Sugyo is very proud of. But life in Austria was not easy for the Indonesian man; he could not find a

job and felt isolated. His girlfriend had to work to earn a living for their little family. While Sugyo was supposed to care for their child, he got drunk and neglected his duties. Their relationship deteriorated. He stole money from his girlfriend, left Austria and traveled through Europe. Finally he returned home to Yogyakarta. Years later, his girlfriend showed up in town again. They made up—for the sake of their son, as Sugyo says. However, both decided to live separately: the woman and the child stay in Austria and visit Yogyakarta once a year. Sugyo is depressed because of this situation. He feels that he fails as a father, but cannot do without his friends in Yogyakarta.

All the street guides who have gone through that kind of disillusioning experience in the "promised land" regard their return as a failure. They keep yearning for a better life in the West and advise their friends to seize their chances whenever they arise, be smarter and become a successful businessman abroad. Street guides who are growing older, without being able to realize their dream, change their tune. They start dreaming of accumulating enough money to start their own enterprise: a shop, cafe, restaurant, *losmen*, boutique, or atelier to become a "boss" in the backpacker area of the city—preferably through marrying a "rich" tourist.

Turning to Lombok, it is striking to learn how many beach boys have already visited Europe or Australia in the wake of that one "true" love. However, in contrast to their counterparts in Yogyakarta, leaving their own surroundings and peer group forever to get married and settle down abroad is not the first priority of the beach boys of Senggigi. When they go abroad, they consider their stay in Europe as a temporary escape from their home situation, as a way of satisfying their curiosity for Western lifestyles, as a holiday paid by their girlfriend. A steady relationship with a foreign woman is used as a vehicle to start a business. While she is providing the money, the man is becoming a business associate providing the access to the Indonesian bureaucracy and to local networks. A striking example is set by a local guide who used to combine guiding and flirting with female tourists and playing guitar in front of his house until he, now already 13 years ago, met his present wife from Canada. Together they started a homestay that developed into one of the most popular mid-range accommodations in Senggigi. That he is not the only one who succeeded in becoming a businessman is shown by the growing number of small and medium-size enterprises in Senggigi—and also on the Gili Islands—that are the result of mixed marriages. Becoming a successful entrepreneur in tourism, still hanging out with their old guiding friends, but leaving behind their "odd-jobber" life is the dream of all the beach boys. But only a few are able to make this dream come true. What is left for the others, easily the majority, is a life in the margins of the tourism industry.

For those guides who aspire to a Western lifestyle, but reject or fail to reach this goal through an intimate relationship with a female tourist, there is another opportunity for a better future that is less fragile and uncertain than a relationship with a female tourist. Some guides focus on developing long-standing relationships with tourists in general. What can be observed is the so-called *orang tua angkat* (adopted parents) phenomenon (Dahles & Bras, 1999). After a pleasant stay to which the local guide contributed significantly, tourists express the desire to stay in touch with their new friend. Older couples without children of their own sometimes decide to "adopt" a local guide. They send him letters and presents, support his family, pay for his studies, and sometimes even invite him to their home country. Contacts like these can be quite beneficial for the local guide, but normally they will only lead to occasional visits to Europe or Australia.

Conclusions

"Ask a local in a Third World tourist destination [what tourism means to them], and they may well tell you that it's about selling: selling their environment, their culture and their services to the guest" comments the earlier-quoted Australian journalist (Wolf, 1993, p. 13). One may argue that this attitude characterizes what sociologists have defined in terms of prostitution: emotionally neutral, indiscriminate, specifically remunerated sexual services (quoted in Cohen, 1993). As Cohen (1971, 1982b, 1986, 1993) and Crick (1992) have observed in various cultural contexts, the concept of prostitution does not adequately convey the meaning of the relationships emerging from sexual encounters between tourists and locals as described here. Cohen (1993) suggests to apply the concept of "open-ended" prostitution to characterize a kind of relationship between a prostitute and her (sic!) customer, which, though it may start as a specific neutral service, rendered more or less indiscriminately to any customer, may be extended into a more protracted, diffused, and personalized liaison, involving both emotional attachment and economic interest. The same applies to the street guides of Yogyakarta and the beach boys of Lombok. The term gigolo—in the sense of male prostitute—is not quite a literal one here. These boys are not paid for their services as such, but relationships with tourists entail improved financial security.

If prostitution is not the right concept to characterize these relationships, love is not the right concept either. It is true that the young men underplay the commercial side of the relationship from the beginning, stage affection, change their identity, and—if necessary—hide other emotional or even marital obligations. But different from Cohen's (1993) continuum of "open-ended" prostitution, which is characterized by a shift from a "mercenary" through a "staged" to an "emotional" phase, the relationships of the guides discussed here are not characterized by such a phasing. These young men are risk-taking, small-scale entrepreneurs who have to seize their opportunity under pressing limits of time and fierce competition from their peers. One of our informants called them "multifunctional guides": they offer companionship, entertainment, and sex; and, in return, they expect to "experience a white woman, which they regard as a meaningful opportunity to capture the love and money they desire" (Pruitt & Lafont, 1995, p. 428).

Tourists visiting Yogyakarta usually stay in town for only one or two nights. There is no time to "develop" a relationship. Within this short span of time, the young men strive to benefit as much as possible from this relationship, and as long as it remains beneficial they are willing to continue for weeks, months, and—perhaps—even years. But when the profit drops, they break off the relationship easily, and enter into another one without hesitation when the opportunity arises. They keep a number of relationships going simultaneously. The guides of Lombok can profit from an average stay of 3 to 5 days to build up a romantic relationship. In particular, newly arrived tourists are an interesting and often easy prey. They can expect a complete "treatment": two or three day trips, an evening program, and all kinds of additional services. But the guides will only invest time when the guest is worth the effort. They are pragmatic in their contacts with tourists. As long as the tourist will yield the expected amount of money or provide access to other sources of income, or whenever there is a possibility for a sexual interlude, guides will do everything in their power to come up with a special program and build up longer-lasting relationships.

The guides' position is insecure, their income is irregular, mostly commission based or depending on tips and gifts received from their tourist friends. Windfalls are made, but they may go for days without business. They spend a lot of money, partly on the tourist lifestyle in which they must to some extent participate, partly because of their social obligations in their peer group living up to their role models, the Kuta cowboys, which have proven to be the most successful presentation of self in the field of romancing the tourist. Having money entails the obligation to share it, to spend it on parties, drinks, and drugs with other guides. They do not save money and they do not invest in any long-term scheme to improve their situation permanently. They perceive any obligation—like a steady job or a marriage that ties them down—as a loss of freedom (Dahles, 1998a). Street guides and beach boys decline any obligations and ties that are difficult to combine with the manifold activities, incidental jobs, and businesses that they are engaged in. As small entrepreneurs, they spread themselves thin over a wide range of deals rather than plunge deeply on any one. In the tourism industry, being a very precarious trade, it would be foolish to put all of one's eggs in a single basket. Small-scale peddling and guiding tourists are flexible jobs that fit in with busy tourist seasons and calm off-season trade. However, more research is needed on the—diverse— cultural background of local guides to provide a better understanding of the way in which their upbringing, family ties, class position, religion, and ethnicity influence their attitudes towards tourist culture.

The earlier-quoted analysis of both destinations in terms of Butler's tourist area life cycle showed that the nature of the location demands different requirements and offers different possibilities. The dispersed attractions situated at rather inaccessible places in the countryside of Lombok make the beach boys dependent on facilities and the infrastructure of the formal tourism industry. These guides, in order to be successful, have to be able to develop a network that will give them access to transportation, accommodation, and sites. Given the fact that every high season there is a shortage of tourist guides, it is not surprising that the more successful beach boys operate partly in the formal tourism industry. As the island of Lombok only recently entered the tourism stage, government regulations regarding licenses are less strictly enforced than in areas with a developed tourism industry. In Yogyakarta the formal and informal tourism sectors are more clearly delimited. As government control is vigorous, the informal sector operates under harsher conditions. Infrequent police raids of the major tourist attractions and shopping areas impose restrictions on their strategies of approaching tourists and make the formal tourism industry inaccessible for them (Dahles, 1998b). Yogyakarta's street guides mostly rely on their contacts within their own peer group or operate independently. The compact tourism center of Yogyakarta makes guiding a highly individual activity. A limited network, therefore, does not inhibit the street guides from doing their job.

Another important difference between the romantic entrepreneurs of Yogyakarta and Lombok is their long-term goal. Both develop intimate relationships with female tourists to improve their personal situation. In Yogyakarta their main goal is to get away, to acquire a ticket to another life in a different, Western world. White girlfriends are seen as vehicles to make these dreams come true. On Lombok the female tourists are regarded as potential business associates who bring in the money to start a tourist enterprise on the island. Further research has to reveal in what way and to what extent these different future perspectives are related to the diverging cultural background of the young males. It can be hypothesized that the ethnic identity and religious obligations of young Sasak men establish a close bond with their home island, whereas young people in Yogyakarta are more detached, partly because city life is more anonymous, and partly because they are migrants and Yogyakarta is not their home town after all. Clear is that the different future perspectives are related to the opportunities and restrictions in terms of Butler's tourist area life cycle. The availability and access to economic capital in terms of "rich" tourists and the investment opportunities for this capital differ between both destinations. Tourism in Lombok is experiencing a rapid growth due to the fact that the island has been included in the government's *Beyond Bali* campaign. As a consequence, there is a serious shortage of skilled labor for tourism jobs. Although the provincial government is making efforts to professionalize the sector, there is still a demand for low-skilled employees. Guiding is open for anyone. As long as local guides, with their knowledge of tourism, strategically grasp the opportunities that come their way, they can become successful entrepreneurs in tourism. Acting as romantic entrepreneurs provides them with the capital they require to start their business careers.

In Yogyakarta, however, conditions are different. Yogyakarta is in the consolidation phase of its tourism development. The growth rate in the number of tourist arrivals and the length of stay are stagnating, and many (new) businesses fail. As Yogyakarta is losing its position as the second tourism area in Indonesia through recent government planning, but at the same time depending on tourism more than ever, it may be that the future prospects of small entrepreneurs in tourism are gloomy. Street guiding is a specific economic and social niche within the tourist sector that is generated and sustained because of the growing influx of international tourists. The city of Yogyakarta is a Third World city characterized by a high unemployment rate, and a high birth rate combined with immigration from rural areas, and its self-employed young males are attracted to Western consumer culture. Tourists enact the dream of Western consumerism and hold the promise of a ticket to a better life.

Glossary

Alun alun: big square

Arisan: rotating credit organizations

ASITA: Association of Indonesian Tour and Travel Agencies

Banjar: Balinese: neighborhood organization concerned with social control, public order, and religious ceremonies

Bapak angkat: lit.: adopted father (i.e., subcontracting relations between a large and a small business)

BPHN: *Badan Pusat Hotel Negara*: National Hotel Association

Bahasa: language

Bahasa Indonesia: Indonesian language

Bankrut: broke

Becak: pedicab

Bebas: free

Bemo: *becak bermotor*: small motorized vehicle used for transportation

Bintang: star

Bupati: governor

Depparpostel: *departemen pariwisata, pos dan telekomunikasi*: the ministry of tourism, post, and telecommunication

Desa: village

Diparda: *dinas pariwisata*: the provincial tourism department

Dusun: hamlet

Gondrong: long-haired man

Gunung: mountain

HGU: *Hak Guna Usaha*: right of customary use

HPI: *Himpunan Pramuwisata Indonesia*: Indonesian guide association

Ibu: mother, married woman

Idul Fitri: last day of Ramadan, the month of fasting

Ikat: woven cloth

Ikut-ikutan: lit.: going along with whatever happens to be the prevailing view; imitation

KADIN: *Kamar Dagang dan Industri*: the chamber of commerce and industries

Kampung: (low-class) neighborhood

Kabupaten: regency, administrative unit below the province

Kantor pos: post office

Kanwil: *kantor wilayah*: provincial government office

Liar: wild, unlicensed

Losmen: bed and breakfast accommodation

Mandi: Indonesian bath: water is taken from a basin with a dipper and poured over the body

Melati: jasmin flower

Orang besar: rich man

Orang jalan: lit.: people of the street

Orang tua angkat: adopted parents

Paguyuban: association

Pemda: *pemerintah daerah*: local government

Pengelola: management

Penginapan: lit.: lodging for the night; small pension

Pondok wisata: accommodation with less than five rooms

Pos: post

PT.: *perseroan terbatas*: Inc., Ltd.

Repelita: *rencana pembangunan lima tahun*: Five-Year Development Plan

Rupiah: Indonesian currency; in 1995–1996 1,000 *rupiah* was worth about US$0.40

Sarong: cloth worn as skirt or trousers by women and men

Senang: happy

Tukang becak: pedicab man

Tukang becak liar: unlicensed pedicab man

Tukang catut: ticket shark

Turis: tourist

Wartel: *warung telpon*: commercial telecommunication office

Wayang: puppet

Wayang kulit: leather puppet

Wetu telu: indigenous variant of Islam among the Sasak in Lombok

Wisma: guesthouse

Contributors

Karin Bras is a cultural anthropologist who graduated from the University of Amsterdam, The Netherlands in 1991. Her M.A. thesis deals with rural integrated tourism in the Basse-Casamance, Senegal. She is currently finishing her Ph.D. thesis at the Department of Leisure Studies, Tilburg University. Her dissertation is about the role of local tourist guides in the social construction of tourist attractions on the island of Lombok, Indonesia.

Heidi Dahles received her Ph.D. in cultural anthropology from the University of Nijmegen, The Netherlands. She worked in the field of tourism and leisure studies at Tilburg University and was senior fellow at the International Institute for Asian Studies in 1998. Currently she teaches in the Department of Business Anthropology, Vrije Universiteit Amsterdam, and holds a postdoctoral fellowship at the Centre for Asian Studies Amsterdam (CASA). Her research interests include entrepreneurial culture, brokerage, and patronage in Southeast Asian countries, in particular in the tourism industry.

Theo Kamsma is a cultural anthropologist who graduated from the Vrije Universiteit Amsterdam, The Netherlands in 1991. His M.A. thesis deals with youth tourism in Amsterdam. He has been actively involved in the tourism industry in Amsterdam for many years. At present, he is a freelance journalist writing about tourism, leisure, and Indonesia.

Saskia Peeters graduated from Tilburg University, Department of Leisure Studies in 1996. Her M.A. thesis is about tourist motivation and budget accommodation in Yogyakarta, Indonesia. At present, she is involved in welfare work.

Sandra Stam graduated from Tilburg University, Department of Leisure Studies in 1997. In her M.A. thesis she focuses on the relation between tourists and local tourist guides in the Rinjani area on the island of Lombok, Indonesia. At present she is working for a refugee organization.

Karin ter Steege graduated from Tilburg University, the Department of Leisure Studies in 1997. In her M.A. thesis she focuses on the relation between tourists and local tourist guides in the Rinjani area on the island of Lombok, Indonesia. At present she is a travel advisor for a Dutch tour operator.

Jolanda Urru graduated from Tilburg University, Department of Leisure Studies in 1996. Her M.A. thesis is about tourist motivation and budget accommodation in Yogyakarta, Indonesia. At present, she is a researcher for a publisher of professional information about tourism.

Eveline van der Giessen graduated from Tilburg University, Department of Leisure Studies in 1996. In her M.A. thesis she compares the small-scale accommodation in two tourist destinations on the island of Bali, Indonesia. After working as a management trainee in the accommodation sector, she has recently accepted a job as an account manager.

Hanneke van Gemert graduated from Tilburg University, Department of Leisure Studies in 1996. Her M.A. thesis is about the activities of pedicab men in the major tourist areas in the city of Yogyakarta, Indonesia. At present she lives in Bandung and is employed by a Dutch trading company.

Esther van Genugten graduated from Tilburg University, Department of Leisure Studies in 1996. Her M.A. thesis is about the activities of pedicab men active in the major tourist areas in the city of Yogyakarta, Indonesia. She currently works as a human resources manager for a Dutch broadcasting company.

Marie-Chantal van Loo graduated from Tilburg University, Department of Leisure Studies in 1996. Her M.A. thesis focuses on small-scale accommodation in two tourist destinations on the island of Bali, Indonesia. She is a travel advisor for a Dutch tour operator.

Bibliography

Alexander, J. (1987). *Trade, traders and trading in rural Java*. Singapore: Oxford University Press.

Alexander, P. (1989). Introduction. In P. Alexander (Ed.), *Creating Indonesian cultures* (pp. i-vii). Sidney: University of Sidney, Oceania Publications.

Anderson, B. (1990). *Language and power. Exploring political cultures in Indonesia*. Ithaca/London: Cornell University Press.

Balai Pendidikan dan Latihan Pariwisata Bali (n.d.). *The tour guide*. Unpublished course book.

Balinese sociocultural values at stake. (1996, May 14). *Jakarta Post*.

Bali's economic success is environment's loss. (1996, April 30). *Bali Post*.

Bali Tourism Directory. (1995). Denpasar: Bali Government Tourism Office.

Bara Pariwisata Gili Trawangan Berkobar. (1995, April, 20-22). *Bali Post*.

Berger, P. (1973). "Sincerity" and "authenticity" in modern society. *Public Interest*, 81-90.

Berry, A., & Mazumdar, D. (1991). Small-scale industry in the Asian-Pacific region. *Asian-Pacific Economic Literature*, 5(2), 35-67.

Beterams, P. (1996). *Life in the eye of a hurricane. Effects of tourism on the village of Senaru, gate-way community of Rinjani National Park*. Unpublished thesis in Development Studies, Third World Center, Catholic University of Nijmegen.

Boissevain, J. (1974). *Friends of friends. Networks, manipulators and coalitions*. Oxford: Basil Blackwell.

Boissevain, J. (1997). Small European entrepreneurs. In M. Rutten & C. Upadhya (Eds.), *Small business entrepreneurs in Asia and Europe. Towards a comparative perspective* (pp. 301-324). New Delhi/Thousand Oaks/London: Sage Publications.

Boorstin, O. J. (1964). *The image: A guide to pseudo-events in America*. New York: Harper and Row.

Booth, A. (1990). The tourism boom in Indonesia. *Bulletin of Indonesian Economic Studies*, 26(3), 45-73.

Bourdieu, P. (1977). *Outline of a theory of practice*. Cambridge: Cambridge University Press.

Bowman, G. (1989). Fucking tourists: Sexual relations and tourism in Jerusalem's Old City. *Critique of Anthropology*, 9(2), 73-93.

Bowman, G. (1996). Passion, power and politics in a Palestinian tourist market. In T. Selwyn (Ed.), *The tourist image: Myth and myth making in tourism* (pp. 83-103). Chichester: Wiley,

Biro Pusat Statistik. (1991). *Statistik Kunjungan Tamu Asing 1991*. Jakarta: Author.

Biro Pusat Statistik. (1994). *Statistik Kunjungan Tamu Asing 1994*. Jakarta: Author.

Biro Pusat Statistik. (1995). *Statistik Kunjungan Tamu Asing 1995*. Jakarta: Author.

Biro Pusat Statistik. (1996a). *Statistik Kunjungan Tamu Asing 1996*. Jakarta: Author.

Biro Pusat Statistik. (1996b). *Small scale manufacturing industry statistics 1996*. Jakarta: Author.

Bras, K. (1991). *"De Diola als Attractie"—Het geïntegreerd ruraal toeristisch project in de Basse-Casamance Senegal*. Unpublished M.A. thesis, Cultural Anthropology, University of Amsterdam.

Bras, K. (1994). Toerisme: de ontdekking van het echte Afrika. Het dagelijks leven van de Diola in de Basse-Casamance (Senegal) als toeristisch attractie. *Vrijetijd en Samenleving, 12*(1/2), 15-29.

Bras, K. (forthcoming). *Lombok and the art of guiding. The social construction of a tourist destination in Indonesia.* Unpublished Ph.D. thesis, Department of Leisure Studies, Tilburg University.

Bras, K., & Dahles, H. (1998). Women entrepreneurs and beach tourism in Sanur, Bali. Gender, employment opportunities and government policy. *Pacific Tourism Review, 1*(3), 243-256.

Breda, A. van. (1997). Kleinschalig Toerisme op Lombok onder Druk. *IFM*, maart, 16-17.

Brent Ritchie, J. R., & Goeldner, C. F. (Eds.) (1987). *Travel, tourism and hospitality research. A handbook for managers and researchers.* New York: Wiley.

Britton, C., & Clark, W. (Eds.) (1987). *Ambiguous alternatives: Tourism in small developing communities.* Suva, Fiji: University of South Pacific.

Britton, S. (1989). Tourism, dependency and development. A mode of analysis. In Singh Tej Vir, H. L. Theuns, & F. M. Go (Eds.), *Towards appropriate tourism: The case of developing countries* (pp. 93-116). Frankfurt: Peter Lang Verlag.

Brohman, J. (1996). New directions in tourism for Third World development. *Annals of Tourism Research, 23*(1), 48-70.

Butler, R. W. (1980). The concept of a tourist-area cycle of evolution and implications for management. *The Canadian Geographer, 24*, 5-12.

Butler, R. W. (1991). Tourism, environment and sustainable development. *Environmental Conservation, 18*(3), 201-209.

Cederroth, S. (1981). *The spell of the ancestors and the power of Mekkah. A Sasak community on Lombok.* Gothenburg Studies in Social Anthropology 3. Acta Universitatis Gothoburgensis.

CISED—Center for Indonesian Studies on Eco-development. (1995). *Summary of the prepatory research for the Rinjani Eco-development Project.* Mataram, NTB, Indonesia.

Chan, A., & Go, F. M. (1996). *Marketing cultural assets to sustain the competitiveness of tourism destinations in Southeast Asia.* Paper presented at the 12th Annual Academy of International Business South East Asia Regional Conference Dunedin and Queenstown, New Zealand, 17-20 June.

Chowdhury, A., & Islam, I. (1993). *The newly industrialising economies of East Asia.* London/New York: Routledge.

Clapham, R. (in cooperation with R. Strunk, H. G. H. Schaldach, & G. Clapham) (1985). *Small and medium entrepreneurs in Southeast Asia.* Research Notes and Discussion Paper No. 49, Institute of Southeast Asian Studies, Singapore.

Cohen, E. (1971). Arab boys and tourist girls in a mixed Jewish-Arab community. *International Journal of Comparative Sociology, 12*(4), 217-233.

Cohen, E. (1979). A phenomenology of tourist experiences. *Sociology, 13*, 179-201.

Cohen, E. (1982a). Marginal paradises: Bungalow tourism on the islands of Southern Thailand. *Annals of Tourism Research, 9*(2), 189-205.

Cohen, E. (1982b). Thai girls and farang men: The edge of ambiguity. *Annals of Tourism Research, 9*(3), 403-428.

Cohen, E. (1982c). Jungle guides in Northern Thailand. The dynamics of a marginal occupational role. *Sociological Review, 30*(20), 234-266.

Cohen, E. (1985). The tourist guide: The origins, structure and dynamics of a role. *Annals of Tourism Research, 12*(1), 5-29.

Cohen, E. (1986). Lovelorn farangs: The correspondence between foreign men and Thai girls. *Anthropological Quarterly, 59*(3), 115-127.

Cohen, E. (1993). Open-ended prostitution as a skilful game of luck. Opportunity, risk and security among tourist-oriented prostitutes in a Bangkok soi. In M. Hitchcock, V.T. King, & M. J. G. Parnwell (Eds.), *Tourism in South-East Asia* (pp. 155-178). New York/London: Routledge.

Cohen, E. (1996). *Thai tourism. Hill tribes, islands and open-ended prostitution.* Studies in Contemporary Thailand No. 4. Bangkok: White Lotus Co., Ltd.

Cooke, P. (1983). *Theories of planning and spacial development.* London: Hutchinson.

Crang, Ph. (1997). Performing the tourist product. In Ch. Rojek & J. Urry (Eds.), *Touring cultures. Transformations of travel and theory* (pp. 137-154). London: Routledge.

Crick, M. (1992). Life in the informal sector: Street guides in Kandy, Sri Lanka. In D. Harrison (Ed.), *Tourism & the less developed countries* (pp. 135-147). London: Belhaven Press.

Crush, J., & Wellings, P. (1983). The Southern Africa pleasure periphery, 1966-1983. *Journal of Modern African Studies 21*(4), 673-698.

Cukier, J. (1996). Tourism employment in Bali: Trends and implications. In R. Butler & T. Hinch (Eds.), *Tourism and indigenous peoples* (pp. 49-75). London: International Thomson Press.

Cukier-Snow, J., & Wall, G. (1993). Tourism employment: Perspectives from Bali. *Tourism Management, 14*(3), 195-201.

Dahles, H. (1996). "Hello Mister!": De rol van informele gidsen in Yogyakarta. *Derde Wereld, 15*(1), 34-48.

Dahles, H. (1997a). The new gigolo. Globalization, tourism and changing gender identities. Focaal. *Tijdschrift voor Antropologie, 30/31* (Special Issue: Globalization/Localization: Paradoxes of Cultural Identity), 121-137.

Dahles, H. (1997b). Urban tourism and image management in Yogyakarta: National development, cultural heritage and the presentation of a tourist product. In M. P. Gunawan (Ed.), *Pariwisata Indonesia. Berbagai Aspek dan Gagasan Pembangunan* (pp. 5-28). Bandung: Pusat Penelitian Kepariwisataan, Lembaga Penelitian, Institut Teknologi Bandung.

Dahles, H. (1998a). Of birds and fish. Streetguides, tourists and sexual encounters in Yogyakarta, Indonesia. In M. Oppermann (Ed.), *Sex tourism and prostitution* (pp. 30-41). New York: Cognizant Communication Corporation.

Dahles, H. (1998b). Tourism, government policy and petty entrepreneurs in Indonesia. *South East Asia Research.* School of Oriental and African Studies. University of London, 6(1), 73-98.

Dahles, H., & Bras, K. (1999). Entrepreneurs in romance. Tourism in Indonesia. *Annals of Tourism Research, 26*(2), 267-293.

Dalton, B. (1991). *Indonesian handbook.* Moon Publications.

Darling, D. (1994). The benefits of tourism. In A. Vickers (Ed.), *Travelling to Bali. Four hundred years of journeys* (pp. 273-278). Kuala Lumpur: Oxford University Press.

De Kadt, E. (1979). *Tourism—passport to development? Perspectives on the social and cultural effects of tourism in developing countries.* New York: Oxford University Press for the World Bank and UNESCO.

De Kadt, E. (1995). Tourism policy management after structural adjustment. In *Plenary V. International Tourism, Development, and Policy-Making. International Conference on Cultural Tourism,* Indonesian-Swiss Forum on Culture and International Tourism, Yogyakarta.

Dibnah, S. P. (1992). *An assessment of spatial arrangement plans for tourist areas in Bali.* Research paper No. 39, Bali Sustainable Development Project.

Dinas Pariwisata Prop. DATI I NTB. (1995a). *Petunjuk Pelaksanaan Pembinaan dan Penertiban Pramuwisata Nusa Tenggara Barat.* 1995-1996.

Dinas Pariwisata Prop. DATI I NTB. (1995b). *Selected tourism data 1988-1995.* Nusa Tenggara Province Mataram, November 1995.

Dinas Pariwisata Prop. DATI I NTB. (1996). *Kepariwisataan.* Nusa Tenggara Barat Dalam Angka

1995.

Diparda. (1995). *Statistik Pariwisata*. Daerah Istimewa Yogyakarta. Dinas Pariwisata.

Dove, M. (1988). Introduction: Traditional culture and development in contemporary Indonesia. In M. Dove (Ed.), *The real and imagined role of culture in development. Case studies from Indonesia* (pp. 1–40). Honolulu: University of Hawaii Press.

Drakakis-Smith, D. (1987). *The Third World city* (Routledge Introductions to Development). London/New York: Routledge.

Echtner, C. M. (1995). Entrepreneurial training in developing countries. *Annals of Tourism Research, 22*(1), 119–134.

Evers, H. D. (1981). The contribution of urban subsistence production to incomes in Jakarta. *Bulletin of Indonesian Economic Studies, XVII*(2), 89–96.

Evers, H. D. (1991). Shadow economy, subsistence production and informal sector: Economic activity outside of market and state. *Prisma, 51*, 34–45.

Evers, H. D., & Mehmet, O. (1994). The management of risk: Informal trade in Indonesia. *World Development, 22*(1), 1–9.

Firat, F. A. (1994). Gender and consumption: Transcending the feminine? In J. A. Costa (Ed.), *Gender issues and consumer behavior* (pp. 205–228). Thousand Oaks/London/New Delhi: Sage Publications.

Geertz, C. (1963). *Peddlers and princes. Social development and economic change in two Indonesian towns*. Chicago/London: University of Chicago Press.

Gilbert, A., & Gugler, J. (1992). *Cities, poverty and development. Urbanization in the Third World*. Oxford: Oxford University Press.

Go, F. M. (1997). Entrepreneurs and the tourism industry in developing countries. In H. Dahles (Ed.), *Tourism, small entrepreneurs, and sustainable development. Cases from developing countries* (pp. 5–22). Tilburg: ATLAS.

Gorter, P. (1997). The social and political aspirations of a new stratum of industrialists: Local politics on a large industrial estate in West India. In M. Rutten & C. Upadhya (Eds.), *Small business entrepreneurs in Asia and Europe. Towards a comparative perspective* (pp. 81–114). New Delhi/Thousand Oaks/London: Sage Publications.

Graburn, N. H. H. (1983). Tourism and prostitution. *Annals of Tourism Research, 10*(3), 437–442.

Greenfield, S. M., Strickon, A., & Aubey, R. T. (Eds.) (1979). *Entrepreneurs in cultural context*. Albuquerque: School of American Research Book, University of New Mexico Press.

Guinness, P. (1994). Local society and culture. In H. Hill (Ed.), *Indonesia's new order. The dynamics of socio-economic transformation* (pp. 267–304). London: Allen and Unwin.

Gunawan, M. (1997) Pariwisata di Indonesia: Dulu, kini, dan yang akan datang. In M. P. Gunawan (Ed.), *Prosiding Pelatihan dan Lokakarya. Perencanaan Pariwisata Berkelanjutan* (pp. 19–34). Bandung: Penerbit ITB.

Gurung, G., Simmons, D., & Devlin, P. (1996). The evolving role of tourist guides: The Nepali experience. In R. Butler & T. Hinch (Eds.), *Tourism and indigenous peoples* (pp. 107–128). London: International Thomson Business Press.

Hall, D. R. (1992). Sex tourism in South-east Asia. In D. Harrison (Ed.), *Tourism & the less developed countries* (pp. 102–120). London: Belhaven Press.

Hamengku Buwono X, Sri Sultan. (1992). Revitalization of cultural heritage within the context of tourism. In *International Conference on Cultural Tourism, "Universal Tourism: Enriching or Degrading Culture,"* Yogyakarta, November 24–26.

Harrell-Bond, B. (1978). *A window on the outside world, tourism and development in the Gambia*. American Universities Field Staff Report No. 19. Hanover, New Hampshire.

Harrison, D. (Ed.) (1992). International tourism and the less developed countries. In *Tourism and the less developed countries*. London: Belhaven Press.

Hart, K. (1973). Informal income opportunities and urban employment in Ghana. *Journal of Modern African Studies, 11*.

Hart, K. (1993). Markt en staat na de Koude Oorlog—De informele economie opnieuw beschouwd. *Derde Wereld, 12*(2), 87–103.

Harvey, D. (1989). *The conditions of postmodernity. An enquiry into the origins of cultural change*. Oxford: Basil Blackwell.

Hellingwerf, E. (1996). *Overstanding Cahuita. Social relations in Costa Rican tourist town*. Unpublished M.A. thesis, Tilburg University.

Hill, H. (1996). *The Indonesian economy since 1966: Southeast Asia's emerging giant*. Hong Kong: Cambridge University Press.

Holloway, J. C. (1981). The guided tour. A sociological approach. *Annals of Tourism Research, VIII*(3), 377–402.

Hull, T. H., & Jones, G. W. (1994). Demographic perspectives. In H. Hill (Ed.), *Indonesia's new order. The dynamics of socio-economic transformation* (pp. 123–178). London: Allen and Unwin.

Hussey, A. (1989). Tourism in a Balinese village. *Geographical Review, 79*(3), 311–325.

Jafari, J. (1989). Sociocultural dimensions of tourism. An English language literature review. In J. Bustrzanowski (Ed.), *Tourism as a factor of change: A sociocultural study* (pp. 17–60). Vienna: Economic Coordination Centre for Research and Documentation in Social Sciences.

Jellinek, L. (1991). *The wheel of fortune. The history of a poor community in Jakarta*. Sidney: Allen and Unwin.

Kadiparda Loteng Siap Tertibkan "Guide" Nakal. (1996, March 29). *Bali Post*.

Kamsma, M. J. (1996, November 23). Grof geweld in het Paradijs. *De Volkskrant*.

Karch, C. A., & Dann, G. H. S. (1981). Close encounters of the Third World. *Human Relations, 34*, 249–268.

Kartodirdjo, S. (1981). *The pedicab of Yogyakarta. A study of low cost transportation and poverty problems*. Yogyakarta: Gadjah Mada University Press.

Kermath, B. M., & Thomas, R. N. (1992). Spatial dynamics of resorts, Sosua, Dominican Republic. *Annals of Tourism Research, 19*, 173–190.

Kinnaird, V., Kothari, U., & Hall, D. (1994). Tourism: Gender perspectives. In V. Kinnaird & D. Hall (Eds.), *Tourism: A gender analysis* (pp. 1–34). Chichester: Wiley.

Koetsier, P. (1989). *The role of the becak in the urban public transport system of Bandung*. Unpublished thesis, University of Amsterdam, Department of Human Geography.

Kruhse-Mount Burton, S. (1995). Sex tourism and traditional Australian male identity. In M. F. Lanfant, J. B. Allock, & E. M. Bruner (Eds.), *International tourism. Identity and change* (pp. 192–204). London: Sage Publications.

Kumorotomo, W. (n.d.). *The key issues in cultural tourism management in Bali-Indonesia*. Unpublished manuscript.

Lea, J. (1988). *Tourism and development in the Third World*. London/New York: Routledge.

Lee, W. (1991). Prostitution and tourism in South-East Asia. In N. Redclift & M. T. Sinclair (Eds.), *Working women: International perspectives on gender and labour ideology* (pp. 79–103). London/New York: Routledge.

Leheny, D. (1995). A political economy of Asian sex tourism. *Annals of Tourism Research, 22*(2), 367–384.

Leiper, N. (1990). Tourist attraction systems. *Annals of Tourism Research, 17*, 367–384.

Leser, D. (1997). Farewell my lovely. *Contours, 7*(10), 19–27.

Long, V. H., & Kindon, S. L. (1997). Gender and tourism development in Balinese villages. In M. T. Sinclair (Ed.), *Gender, work & tourism* (pp. 91–119). London/New York: Routledge.

Lübben, Ch. (1995). *Internationaler Tourismus als Faktor der Regionalentwicklung in*

Indonesien: untersucht am Beispiel der Insel Lombok. Berlin: Dietrich Reimer Verlag.

Mabbett, H. (1987). *In praise of Kuta. From slave port to fishing village to the most popular resort in Bali.* Wellington: January Books.

Mabbett, H. (1989). *The Balinese. All about the most famous island in the world* (2nd ed.). Wellington: January Books.

MacCannell, D. (1976). *The tourist—a new theory of the leisure class.* New York: Shocken.

Massey, D. (1983). Industrial restructuring as class restructuring: Production, decentralisation and local uniqueness. *Regional Studies, 17,* 73-90.

Massey, D. (1984). *Spatial divisions of labour: Social structures and the geography of production.* London: Macmillan.

Mazumdar, D. (1989). *Government interventions and urban labour markets in developing countries.* EDI working papers. Washington, DC: World Bank.

McCarthy, J. (1994). *Are sweet dreams made of this? Tourism in Bali and Eastern Indonesia.* Northcote: Indonesia Resources and Information Program (IRIP).

McGee, T. G. (1982). *Labor markets, urban systems, and the urbanization process in Southeast Asian countries.* Honolulu: East-West Center.

McTaggert, W. D. (1977). Aspects of the tourist industry in Indonesia. *The Indonesian Quarterly, 4,* 62-74.

McVey, R. (1995). Shaping the Sasak. Religion and hierarchy on an Indonesian island. In B. Werler & S. Wälty (Eds.), *Kulturen und Raum. Theoretische Ansätze und empirische Kulturforschung in Indonesien* (pp. 311-351). Chur/Zurich: Verlag Rüger A.G.

Meisch, L. A. (1995). Gringas and Otavalenos. Changing tourist relations. *Annals of Tourism Research, 22*(2), 441-462.

Mengapa terjadi Tragedi Trawangan yang menumpahkan air mata? (1995, April 26). *Suara Nusa.*

Midgley, J. (with A. Hall, M. Hardiman, & D. Narine) (1986). *Community participation, social development and the state.* London/New York: Methuen.

Miller, D. B., & Branson, J. (1989). Pollution in paradise: Hinduism and the subordination of women in Bali. In P. Alexander (Ed.), *Creating Indonesian cultures* (pp. 91-112). Sidney: University of Sidney, Oceania Publications.

Momsen, J. H. (1991). *Women and development in the Third World.* New York: Routledge.

Momsen, J. H. (1994). Tourism, gender, and the development of the Caribbean. In V. Kinnaird & D. Hall (Eds.), *Tourism: A gender analysis* (pp. 106-120). New York/Chichester: Wiley.

Mucipto, I. (1994). *Development for whom? The tourism industry in Lombok, Indonesia.* Unpublished manuscript, Center for Indonesian Studies on Eco-Development (CISED), Mataram, NTB, Indonesia.

Murphy, P. E. (1985). *Tourism: A community approach.* London: Methuen.

Murphy, P. E. (1994). Tourism and sustainable development. In W. F. Theobald (Ed.), *Global tourism. The next decade* (pp. 274-290). Oxford: Butterworth-Heinemann Ltd.

Norris, J. N. E. (1994). *Gender and tourism in rural Bali: Case study of Kedewatan Village.* A thesis presented to the Faculty of Graduate Studies of the University of Guelph.

O'Malley, J. (1988). Sex tourism and women's status in Thailand. *Loisir et Société, 11*(1), 99-114.

Operations Review Unit. (1988). *Women entrepreneurs. Development prospects for women entrepreneurs in small and micro scale industry.* (Place of publication and name of publisher unknown.)

Parapak, J. (1995). *The curricula in tourism education and training. The case study of Indonesia.* A paper by the Department of Tourism, Post and Telecommunication, Republic of Indonesia for the Education and Training for Industry Growth Conference, July, 17-18.

Pearce, L. (1984). Tourist-guide interaction. *Annals of Tourism Research, 11*(1), 129-146.

Peeters, S., & Urru, J. (1996). *Homestays: Een glimp van het echte Javaanse leven? Een onderzoek naar de budget-accommodatie sector in Yogyakarta, Indonesië.* Unpublished M.A. thesis, Department of Leisure Studies, Tilburg University.

Periplus. (1991). *Java.* Berkeley/Singapore: Periplus Editions.

Penuturan Seorang "Guide" tanpa Lisensi. Disebut Gigolo, Saya Pasrah. (1996, June). *Bali Post.*

Picard, M. (1993). Cultural tourism in Bali: National integration and regional differentiation. In M. Hitchcock, V.T. King, & M. J. G. Parnwell (Eds.), *Tourism in South-East Asia* (pp. 71-98). London: Routledge.

Picard, M. (1996). *Bali. Cultural tourism and touristic culture.* Singapore: Archipelago Press.

Pruitt, D. (1993). *"Foreign mind": Tourism, identity and development in Jamaica.* Ph.D thesis, University of California, Berkeley.

Pruitt, D., & LaFont, S. (1995). "For love and money." Romance tourism in Jamaica. *Annals of Tourism Research, 22*(2), 422-440.

Rodenburg, E. (1980). The effects of scale in economic development: Tourism in Bali. *Annals of Tourism Research, 7*(2), 177-196.

Roebuck, J., & McNamara. P. (1973). Ficheras and free-lancers: Prostitution in a Mexican border city. *Archives of Sexual Behaviour, 2*(3), 231-244.

Rotge, V. L. (1991). *Addressing Regional Development and Rural Employment Creation in the Context of Rising Rural-Urban Linkages.* Second country seminar on regional development in the special province of Yogyakarta, Indonesia, September 3-6.

Rutten, M. (1997). Cooperation and differentiation: Social history of iron founders in central Java. In M. Rutten & C. Upadhya (Eds.), *Small business entrepreneurs in Asia and Europe. Towards a comparative perspective* (pp. 173-210). New Delhi/Thousand Oaks/London: Sage Publications.

Saglio, C. (1979). Tourism for discovery: A project in Lower Casamance, Senegal. In E. De Kadt (Ed.), *Tourism—passport to development? Perspectives on the social and cultural effects of tourism in developing countries* (pp. 321-335). New York: Oxford University Press for the World Bank and UNESCO.

Sammeng, A. M. (1995). Tourism as a development strategy. Plenary address. In *Plenary V: International Tourism, Development, and Policy Making.* The 1995 Indonesian-Swiss Forum on Culture and International Tourism. Universitas Gadjah Mada, Yogyakarta, Indonesia.

Schlechten, M. (1988). *Tourisme balnéaire ou tourisme rural intégré? Deux modèles de développement sénégalais.* Editions Universitaires Fribourg Suisse.

Schoch, L. N. (1985). *Kaki lima and streethawkers in Indonesia.* Jakarta: PT. Indira.

Schumpeter, J. A. (1942). *Capitalism, socialism and democracy.* Boston: Harvard University Press.

Schuurman, F. (1993). Introduction: Development theory in the 1990s. In F. Schuurman (Ed.), *Beyond the impasse. New directions in development theory* (pp. 1-48). London/New Jersey: Zed Books.

Scures, J. S. (1994). *Culture contact and social change through tourism: Crossroads of an international village on Bali.* Unpublished Ph.D. thesis, University of California, San Diego.

Sensus. (1995). *Penduduk Daerah Istimewa Yogyakarta.*

Shaw, G., & Williams, A. M. (1994). *Critical issues in tourism. A geographical perspective.* Oxford/Cambridge: Blackwell.

Simmons, D. G. (1994). Community participation in tourism planning. *Tourism Management, 15*(2), 98-108.

Sinclair, M.T. (1997). Issues and theories of gender and work in tourism. In M.T. Sinclair (Ed.), *Gender, work & tourism* (pp. 1-15). London/New York: Routledge.

Smith, V. (1994). Privatization in the Third World: Small-scale tourism enterprises. In W. F. Theobald (Ed.), *Global tourism: The next decade* (pp. 163-173). Oxford: Butterworth-Heinemann.

Smith, V., & Eadington, V. (Eds.) (1992). *Tourism alternatives: Potentials and problems in the development of tourism.* Philadelphia: University of Pennsylvania Press.

Smithies, M. (1986). *Yogyakarta. Cultural heart of Indonesia.* Singapore/Oxford/New York: Oxford University Press.

Soedarso, S. (1992). *The role of visual arts in cultural tourism development in Central Java and the special district of Yogyakarta.* Regional Office for Science and Technology for Southeast Asia, Office for the UNESCO Representative to Indonesia and the Philippines.

Soedjarwo, A. (1991). *Social Aspects of the Special Province of Yogyakarta. Some important issues to be considered in the Urban Development and Planning of the Special Province of Yogyakarta.* Second country seminar on regional development in the special province of Yogyakarta, Indonesia, September 3-6.

Soegijoko, B. T. S. (1986). The becaks of Java. *Habitat International, 10*(1/2), 155-164.

Sofield, T. H. B. (1995). Indonesia's national tourism development plan. *Annals of Tourism Research, 22*(3), 690-694.

Stam, S., & Ter Steege, K. (1997). *A travel survival kit. The interaction between mountain guides and nature-based tourists in North-Lombok, Indonesia.* Unpublished M.A. thesis, Department of Leisure Studies, Tilburg University.

Statistik Diparda DIY. (1995). *Statistik Pariwisata Daerah Istimewa Yogyakarta.* Dinas Pariwisata DIY.

Statistik Pariwisata DIY. (1995). *Statistik Pariwisata, Pos dan Telekomunikasi, Daerah Istimewa Yogyakarta Tahun 1995.* Diterbitkan oleh: KANWIL VIII Departemen Pariwisata, Pos dan Telekomunikasi, Daerah Istimewa Yogyakarta.

Statistik Indonesia. (1995). *Statistik Indonesia 1995.* Jakarta: Biro Pusat Statistik.

Suardika, I Wayan. (1996a, February 25). Wanita Bule di Sarang Gigolo. *Nusa Tenggara Minggu.*

Suardika, I Wayan. (1996b, February 25). Mengikat Gigolo lewat Anak. *Nusa Tenggara Minggu.*

Suhartono, R. B. (1995). Small and medium-scale industries in Indonesia. *Asian Development Review,* 41-69.

Sullivan, J. (1992). *Local government and community in Java. An urban case-study.* South East Asian Social Science Monographs. Singapore: Oxford University Press.

Sullivan, N. (1989). The hidden economy and Kampung women. In P. Alexander (Ed.), *Creating Indonesian cultures* (pp. 75-90). Sidney: University of Sidney, Oceania Publications.

Sutherland, A. (1986). *Caye Caulker, economic success in a Belizean fishing village.* Boulder: Westview Press.

Swain, M. B. (1995). Gender in tourism. *Annals of Tourism Research, 22*(2), 247-266.

Telfer, D., & Wall, G. (1996). Linkages between tourism and food production: An Indonesian example. *Annals of Tourism Research, 23*(3), 635-653.

Timothy, D. J., & Wall, G. (1997). Selling to tourists. Indonesian street vendors. *Annals of Tourism Research, 24*(4), 322-340.

Truong, T. D. (1983). The dynamics of sex tourism: The cases of South-East Asia. *Development and Change, 14*(4), 533-553.

Truong, T. D. (1990). *Sex, money and morality: Prostitution and tourism in South-East Asia.* London: Zed Press.

Turner, P., Delahunty, B., Greenway, P., Lyon, J., McAsey, Ch., & Willett, D. (1995). *Indonesia, a Lonely Planet travel survival kit.* Hawthorne/Australia: Lonely Planet Publications.

Upadhya, C. (1997). Culture, class and entrepreneurship: A case study of coastal Andhra Pradesh, India. In M. Rutten & C. Upadhya (Eds.), *Small business entrepreneurs in Asia and Europe. Towards a comparative perspective* (pp. 47-80). New Delhi/Thousand Oaks/London: Sage Publications.

Upadhya C., & Rutten, M. (1997). In search of a comparative framework: Small-scale entrepreneurs in Asia and Europe. In M. Rutten & C. Upadhya (Eds.), *Small business entrepreneurs in Asia and Europe. Towards a comparative perspective* (pp. 13-46). New Delhi/Thousand Oaks/London: Sage Publications.

Urry, J. (1990). *The tourist gaze. Leisure and travel in contemporary societies.* London: Sage Publications.

Urry, J. (1995). Tourism, travel and the modern subject. In J. Urry (Ed.), *Consuming places* (pp. 141-151). London/New York: Routledge.

Van der Duim, R. (1997). The role of small entrepreneurs in the development of sustainable tourism in Costa Rica. In H. Dahles (Ed.), *Tourism, small entrepreneurs, and sustainable development. Cases from developing countries* (pp. 35-48). Tilburg: ATLAS.

Van der Giessen, E., & van Loo, M. C. (1996). *Bali, a 'paradise' with two faces. A study of low-budget accommodation in Kuta and Ubud on the island of Bali in Indonesia.* Unpublished M.A. thesis, Tilburg University.

Van Diermen, P. (1997). *Small business in Indonesia.* Aldershot/Brookfield/HongKong/Singapore/Sidney: Ashgate.

Van Genugten, E., & van Gemert, H. (1996). *Tukang Becak. A study of becak drivers who operate in the tourist sector of Yogyakarta, Indonesia.* Unpublished M.A. thesis, Tilburg University.

Van Schaardenburgh, A. (1995). *Local participation in tourism development. A study in Cahuita, Costa Rica.* Unpublished manuscript, Tilburg University.

Verschoor, G. (1992). Identity, networks, and space: New dimensions in the study of small-scale enterprise commoditization. In N. Long (Ed.), *Battlefields of knowledge: The interlocking of theory and practice in social research and development* (pp. 171-188). London: Routledge.

Vickers, A. (1989). *Bali: A paradise created.* California: Periplus Editions Inc.

Wagner, U. (1977). Out of time and place—mass tourism and charter trips. *Ethnos, 42*(I-II), 38-52.

Wagner, U., & Yamba, B. (1986). Going north and getting attached: The cases of Gambians. *Ethnos, 51,* 3-45.

Wall, G. (1995). *People outside of the plans.* Address to the Indonesian-Swiss Forum on Culture and International Tourism, Gadjah Mada University, Yogyakarta.

Wall, G. (1996). Perspectives on tourism in selected Balinese villages. *Annals of Tourism Research, 23*(1), 123-137.

Wall, G. (1997). Indonesia: The impact of regionalization. In F. M. Go & C. L. Jenkins (Eds.), *Tourism and economic development in Asia and Australasia* (pp. 138-149). London/Washington: Cassell.

Wall, G., & Long, V. (1996). Balinese homestays: An indigenous response to tourism opportunities. In R. Butler & T. Hinch (Eds.), *Tourism and indigenous peoples* (pp. 27-48). London: International Thomson Business Press.

Warren, C. (1989). Balinese political culture and the rhetoric of national development. In P. Alexander (Ed.), *Creating Indonesian cultures* (pp. 39-54). Sidney: University of Sidney, Oceania Publications.

Wheeler, T., & Lyon, J. (1992). *Bali & Lombok—a travel survival kit* (4th ed.). Hawthorn, Australia: Lonely Planet Publications.

Wilkinson, P. F., & Pratiwi, W. (1995). Gender and tourism in an Indonesian village. *Annals of Tourism Research, 22*(2), 283-299.

Wolf, Y. (1993, June). The world of the Kuta cowboy. A growing subculture of sex, drugs and alcohol is evident among male youth in the tourist areas of Bali and Lombok as they seek an alternative to poverty. *Inside Indonesia*, 15-17.

Wood, R. E. (1997). Tourism and the state: Ethnic options and constructions of otherness. In M. Picard & R. E. Wood (Eds.), *Tourism, ethnicity, and the state in Asian and Pacific societies* (pp. 1-34). Honolulu: University of Hawaii Press.

World Tourism Organisation. (1987). *Tourism development planning study for Nusa Tenggara. Tourism development plan package A—Lombok.* United Nations Development Programme/ Directorate General of Tourism Jakarta, Indonesia. Madrid: Author.

Index